THE BRITISH EMPIRE
1784—1939

THE
BRITISH
EMPIRE
1784–1939

James Truslow Adams

DORSET PRESS
New York

Originally published as
Empire on the Seven Seas

Copyright © 1940 by Charles Scribner's Sons
All rights reserved.

This edition published by Dorset Press,
a division of Marboro Books Corporation,
by arrangement with
Charles Scribner's Sons Reference Books,
an imprint of Macmillan Publishing Co.
1991 Dorset Press

ISBN 0-88029-706-9

Printed in the United States of America
M 9 8 7 6 5 4 3 2 1

PREFACE

IN RECENT centuries the greatest political factor in the modern world has been the British Empire. This is particularly true of the last hundred and fifty years. It is not merely that the Empire rules a quarter of the globe territorially, and a quarter—500,000,000—of its inhabitants. Its trade and financial influences have been equally important, and above all its political. "The Mother of Parliaments" in London has brought into being the free governments in all quarters of the earth which now make up the British Commonwealth of Nations. Its story, with all its shadows, is the story of the steadily increasing freedom of the individual citizen and of the free human spirit.

The volume now presented opens with the defeat of the Empire against a European world in arms, and the loss of the colonies which have since grown into the United States of America. The loss seemed overwhelming but from apparent ruin the British built up a still greater empire, the greatest the world has ever seen.

After the losses, the frivolities and scandals of the earlier Hanoverian rulers, there suddenly and unexpectedly rose the sun of the Victorian Era, the greatest in English history next to the Elizabethan. A succession of statesmen, such as Lord Palmerston, Lord Grey, Russell, Disraeli, Gladstone, Salisbury and others, not only brought Britain to her highest pinnacle of power and prestige, but nursed the old liberties into the forms of modern democracy. Crisis after crisis, national and international, arose and were met in the age-old muddling way but conquered in the end.

The scenes and actors constantly shift. France, with Napoleon at its head, was the first great menace to liberty in the period. In the crisis of the world today, with its ruthless dictatorships, no previous period offers a closer parallel or a more interesting comparison than the Napoleonic. For twenty years Britain fought on, more than once deserted by every Continental Ally, until at long last the would-be Dictator of Europe was carried to life exile on a British battleship.

Problems at home called for revolution but there was none. Instead, in British ways, there were compromise, conciliation, and such great Reform Bills as those of 1832 and 1867, with all the social legislation which followed. Overseas, the first empire had been lost largely because of inflexible ideas as to government. There followed a long period of comparative indifference to overseas possessions, together with the ferment of the new ideas of imperial reformers. In the latter part of the nineteenth century came the race for world empire which can be compared only with that of the Elizabethan period of expansion of European populations and energies. From that developed the tensions which led to the World War and again to the war of today.

At present, the Empire is once more facing fearful odds, perhaps the greatest crisis in its, and our, history. What has happened in the conquests made by Germany and Russia in the past year or so, as well as the crushing of freedom of thought and speech in their own lands for some years, shows all too well what would happen to the world if the ambitions of Hitler and Stalin could be achieved. Aided by France, the one great opponent to the coming of a new Dark Age to the soul and mind of man is the British Empire. Our own fate is more at stake than many realize. The Hitler-Stalin conquests mean more than mere annexations of territory and population in the old sense. They mean the wiping out of freedom and the type of western civilization which Europe and America have slowly achieved during centuries.

We in America were not only a part of the British Empire for a longer period than we have been independent, but since achieving independence our history touches that of the Empire at almost every point, decade by decade. The greatest Dominion in the Empire is our next-door neighbor, our younger sister with whom we divide almost the whole of the North American continent in friendliness and without a dollar spent for defense along a boundary of some 5000 miles.

Whatever may be the feelings of any individual reader, we are linked to the future of the Empire as to that of no other nation. Its history and destiny have a deeply intimate relation to ourselves. If, in a world tossing on the wild waves of chaos, and in which distance no longer means safety, we ever need a friend whose ideals of life and liberty agree with ours, whom among the great powers can we turn to with more understanding or more hope of being understood?

In the writing of this volume I have been especially indebted to the courteous help of Doctor Will D. Howe of Charles Scribner's Sons and Mr. William G. Wilbur of Columbia University for reading the manuscript and the proof and offering valuable suggestions, although obviously they are not responsible for any errors of fact or judgment, which are my own.

J. T. A.

Southport, Connecticut,
March 1, 1940.

CONTENTS

CONTENTS

CONTENTS

THE BRITISH EMPIRE
1784—1939

CHAPTER I

THE NEW ERA

I. A Fresh Start

THE YEAR 1783 was one of gloom in Great Britain. She had just emerged from a long and exhausting war against a world in arms against her. The independence of the United States had had to be acknowledged and the work of some two centuries of exploration and colonization appeared to have been largely lost. Between the as yet unappreciated colony of Canada, with its almost unknown territory and resources, and the remaining islands in the West Indies, she had lost all her possessions on the Atlantic seaboard, with over 3,000,000 of citizens and lucrative markets. The nation, bitter and anxious, could not foresee that in the next century a new Empire would be formed which would rise to the pinnacle of power, wealth and prestige.

But if there is one lesson which the two millenniums of British history teach, it is that the race is never so great as in defeat and when all seems lost. There is an old saying, which has been proved again and again, that England loses all battles but the last one. Tenacity, courage, the refusal to admit defeat have somehow always pulled her through. Again and again she has faced apparent extinction,—at the hands of the Saxons and Danes, of William the Norman, of empires such as those of Spain, of Louis XIV, of Napoleon, of Germany,—but if she has not had the imagination to prepare for a crisis, neither has she had the imagination to admit defeat. If she has never yet suffered a permanent one, it may well be because of this lack and of the belief, sometimes so annoying to foreigners, in her own superiority. This volume begins with a heavy loss and ends with the threat of another mighty struggle; but it also ends with the British Empire, with its ownership of a quarter of the globe and with 500,000,000 citizens, as still the greatest political factor that the world has ever known.

At the beginning of the period which this book covers, Great Britain, like the rest of the world, was in the grip of forces it could neither recognize nor understand but which were to push the human race along the most bewildering and fantastic stretch of road it has ever encountered in its long journey. The changes which will have to be briefly chronicled in the next century and a half were to prove greater for the lives of ordinary British people than all those of the twenty centuries before. Perhaps, in the turmoil following the peace, the dilettante Horace Walpole showed more prescience than any of the statesmen when he wrote that, when asked " 'How all this would end?,' I answered 'How will it begin?' " There was indeed much beginning which would eventually affect the inhabitants of the entire globe in every quarter, and which has brought us of this generation to possibly the greatest crisis in the history of mankind.

Britain, which, like a wounded lion with a great gash in its side, faced the world and the future, was numerically inferior to many of its continental neighbors. Its population even at the opening of the nineteenth century, when the first official census was taken in 1801, was approximately that of Italy and considerably less than those of Russia or France. One of the striking features of the period of this chapter, however, was the great increase in the fifty years preceding our first accurate statistics. A proposal to enumerate the people in 1753 had been objected to in Parliament as "totally subversive of the last remains of English liberty" and as demonstrating the weakness of the nation to its enemies. However, in the second half of the century population rose from 6,500,000 to over 8,000,000.

This increase, which marked the beginning of the "rise of the masses," has no undisputed explanation. The industrial revolution

2

had not yet developed into its later phase, and the increases were not confined in any case to England but were almost equally notable in Ireland and on the Continent. This was probably due, not to many of the causes which have been suggested, but largely to the decrease in infant mortality owing to improvement in midwifery and medical science in general. The latter, combined with better sanitation and living conditions, tended also to prolong the life of adults. The fact, however, that by 1801 (eleven years, it may be noted, after the first official census was taken in the United States) the population of the British Isles had risen with amazing rapidity to around 15,000,000, is of very considerable influence in our story. It affected economic, political and class thinking to a marked degree. Moreover, in considering the evils of the machine age it must be recalled that with the increasing population trend, which began before the real industrial revolution, it would have been impossible to support the new masses without the employment, transportation and other effects of the machine on society, evil as many of the aspects of the new social order were to be.

Before considering the life of this population more in detail, we may note that by the time we have now reached, Britain, in spite of its small territory, its American losses, and its inferiority in numbers, held one trump card. By changes in world trade, England had become the central focus of the most important maritime routes for Europe, America and the Far East. If these could be held by sea power, and if England's nascent manufactures could surpass those of the European powers, she would control the markets of the world and outstrip every competitor for wealth and power. Manufactures, trade markets, lordship of the seas,—those were to be the weapons with which Britain was to win intoxicating success out of humiliating defeat.

England was still aristocratic, with power for the most part in the hands of the upper classes as represented by the nobility, the county families, the squires, clergy and justices of the peace. These controlled not only the making but the administration of the laws, which naturally were almost wholly, and often cruelly, in their own favor. For these and the increasing number of new rich who were allied with them, England, if not the best of all possible worlds, was an exceedingly comfortable one and one in which the ruling classes dreaded to see any change made.

Change, however, although unrecognized by them, was at work, and the beginning of the cleavage into "two Englands," that of the rich and that of the landless poor, had begun. Many factors, closely related, were combining to bring it about. The nation was still 80 per cent agricultural, with London as its one great city, the minor provincial towns lagging far behind. The English village of the old days was not a mere collection of farms but supported a life largely communal and of varied occupations.

Two forces, one realized and the other not, were destined to undermine this ancient rural society. On the one hand, practically all the leaders in agricultural improvement believed enclosures and the private ownership of the land, in large or small amounts, to be essential if farming methods were to be bettered and an increased food supply raised for the increasing population. Although Malthus did not publish his famous *Essay on Population* until 1798, the desire for improvement and the fear of dearth had long been at work. It was true that the old form of communal farming did prevent experimentation and even the use of tools and methods already known. One stubborn or ignorant farmer could block any change, and without enclosures it was impossible to improve the breed of animals or get the best results from the soil.

However, when the change from common to enclosed lands did occur on a large scale there were effects which the reformers had not anticipated. The old method had been wasteful and unprogressive but had provided reasonable security. Under the new system, to a considerable extent, among the lesser farmers there were those who came into possession of bits of land too small to farm properly or who had no capital or were lazy or incompetent. Many, too, were tempted to sell their lands for money soon spent. The extent of the change is indicated by the fact that, although from 1710 to 1760 only 300,000 acres had been enclosed, over 7,000,000 were taken over between the latter date and 1843. Moreover, there was a steady movement from small to large farms, one observer

4

noting in a Dorsetshire village only two farms where twenty years before there had been thirty.

The enormous increase in enclosures, particularly after 1793, was due to both economic and psychological factors. In the famine and war years agricultural produce, particularly wheat, which sold above 126 shillings by 1812, added immensely to the profits of landlords and progressive farmers. The latter found themselves hampered by the old communal system, which prevented them from introducing new ideas and methods unless they could educate and carry with them all their more conservative and stubborn neighbors. They therefore naturally aligned themselves with the enclosure movement so that they might be free to do as they would on their own lands without the need of consultation with those who were not willing to move with the times.

In spite of this, the concentration of landholdings did not in this period go nearly as far as in Ireland or Scotland, and as late as 1851 two-thirds of all the farms in England and even Scotland were less than a hundred acres in extent. Nevertheless, in one way and another a considerable part of the old farming population found themselves worse off, though production for the land as a whole increased. Many became landless and went to swell the ranks of the agricultural labor class as well as the urban population which was to be available for the new industries being developed.

II. The Industrial Revolution

Another factor of an unconscious and impersonal sort was also at work to reduce the comfort and security of the rural population, the so-called Industrial Revolution, which was deeply to affect not only the countryside but towns as well. It is impossible either to define the term or date the movement precisely. Arnold Toynbee found its essence to be "the substitution of competition for the medieval regulations which had previously controlled the production and distribution of wealth." In that aspect we find one of its first great landmarks in the appearance of Adam Smith's *Wealth of Nations*, published in 1776, which advocated freedom in industrial and commercial life instead of regulation or restriction. The book was for long to be of immense influence on the thought of both statesmen and business men and helped to give unbridled scope, in the popular doctrine of *laissez faire*, to the results of the Industrial Revolution in its more usual sense.

What is generally meant by it is the whole complex of changes which have occurred from the inauguration of the machine age. We may date it 1760–1800 or 1760–1840, but, although it has as yet far from worked itself out and some of the new inventions date from earlier in the eighteenth century, the above years mark more or less accurately the overthrow of the old order of life which, with variations, the civilized world had known almost from the first, and the harsh beginning of that new order in which we are still living.

We usually think of the introduction of machinery as the work of certain inventors, but in fact many of these were merely adapting principles long known but which had not been worked out in practical form because the time had not come when they would have any commercial use or value. Many things combined toward the end of the eighteenth century to create a demand for machinery. A larger production than the old hand methods had permitted would have been of no use unless there had also been larger markets, nor would markets have availed unless there were means of transport. Capital was also required, and this was being provided by the introduction of modern banking and the increased use of the corporation, although the latter, as yet, was more notable in the fields of finance, insurance and transportation than in the manufacturing companies which were largely effecting the industrial revolution but which still remained chiefly individualistic. England led the world in the vast transformation then going on in the world not because of her inventions, but the inventions came because she had the markets, capital and raw materials, notably coal and iron, which made new forms of production profitable.

Before considering these points we may note one to which historians have usually paid no attention. If, in spite of known scientific facts and principles from which practical inventions would naturally follow when the time was ripe, machines had to await

6

specific commercial needs, they had also to await another condition. That was the invention and production of the *machine tools* with which large machines could be made. For example, Watt so improved the idea of the steam engine as to make it an assured commercial success provided it could be manufactured. But it could not be, because of lack of tools. These were incredibly crude during most of the eighteenth century, and such as there were were almost wholly for working in wood.

The new machinery demanded tools for working iron and other metals, and Watt's engine could not be built because there was no tool which could bore accurately a cylinder six inches in diameter and two feet long. It was more than ten years before the proper tools could be devised and made so as to build the engine which Watt had conceived of in 1765. The story of the advent of the machine age is usually told in terms of the great inventors, Watt, Arkwright, Hargreaves, Crompton and others, but the inventions of these men would have been of no use had it not been for another group of great men, the tool builders who made the machines possible, and whose names are almost unknown to history, Joseph Bramah, Sir Samuel Bentham, Henry Maudsley (greatest of all), and many more.[1] For some reason, during the period of this chapter and up to about 1850 the English, and in the later portion the Americans, were the finest tool makers in the world. Other nations had ideas, but they could not apply them.

The industry which led in the revolution was the textile and particularly cotton. In 1764 Hargreaves invented the spinning-jenny, in which eight spindles were combined, thus increasing the output of one operator. Five years later Arkwright invented the water-frame, by which water power instead of human labor could be used in the spinning. By 1793, in America, Eli Whitney, with his cotton gin, started the production of American cotton on its amazing upward course. The supply of raw material increased annually by leaps, and at the same time the Far East, particularly England's Indian Empire, afforded an almost illimitable market for manufactured cotton goods. It is an example of how many fac-

[1] *Vide*, Joseph W. Roe, *English and American Tool Builders*, New York, 1926, who has made this field of history practically his own.

tors, including England's insular position, all combined at about the same time to make machinery both necessary and profitable.

Again, the increased demand for iron for machinery and other purposes came at just the period when the wood supply of England, which had been used in the iron works for fuel, was giving out. About 1783, under pressure of this situation, two men almost simultaneously discovered that coal could be treated somewhat as the charcoal makers had treated wood. The great significance of the coking of coal lay in its use for the smelting of iron, thus utilizing two of England's greatest natural resources of the greatest importance in the transition to the machine and factory age. The rapid advance of both the coal and iron industries caused a demand for better transportation of heavy material, and the great era of canal building began. Better internal transport combined with control of the sea routes helped to give England her start on the new path. We cannot recite further in detail how one thing led to another and how all the factors combined soon made England the "work-shop of the world," but must return to the effect on the people of the great change which began toward the end of the eighteenth century.

Going back to the major part of the population, the agricultural, we may note that it was profoundly affected not only by the machine as such, but also by the shifts in industries. The woolen industry over a large part of England had given part time employment to the small farmer with his wife and children within their own homes. The new cotton industry, however, was based on machinery and non-human power. Instead of scattering the work in various stages among people in their farm homes, many of whom were in fact proprietors in a small way in their particular branch of the industry, the cotton trade called for factories and concentration of population near them. The workers ceased to be proprietors and owners of homes, and became mere wage earners in rented rooms.

During the French wars wages and the cost of living were to become almost hopelessly out of balance, and, as Parliament would take no action, efforts at amelioration of the situation were left to the local authorities. In the eighteenth century government by Parliament was not only corrupt and careless of the needs of the working class but it was also clumsy, and it was not until well into the next century that it received that overhauling of methods which was to enable it to function under the new social and economic conditions that were developing. It was still largely Tudor machinery trying to operate under conditions very different from those of Tudor days. The theory of a state-regulated wage, for example, was a hoary idea in English life, running far back of the famous Statute of Laborers under Elizabeth, but Parliament, coming more and more under the influence of the doctrine of *laissez faire*, was to decline at the end of the eighteenth century to meddle with the relations between employer and employed, though the old statutes were still nominally in effect.

The local powers, as represented by the Justices of the Peace, were willing to try to help the agricultural laborers, but unfortunately adopted a wrong method which was to have disastrous results. At a meeting of the Justices of Berkshire at Speenhamland in 1795 they set a scale of wages which were to rise and fall with the price of corn [wheat]. Although they recommended that employers raise wages in accordance with the plan, they also ruled that if the laborer did not receive the agreed amount he should be given the difference from the parish funds, provided that he should first be declared a pauper. As should have been foreseen, employers took advantage of their opportunity and, instead of raising wages, they allowed the parishes to take up the slack, with the result that a large part of the rural population sank to the status of paupers in order to live. As a consequence there was a distinct lowering of their morale. In spite of increase of local taxes, the system was popular with employers. Not only did it stave off the revolution on the part of the laboring class feared by many, but the rise in profits and rents more than covered the rise in taxes. Within a generation the system had spread over practically every county in England and Wales at the cost of much suffering and loss of self-respect on the part of the honest laboring poor.

The full effects of all these forces were not felt until after 1815

9

and the end of the Napoleonic wars, but the process was beginning in the period of this chapter, and two things, the increase in population and the factory, began to show their evil results almost at once. When, in the woolen industry, the work was done in their own homes by a considerable part of the workers there was not that bogey of modern industrialism, the "overhead" cost. But when factories were built and machinery installed there was a heavy investment, and the failure to earn interest on it might spell bankruptcy for the owner who had invested his own or borrowed capital.

Under the old system of cottage industry, risk and profits had been widely distributed in comparatively small shares, but the new system meant concentrated ownership, the possibility of vast wealth for the few, and the reduction of the former independent cottage worker to the position of a mere wage earner dependent on the new factory owner for everything in life. Formerly industrial work in a cottage had been only an adjunct to the food and shelter already assured in countless cases, in spite of much poverty. Now employment and wages, at any level, came to mean for the factory worker life itself on any terms he could make.

The overhead and the desire to get rich quickly by the new methods led most employers, with some notable exceptions, to a ruthless treatment of their labor. In order to use the machines to the utmost of their productive power, labor was speeded up, so that little children were often worked sixteen hours a day, and the prevailing humanitarian minimum was twelve. Had the supply of labor been limited, the position might have been better, but as we have seen at the very beginning of the industrial revolution other forces had been at work to create a surplus labor supply, which was further enlarged by the rapid increase in population. It is true that machine-produced goods quickly fell in price, but the cost of living as a whole did not, largely owing to food cost due to the corn laws and the French wars, of which we shall speak later. Moreover, unjust and overbearing as the old country aristocracy had been, they had, from the long possession of land and relations with tenants, acquired a certain sense of responsibility which was frequently wholly lacking in the new rich of the factory-owning class, who regarded their machines and those who operated them as much the same in the money-making process.

It is impossible accurately to appraise the social conditions of any past period, but, although authorities differ, in general we may say, I think, that in the old England from which we are now passing there had been a closer and more human relation between owners of property or a business, whether between country landlords and tenants who might have lived on their land for generations, or between town tradesmen and the apprentices living in the homes of their masters, than between the new factory owners and the shifting multitude of "hands" whom they might not even know by sight or name. The era of individualism and the cash relationship had begun, for good and evil.

III. THE SOCIAL SCENE

The period of the rapid rise of the large factory towns was still a decade or two ahead, but to get a glimpse of the "two Englands" we may glance at London in this period. The rich and well-to-do were rapidly moving westward from the older portions of the city or building houses facing on the newly developing garden squares. These classes, however, were but a small part of the population, which was about 900,000 in 1801, and we may place the homes of the rest, in a descending economic scale, as on streets, lanes, courts, alleys, yards, and passages.

From novels, diaries, and letters, the home life of the upper classes is fairly well known to every one and, together with the country life of those of the same social grades, usually forms in our minds the picture of Georgian England. We cannot, however, understand either the social or political history of the next century without bringing into the picture the dark shadows of the lives of the poor, and it must be remembered that the wages of what we now call "the white collar class," such as clerks and others, were usually below those of skilled artisans.

In the laboring class of London an entire family commonly occupied only a single room. The poorest lived in dark holes in the cellars; those a little better off in the attics; while those still better off occupied rooms on the first or second floors. Among the poorest, conditions were almost indescribably bad. The several members, sometimes eight or more, of the one-room family would sleep in one bed, the sheets of which, if there were any, would be washed only two or three times a year, and the vermin-infested blankets never. The windows often could not be opened, and the rooms were filled not only with foul air from their unwashed crowded occupants and the cooking but also with the stench from the filthy privies at the bottom of the staircase. Even those who lived on the better floors had to suffer from their fellow-tenants above and below them in the same house. For artisans in the "genteel trades" the standard home was one room, in which frequently the trade was carried on in addition to the life of the family.

There were no cheap means of transportation, and as workmen, therefore, had to live near their work, overcrowding was general. Although we may ascend gradually from the above conditions to those of the comfortably off, we must also descend to yet lower levels for a large part of the population, which lived in the cheapest of lodgings kept by harpies in ruinous old buildings. One of these was a Mrs. Farrell who died in 1765 and was found to have accumulated £6000 by letting out two-penny lodging rooms. In these refuges, and even these were not the lowest, in which a large floating population lived, it was not infrequent to find the bodies of those who had been frozen or starved to death. It is little wonder that under such conditions the working class to a great extent succumbed to the universal plague of gin drinking as the only escape from the intolerable reality of their existence.

We are apt to think of the eighteenth century, in spite of its political favoritism and corruption, as a rather stolid, solid period, but one of its distinct keynotes was uncertainty. Changes in fundamental conditions, such, for example, as we spoke of in agriculture; gambling among the rich; difficulty for the tradesmen in collecting bills; the fear or actuality of unemployment among the poor, all contributed to this uncertainty, and for the debtor there remained only exile or the debtors' prison. Thousands were thrown into these places, such as the Fleet or the King's Bench in London, often with little hope of ever getting out. Sometimes whole families were incarcerated, and children were brought up in them. Here the debtors, honest or fraudulent, and their families had to associate with the vilest of criminals and live among the wildest scenes of debauchery. As late as 1814 it was said that the Fleet was the biggest brothel in the city. Another characteristic of the period was violence, as displayed in looting, rioting, highway robberies and the dangers to be encountered on both country highways and city streets.

We could paint many other black shadows into our picture, but we have said enough to counterbalance the Christmas-card pictures of old Merry England, and it is as easy to overrate the actual human suffering of an earlier period as it is difficult to compare the total of lights and shadows of one period with another. To say this is not to minimize the evils of either past or present, but to point to the fact that not only do ideas and outlooks change, but apparently even the susceptibility to pain and suffering of our nervous systems. It would not only, for example, be considered the height of cruelty today to amputate a man's leg without an anæsthetic, but it may well be questioned whether the man would not actually suffer more than his ancestor of a century ago who had never heard of an anæsthetic, just as we should find it almost intolerably inconvenient to go without many things to which our ancestors never gave a thought because they had never heard of them.

Looking back to the London of the end of the eighteenth century we see its injustices and horrors, but it may well be that those living in it at that time and comparing it with the beginning of the century saw advance. There had, indeed, been progress in many ways, such as water supply, paving, lighting of the streets, with the resultant effect on diminishing street crimes at night, but the greatest advance was in the changed attitude on the part of a large part of the public toward those less fortunate. Modern humanitarianism, as contrasted with medieval charity, was just beginning, and it is through the changed color of the lenses of that movement that we now look back on all past periods, often forgetting, unhistorically, how new these modern humanitarian spectacles are and our increased sensitivity to suffering.

IV. Religion and the Common Man

Another great reform, initiated by an individual about this same time, was that of the prisons. John Howard, who was appointed High Sheriff in Bedfordshire in 1773, was so shocked by the conditions he found in the prisons of his district that for the rest of his life he devoted himself to the study of prisons throughout England and some other countries, and so awoke public opinion that Parliament acted to ameliorate the worst, at least, of the conditions he had discovered and brought to light. As another instance, among many, we may note, in 1787, the formation of the Society for the Abolition of the Slave Trade, for which a large body of private citizens, with William Wilberforce as leader, worked unceasingly until the trade was abolished throughout the Empire twenty years later, a matter of happy augury for all the new possessions which were to become part of the Empire in that century.

One of the most powerful forces operating in English life in this period and which was to bear noble fruit was that of the Evangelical Movement, a recrudescence of that seventeenth-century Puritanism which has always appealed to a large part of the public. Calvinistic in its theology, it differed to some extent from the earlier Wesleyan movement, although it and Methodism had much in common. Both carried religion to the poor, and if the new problems which were to arise from the Industrial Revolution were largely beyond the capacity of Evangelicalism to solve, it did do much to foster, among the upper, the middle and the élite of the working classes, a sense of social duty. To us in this day, that sense may savor of too much complacency and smugness with regard to a social order in which all were expected to know their places and keep them. However, like all Puritan movements, it weighted the scales heavily on the side of personal responsibility, independence and social reform. Also, especially among the workers and lower middle class, it had great influence in lessening violence, sudden changes and the tendency toward revolution. To it was due in no small degree the improved morality of public life and even the development of the Civil Service which were to come with the Victorian era.

These movements got under way as the Industrial Revolution was beginning to change society, but, as we shall see, both were retarded by events across the Channel with which England had nothing to do but the effects of which were profoundly disastrous for her. Before the hurricane of the French Revolution left its traces on all Europe there had been for some decades much reforming zeal. In striking similarity to today, however, there were two theories of the state. Everywhere on the Continent the theory practised was that of despotism, benevolent or otherwise. Reforms in many countries were being enacted, but in all cases they were accomplished by enlightened acts of despots, such as Frederick the Great, Catherine II of Russia and others, and not through any organs of popular opinion. Indeed, the peoples were not supposed to be capable of judging what was for their own good, and for that reason and because one-man government was considered the only possible efficient method, the despots flourished everywhere except in the British Empire. It had been the fear that in trying Bolingbroke's experiment of a Patriot King, George III might extend the Continental system of despotism to his own realms, which had accounted for much of the discontent at home and the revolt of America.

The attempt had not succeeded, thanks to public opinion and the individualism of both those who seceded and those who remained within the Empire. It is too soon to speak of democracy in Britain, but there was much of the democratic process at work, though in view of the disorderly elections, the squabblings of party, and the recent loss of the American colonies, that process might seem to many clumsy and inefficient as contrasted with the smoother working of the neighboring despotisms. It is not without its reassurance to us today, however, to recall that in a few decades most of these despotisms were overturned and their efforts even at reform proved unavailing, while the clumsy popular government of Britain was to prove the enduring victor.

In spite of all the evils of the unreformed Parliament, there was such a thing in England as public opinion, which the Tudors had wisely known and as George III found out. Moreover, there was extreme individualism, a sense of personal independence, and a theory of the state at the opposite pole from that held by the despots. Even if few of the English and scarcely any of the Scots at this time could vote, the state was felt to be in a real sense a *commonweal* in the old English meaning of the word. This was to be a matter of prime importance when the Second Empire was to be established as the *Commonwealth* of British Nations.

The impassable gulf which separated the British idea of popular government from that of the despots, as it still divides the democracies from the dictatorships, was implicit in the pamphlet, *Fragment on Government*, published by Jeremy Bentham in 1776, though the years of his wider influence came later. In this, however, he outlined his thesis that the end of society was "the greatest happiness of the greatest number" with the corollary that "every man is the best judge of his own happiness." This may well be questioned, but if accepted by democracy, it is evident that citizens cannot find happiness in having some one person decide what is best for them, and that they will insist sooner or later on having a voice in their own welfare as they see it. Like the Declaration of Independence, it was a call to men to be free and to make the most of themselves as individuals.

In the decades of reform which we are noting in this chapter we may easily discern the difference between Britain and the Continent. On the latter, reforms were by edict of the despots. In Britain they were the work of innumerable individuals. For example, the movement for the education of poor children working in factories was started by Robert Raikes of Gloucester. As the only free day in the week for the children was Sunday, the schools were called Sunday Schools, though not then devoted to religious education but mostly to reading and writing. The work was soon taken up by the various religious bodies, which in time opened schools for other children on week-days, and the whole vast system which in time grew up was characteristically British. It started with a private individual, appealed to the public and was for long carried on without government aid or control.

In the years before the French Revolution, in spite of the dark shadows, a few of which we have suggested, we can feel fresh winds blowing, and if it had not been for that cataclysm, the history of England and the Empire might have been quite different. The Revolution, in fact, did not come, as is often considered, at the end of an intolerable period. Reform had been in the air for many years both on the Continent and Britain. It had been the Tory Parliament of Lord North which had carried out Howard's prison reforms and, in spite of the ghastly game laws and other blots or blind spots in the English social legislation and outlook, there was a growing sense of social responsibility and of tolerance, as witnessed by the Act of 1779 which released Nonconformist ministers from subscribing to the Thirty-nine Articles of the established Church.

The laboring class, for the most part, looked backward to their former condition as the promised land, and dreamed of a combination of agricultural and industrial work as still possible rather than of combining to better the new and inevitable situation. There was, however, a growing stirring of thought among them, and one, Thomas Spence, a workman of Newcastle, even preached nationalization of all land, though Socialism was as yet an unknown word. Across the Tweed, Robert Burns was writing his songs of lowly life and democracy, and many who probably never read them would have recognized their ideas as their own.

> A prince can mak' a belted knight,
> A marquis, duke, and a' that!
> But an honest man's aboon his might:
> Guid faith, he mauna fa' that.
> For a' that an' a' that,
> Their dignities an' a' that,
> The pith o' sense an' pride of worth
> Are higher rank than a' that . . .
>
> For a' that an' a' that,
> It's comin' yet for a' that,
> That man to man the world o'er
> Shall brithers be for a' that.

The upper classes were not yet alarmed and were willing to go some way toward reforms. In England, if the representation in Parliament was fantastic in its unfairness to much of the population, and if most of the boroughs were "rotten" and in control of a few of the great families, there were some that were not, and there were also London and Westminster, with their democratic franchise, and the counties, in which all who owned land to the value of forty shillings a year could vote. If there was no equality of any sort between classes, there was a certain hilarious friendliness at elections and on other occasions, and the nation, if stratified socially, was nevertheless unified in an odd fashion which only England has been able to achieve. Even with all the yet unrealized problems of the industrial revolution and of the new wealth and the ways in which it was to be made, the situation might have been worked out. At this critical moment came the terrifying eruption of the volcano which France had become.

CHAPTER II

THE EMPIRE AND THE FRENCH REVOLUTION

I. PITT AND FOX

FOR FORTY-ODD YEARS after the death of Queen Anne, the Tories had been excluded from power, and the Whig Party, which meant the great Whig families with their adherents among the Dissenters and business class, had had control of the government. During the deadly struggle of the Seven Years' War, they had been forced to compromise with the elder Pitt, who alone could snatch victory from the dreaded defeat, but when George III came to the throne in 1760 he had decided to rid himself of the Great Commoner and control the government himself as "Patriot King." For the next twenty years or so, as soon as Pitt, who had become the Earl of Chatham, could be dismissed, the monarch employed every means of bribery and corruption, and England was ruled by the "King's Friends."

After the American victory at Yorktown, however, the Whigs had to be called back, led by Rockingham and much chastened by their years in the political wilderness. Nevertheless, the King continued to intrigue in the hope of getting his power back, and, having tried to split the Whigs by favoring Shelburne against Rockingham, he made him Prime Minister on Rockingham's death. Although Shelburne made peace with Britain's enemies, he was unfitted by temperament and abilities for his post, and on his accepting it, Burke, Fox and most of the leading Whigs resigned. In spite of his still unrivalled oratory, the influence of Burke was beginning to decline, and although he had stood forth as the champion of liberty for America, Ireland and India, he was ere long to show the worst side of his nature in the impeachment proceedings against Warren Hastings and in his intense reaction against everything, good and bad alike, which the French Revolution signified to him. It was even to be said that his noble intellect, one of the greatest England had produced, was decaying.

On the other hand, Fox, in spite of his gambling and other notorious faults, was the most popular man in his party, and rightly so. As Burke, of humble origin, was to become more and more reactionary, Fox, the aristocrat, was to become more and more the defender of liberty and reform. Although he was to blunder badly, England owes a great debt to Fox in that he, almost alone with young Grey, kept a section of the Whig Party attached to the liberal principles which were eventually to make Parliamentary reform possible in 1832. Fox made an irretrievable mistake, however, when Shelburne was forced to resign. No leader had a majority, but Fox could control 90 votes in the Commons, and Lord North 120. In view of the bitter attacks on North made by Fox during the American War a coalition between them seemed incredible. Nevertheless it was entered into, and the King had to accept the new Ministry. George III never forgave North for what he considered his lack of gratitude, and Fox never fully regained the confidence of the people for what they considered his lack of principles.

If Fox had honestly believed that his action was the only way to prevent the Crown from regaining undue power, he was to be disappointed, for the new government accomplished little before its unlamented fall a few months later. The King, after straining his prerogative in plotting to defeat his Ministers in the House of Lords on Fox's India Bill, dismissed them at the end of 1783, and appointed the younger Pitt,—then only twenty-five years old,—as Prime Minister. Young as he was, he had already, at twenty-three, served as Chancellor of the Exchequer under Shelburne, and not only had the glamor of his father's great name but was also the hope of the reformers. He was a friend and admirer of Wilberforce and united with him in his attack on the slave trade. He had twice introduced in Parliament measures for the reform of the franchise, which the Coalition Ministry had refused to consider.

He was willing, however, to accept the old Tory doctrine that Ministers could be appointed by the King and not the House of Commons, and he therefore agreed to head a government which had an overwhelming majority against it in the House. Over and over he was outvoted on measures but with decreasing majorities, and remained in office, trusting to the steady decline in popularity of the Coalition to allow him in time to risk a general election. This he did, in April, 1784, when the Coalition forces were completely routed at the polls. The victory which was his might have been Fox's had that statesman been willing to go to the country the year before instead of making the unholy alliance with North. Fox was to remain thereafter a lonely political figure, while Pitt came to believe that he himself alone could save the country and that he must retain power at any cost.

In 1785 Pitt introduced a bill for the purpose of doing away with seventy-seven seats privately owned by paying £1,000,000 for them, and if he and Fox could only have worked together, the half century of the growing pains of political and industrial revolution might have been much ameliorated by a gradual reform of representation. As it was, the bill was defeated, and Pitt never tried again. He had not only striven for Parliamentary reform and that of the slave trade but had also showed how alive he was to the new currents of thought by his efforts to put into effect the doctrine of Adam Smith.

His handling of the government finances was sound, and in his India Bill, which we shall note later, he had to a considerable extent taken appointments, except that of Governor-General, out of politics, thus reducing still further, in line with Burke's bill, the amount of corrupt political management. He had the public behind him, and, except for a brief time when the King had another attack of insanity and it was feared the Prince of Wales might have to become Regent (with the certainty of his replacing Pitt by Fox), his hold on power seemed unquestioned in spite of occasional adverse votes in the Commons. It looked as though, even with the customary English slowness and dislike of anything new, the changes necessary to meet altered social and economic facts might be made in usual British fashion. To a large extent Pitt was supported by the new manufacturing class against the landed Whig families, and with his own desire for reform, it seemed as if he might be the man to lead the nation over the great divide between the old order and the approaching one.

As we have said, England could by no stretch of the term be considered democratic in 1789. Yet a people is likely to remain satisfied, or at least not to resort to violent revolution, if it feels that the privileged classes are doing something for the common welfare, unless living conditions become intolerable. This is a point to be borne in mind today by any nation which wishes to maintain private liberty and property. In general, in the England of this period, though there was ample selfishness among the privileged classes, whether landed aristocrat or new rich in manufacturing, there was also ample work being done by them for the nation. In England, almost alone in that day, public service, whether local or national, had become traditional among the upper classes. If they were rewarded with honors, titles and wealth, they at least did something for them. Even the new business class, harsh as it was in its dealings with the new working class, was considered to be adding to the wealth and so to the power and prestige of the nation. Not a little of England's greatness and successful leadership in the past has been due to her resources of wealth which could be used to subsidize allies or wear out enemies.

II. The Upheaval in France

In France, on the other hand, the privileged had long since ceased to be useful. The people suffered from the extortions of the landed *seigneurs* and the higher clergy with no compensating advantage. At last the social storm broke, and the weak though well-meaning King, Louis XVI, was unable to rule or guide it. When the States-General was called to meet in 1789 for the first time in 175 years, it was to raise money and not to solve the problems of the nation. When the people, who had demanded a constitution, realized this, the mob rose in Paris and captured the great prison fortress of the Bastille, July 14, and through the country districts the peasants burned and sacked the homes of the *seigneurs*. The following month, under pressure, the new National Assembly voted away all the special privileges of the clergy and nobility.

In the autumn the mob marched on Versailles, captured the King and carried him off to Paris, depriving him of all real power in the new doctrinaire constitution now drawn up. On the Continent these events presaged to even the most reforming of the despots the overthrow of the very foundations of social order. In England, however, where the people had always prided themselves on their liberty and, in spite of the misery of many of them, had looked down on the half-starved French, the early stage of the fateful movement now under way was regarded as a sort of counterpart to their own "glorious revolution of 1688." Fox hailed the fall of the Bastille as the greatest and best event in the history of the world. Burke, on the other hand, and he drew Pitt with him to a great extent, was filled with terror at the possible anarchy, which he rightly foresaw. In spite of the magnificent service he had rendered to liberty in the past, he was now completely blind to the causes of the catastrophe. In 1790, in his long pamphlet, *Reflections on the French Revolution*, the publication of which has been called an event equal in importance to the fall of the Bastille itself, he set forth for all time, in his unrivalled rhetoric, the philosophical foundations of the ultra-conservative point of view.

In the extraordinary year of 1776, which had seen the issuance of the Declaration of Independence and the publication of Adam Smith's *Wealth of Nations* as well as Bentham's *Fragment on Government*, Gibbon had printed the first volume of his *Decline and Fall of the Roman Empire*. In that and the succeeding volumes of his immortal work, Gibbon had for the first time established the doctrine of society as a growing and developing organism and of history as not merely a series of disjointed events but as a flowing stream in which past, present and future are inevitably and inextricably linked together. Burke also had this historic sense to the full, and realized that the life and institutions of a nation cannot be suddenly severed from the past; in a word, that the attempt to add an *r* to evolution is fatal to orderly and perhaps even lasting progress. We may note, for example, that the success of the constitution which the revolted American colonies at last framed for themselves as a nation has been due to the fact that, with one or two exceptions, there is nothing in it which the people had not been accustomed to in their earlier colonial relations with England and in their local charters and constitutions. The one attempt which England herself had made to order all things new, under Cromwell, had ended in disaster and a return to the old forms, reformed.

The truth of this lent persuasive strength to Burke's pamphlet, which was marred on the other hand by his unwarranted defense of the old order in France and by the vindictiveness with which the defender of liberty now appeared to oppose not merely reform but any change whatever. He had not become simply conservative but rigidly and dangerously static. In spite of the soundness of part of his views, the extreme and even cruel position which he assumed toward aspirations for any betterment on the part of the poorer classes called for counter-attack.

Among the first of the pamphlets issued on the other side was Mary Wollstonecraft's *Vindication of the Rights of Man* (1790), but of far greater importance was the *Rights of Man* published in two parts (1791-92), by Thomas Paine, who had been the great pamphleteer of the American Revolution. Although many of the measures advocated by him are on the statute books today, such as free public education, a graduated income tax, old age pensions and others, not only did they seem the extreme of radicalism in his own day, but in demanding the abolition of all hereditary parts of the constitution, such as the House of Lords and the Monarchy itself, he made reform depend on republicanism and almost pure democracy. He may be considered as the founder of the first real movement of radicalism among the working classes, but his book was suppressed by the government, and Paine himself forced to flee to France. If Burke, who with many of the Whigs had joined

Pitt, had appealed to reactionary sentiment with his philosophy, Paine was unwittingly even more instrumental in fostering it by his republicanism. He did not realize how deeply rooted was the British attachment to their institutions, even though many called loudly for reform.

The war of pamphlets, not only the above-named, but many more, set men of all classes thinking, but unfortunately it also drowned them in the passions of fear and hatred. These were largely directed against all who desired change of any kind,—the reformers of all sorts, the Dissenters, the nascent labor leaders, and others. In 1791 a mob in Birmingham sacked the house of the noted scientist, Joseph Priestley, because he was a Unitarian, had worked for the repeal of the religious Test Acts, for Parliamentary Reform, and had approved the early stage of the French movement, though he was neither a radical nor a Republican. The rioters continued to destroy other homes of Dissenters and also Dissenting chapels. Fox and his minority of Whigs, who refused to go over like Burke, to the Tories, kept their heads but had no power. Both government and the nation in general abandoned themselves to panic and repression.

These were increased by the rapid movement of events in France. Many French nobles had fled over the borders, and in 1792 the National Assembly, then under control of the Girondists, declared war against Austria and Prussia. In September a Paris mob stormed the prisons and massacred many of the prisoners, while a little later the French Convention, then in power, condemned the King to death. The French arms had been successful, and the Convention had also offered its help to all nations to destroy feudal rights and proclaim the sovereignty of the people. When on January 21, 1793, the head of Louis was severed by the guillotine, a thrill of horror and fear of the overturn of all civilized society ran over the countries of Europe. With the execution of the Queen in October began the hideous Reign of Terror which lasted for seven months until Robespierre himself went to the scaffold.

Meanwhile a minor reign of terror, cruel but not bloody, had been carried on in Scotland and England. Trials for sedition were held in the former country, under the brutal judge, Lord Braxfield, of people whose only crime had been that of membership in societies for the reform of Parliamentary representation. A young lawyer, Thomas Muir, was sentenced to fourteen years' transportation; Thomas Palmer, a Unitarian minister, to seven; and several others to fourteen each. The fifty or more organizations for Parliamentary reform were totally and ruthlessly crushed out of existence.

In England, in 1792, an organization called "Friends of the People" had been formed by the then Charles Grey, who in 1832 as Lord Grey and Prime Minister was to carry the great Reform Bill. Charles Fox had the courage to join him, ruining his own career in his lifetime but winning his highest place in history. With him went what was left of the Whig Party, and thus was founded what was later to be the Whig-Liberal Party of the next generation. Repudiating Paine and his doctrines, they continued to stand for the reform of Parliament, forlorn as the hope was. Although hated by government, most of their own class, and much of the nation, the "Foxites" from their position could escape persecution where lesser folk could not.

In the middle class, Major Cartwright, Horne Tooke and others revived the moribund "Society for Constitutional Information," and, in 1792, a London shoemaker, Thomas Hardy, organized the first distinctively labor-class political organization, called the "London Corresponding Society" and made up of skilled workmen. It was organized to secure reform, including universal suffrage and annual Parliaments, and was chiefly educational, disavowing any illegal or violent actions. The two societies were in touch with one another, and the movement quickly spread throughout England. The government pretended, and perhaps believed, that preparations were being made for a general uprising and threw Tooke, Hardy and some of the other leaders into jail. Although the jury refused to convict, the societies were practically destroyed because some of the leaders were lost to them, and most of the members were sufficiently frightened to cease their active connections.

In 1794 Pitt secured the suspension of *habeas corpus,* and in the following year the people had an opportunity to express their anger. As the King drove in his coach to open Parliament the starving crowds cried "No Pitt! No War! Bread! Bread! Peace! Peace!", and a stone was thrown at the window of the royal coach. The episode was magnified by Pitt and the reactionaries, and the Prime Minister forced through Parliament two bills, which it was said his father would have cut off his right hand sooner than sign. One of these declared that the writing or speaking against the King's authority was treason, and even the stirring up of hatred against the government or constitution was a misdemeanor. The other forbade all public meetings unless advertised in advance and gave the right to any two justices of the peace to disperse them when held, if considered dangerous.

In the debates on the bills the remark which had perhaps the most influence and most deeply stirred resentment was that of the Bishop of Rochester, who said "he did not know what the mass of the people in any country had to do with the laws but to obey them." Grey, however, opposed the legislation with all his power, and Fox remarked that a man could now be sent to Botany Bay if he suggested that Manchester ought to have as many representatives in Parliament as Old Sarum. When the bills passed, open political discussion died and fear bound all men's tongues. It may be noted that panic was general not in England alone, and the above two bills remind an American of the Alien and Sedition Acts passed by Congress in 1798. If the Congress of republican America could be thus terrified, it is not strange that the wealthy and conservative in England, speaking almost under their breath of the anarchy only a few miles from them over the Channel, should have felt that the end of their own comfortable world might be at hand. Parliament had their support, and in 1799 further declared that all national associations with branches or corresponding with local associations were illegal. The following year it suppressed all forms of Trade Unionism.

Thus almost at the beginning of the industrial revolution and of the twenty years of the greatest armed struggle in Europe until the World War, with the ensuing alteration of social and economic conditions, both the middle and working classes were estopped from securing the desired representation in Parliament or from improving their condition through voluntary organization. The result was to bring on the people misery and suffering which might otherwise have been minimized and to lessen in time the old solidarity of classes.

III. WAR WITH FRANCE

Pitt had desired a policy of peace with France, although he had remonstrated when the French threatened to invade the Dutch Netherlands, England having always refused to allow the coasts of the Low Countries to be under control of any great power. France, having determined on the invasion and having already had a taste of that military success which was to be her ruin for a century or so, settled Pitt's policy for him by declaring war on both Holland and Great Britain in 1793.

Pitt had little of his father's genius for conducting war on the grand scale and also failed to realize that this was the first war not between governments but peoples. The French government was weak, bankrupt and inefficient, but the people were inspired by their new dream of liberty and equality for those of all nations. The heady doctrine to an unforeseen extent offset, for the French themselves and as propaganda in other countries, the lack of the money, resources and strong centralized government which Pitt expected would ruin them in a couple of campaigns. The war, however, which passed through four phases might have destroyed France and long delayed the coming of democracy and nationalism, had it been properly planned and conducted. For the first two years of the struggle Britain had as allies Prussia, Austria, Spain, and Piedmont. Had they struck with all their force directly at Paris against the undisciplined troops of their enemy, they might well have conquered and stamped out the revolution. The failure to do so altered the history of the entire world and, for better and worse, began the unrolling of that scroll of fate which we are today endeavoring to decipher in terror for the future.

Pitt determined to follow the lines laid down by his father, sending few troops to the Continent, subsidizing his allies, and trusting to the navy. He did not, however, carry it out completely or with success. The army was honeycombed with official rottenness, and the force which was sent to Flanders under the Duke of York was defeated. In addition Pitt sent so large a force to the West Indies that in three years, owing to the climate, disease and improper medical treatment and commissariat, 80,000 were dead or rendered unfit for service. This ill-designed if not fatal move was due in part to his wish to save the settlers there from the horrors of slave uprisings but also to the desire to capture additional islands to recoup the British taxpayer for the cost of the war. In the latter respect, at least, it was a short-sighted policy, for the capture of Paris might have saved the cost of twenty years of war instead of two or three. As for the allies, the huge sums given to Prussia in particular were largely spent in conquering Poland instead of France, the former country being divided among Prussia, Austria and Russia with no gain to the British or loss to the French. Prussia withdrew to enjoy her new possessions, and by 1796 only Britain and Austria were left in the coalition to fight the real enemy.

So liberally had Pitt handed money to his allies—£4,000,000 to Austria alone in 1796—that even English resources were strained to the extent that the following year the Bank of England had to suspend gold payments, remaining on a paper basis for the next twenty-four years. In large degree it was the new wealth from trade, markets and manufactures that carried Britain through. So disappointing, however, had been the results of the contest that Pitt actually sued for peace, provided that France would give up her conquests in the Austrian Netherlands and in Italy. Meanwhile France had secured the necessary time to reorganize her army under Carnot, and the rising genius of Napoleon was beginning to shine. The answer to England was the attempted invasion of Ireland by 20,000 French troops, which was only prevented by the storm winds over the Channel, which have so often saved England at moments of crisis but which in our own day no longer afford their boisterous protection.

The year 1797 was one of almost unalloyed gloom. Not only had the Bank of England suspended gold payments, but Spain and Holland had become allies of France while Austria had made her peace. In view of the threat of a combined naval attack against England, Admiral Sir John Jervis decided to anticipate it by one on the Spanish Fleet off Cape St. Vincent in which a decisive victory was won, largely by the genius and intrepidity of Nelson, who turned a possible defeat into victory by disobeying orders. This victory, the one bright spot in the operations of the year, which was darkened also by the conditions in Ireland to which we shall refer later, was followed by mutinies in the fleets at Spithead and on the ships stationed to guard the entrance to the Thames at the Nore. Again Pitt offered to make terms with the French, even agreeing to Austrian cession of her Netherland provinces and to the transfer to France of some of the British West India Islands. On her refusal, Britain found herself facing the world alone.

Meanwhile, Napoleon had become the military leader of France, and was indulging in his first great romantic fantasy, which, like his later one of conquering Russia, was to prove almost a fatal failure. The French had tried to strike a blow at England by way of disaffected Ireland, which was a reasonable enough plan, but now Napoleon, with the dream of Oriental conquest, which has lured so many from Alexander the Great to the Germans in our own century, decided to pass by way of conquest of Egypt to India to take advantage of the situation there, which we shall mention in the next chapter.

In spite of the almost impossible odds against Britain, Pitt had determined again to send a fleet into the Mediterranean, which France was threatening to make a French "lake." With Lord Spencer, who was at the head of the Admiralty, he chose, by stroke of luck or ability in sizing up men, one of the youngest flag-officers in the service, the young Horatio Nelson, to hold the Mediterranean open. Part of the Spanish fleet was still afloat, and the French fleet was supposed to be in Toulon. There was danger in the enterprise and meanwhile Napoleon had sailed with his army. Nelson cruised, uncertain where to find his enemy, and did not do so until Napoleon had landed safely and conquered the lower part of Egypt. Then the British Commander found the French fleet anchored in Aboukir Bay, but it was so near dusk that it was uncertain whether light would last for the lines to form.

The fleet was anchored rather close to shore, and Nelson had no good chart of the harbor. However, he was prepared, though he moved with caution, having that rare ability to realize that "five minutes are at once the most important and the least important of considerations." Before morning practically the entire French fleet had been destroyed or captured, in what the leading naval authority in the world has called "unquestionably the most nearly complete and decisive (victory) ever gained by a British fleet."[1]

The details of the battle belong to the specialist, but we may note a few points. In spite of the harsh and often inhumane treatment of the so-called "lower classes," and, notably in the eighteenth century, the gross corruption in government, the British Empire has been built up and saved, bit by bit and over and over again, by the dogged courage and patriotism of the ordinary man and the brilliant leadership of the extraordinary one. Nelson was one of the latter, but he was sincere in the general order of thanks he issued the day after the battle in expressing appreciation and gratitude to the men of every rank, mentioned by name, in his ships. His men had both the deepest respect and affection for him, as he had also for them. He had been severely wounded in the fight, by a flying piece of iron which cut the skin and flesh off his forehead so it hung down over his face, covering his one good eye, but although he thought he had been mortally wounded, he refused any aid from the surgeon until those waiting ahead of him had had their turn first. Genuinely religious, he ordered a service of thanksgiving to be held the morning after the victory, on the bloodstained decks and amid the confusion of damage on his flagship. Six hundred men took part, and it is said that the French prisoners on board were deeply impressed, not by the service but by the quiet discipline displayed by all, and, as Admiral Mahan has pointed out, nothing could have been better calculated to "facilitate the transfer

[1]Admiral A. T. Mahan, *The Life of Nelson*, 1897, Vol. I, p. 361.

from the excitement of battle to the resumption of daily life." It is an incident and a trait worth noting for our story.

The news of Nelson's victory took two months to reach London, but its effect was far-reaching. Not only was new spirit infused into the British people and government but Austria and Russia joined Britain in a new coalition against France, and the Austrians soon drove a French army across the Rhine and defeated others in two great battles in Italy. Napoleon, meanwhile, had continued his campaign into Syria in spite of the loss of his fleet, but having learned of the changed situation in Europe, he returned to Egypt, abandoned his army, and succeeded in reaching France, almost alone.

The French were not merely discouraged by military disaster but were also tired of the disorder and anarchy which the Directory had shown itself incapable of controlling. The revolution had been accomplished but without the replacing of the old government by any strong and efficient new one. The situation was ripe for a dictator, and Napoleon met with practically no opposition when he declared himself First Consul and took all power into his own hands. The overturn of the old régime in 1789 had been justified, but the French had tried to sever the new society wholly from the old by a river of blood. As we have pointed out, no such complete severance is possible, and France and the world were to pay the penalty for the renewed experiment.

France needed a master and had found him. He was more than merely one of the greatest military geniuses of all time. He was also an organizer of the first rank, and was to reorganize French law, government and society into the form which, fundamentally, they have ever since retained. In view of the interest and ability which he showed in such tasks, the year 1799 offers one of the fascinating "ifs" in history, for one of his first acts after assuming supreme power was to offer peace to England, which was refused with scorn. As after the ensuing military operations, which included the almost immediate reconquest of Italy and the great victory of Hohenlinden, he carried out no great military operations outside the frontiers of the enlarged France for five years, it might have been that he would have devoted himself to the consolidation of his own power and that of France inside her new boundaries, though such is not the way of dictators. In any case, he had destroyed the second coalition, and Austria and Russia retired to leave Britain again alone.

She was worse than alone, for Napoleon's diplomacy, added to the ambitions and vagaries of the madman, Paul, who was Czar of Russia, built up an alliance against England of Russia, Prussia, Sweden and Denmark in a League of Armed Neutrality. Although each country had its separate motives and ambitions, the ostensible object of the League was to protest by force of arms against the claim of England to search neutral vessels for contraband. The peculiar nature of the British Empire as one scattered overseas, as well as her preference to fight on sea rather than on land, has always brought this question to the fore when England has been hard pressed. Never finally settled, it was temporarily determined in this case when Nelson, second in command under the incompetent Admiral Sir Hyde Parker, captured the Danish fleet in spite of the protection of the guns of Copenhagen. Although these were finally silenced by Nelson's ships, it was against the orders of the timorous Parker, who had signalled to Nelson to withdraw, and it was on this occasion that the well-known incident occurred of Nelson putting his telescope to his blind eye and declaring that he could see no signal flying.

Meanwhile, owing to events in Ireland, Pitt had been forced to resign in 1801, and the mediocre Henry Addington had become Prime Minister. A year later he succeeded in signing the peace treaty with France which the people had long demanded. Pitt's policies, in spite of the genius of Nelson, had led nowhere and there seemed no prospect of being able to force France to change her government, restore the Bourbons, or give up her conquests. On the other hand, by the Treaty of Amiens, 1802, Britain relinquished her own recent acquisitions beyond the seas, including the Cape of Good Hope to the Dutch, but excluding Ceylon and Trinidad, and also consented to restore Malta to the Knights if there should be a guarantee by the Great Powers. Although she had defeated the French in Egypt, she made no effort to maintain even a sphere of influence there, as that country had as yet no importance as a sea-way to India. All traffic to the Far East rounded the Cape, and the yielding up of that conquest was of far more significance than the ignoring of Egypt.

Thus ended, ingloriously, the first war with France of this period. Britain, proud of her own freedom, had been allied with the despots, who had preferred their own selfish purposes to the success of the general cause. That cause had been obscured by the excesses of the French, who had given themselves over to crime in the name of liberty.

On the other hand, the Revolution and subsequent events, including the Napoleonic wars, were to write indelibly across Europe the idea of "peoples" instead of "governments," and that idea, although it was to foster those of freedom and nationality, was to eventuate in what we have to contend with today, nationality based on force, fed by force, and sucking the lifeblood of citizens by force. The English and American revolutions hewed close to the lines of precedent and human nature, and, in spite of the faults of both the Empire and the United States, individual freedom and self-government have developed and been maintained.

Yet one cannot write up a balance sheet of history and humanity as of a business concern. If the Revolution was followed by a period of reaction and arrested reform, it nevertheless marked the end of an era of many abuses. The claim has been made that for Europe it was more important than the English Revolution of 1688 or the American of 1776. At any rate, it marked the doom of class and privilege and was to prepare in time for the turn to democracy. On the other hand, it was also to prepare the world, only a century or so later, for the philosophy of the conquering State, of totalitarianism and of the dictatorships with their Napoleonic dreams of conquest. If today the world is in the throes of a deadly struggle between democracy and tyranny, the seeds of both were largely sown in the French Revolution and the Napoleonic wars.

CHAPTER III

THE EXPANDING EMPIRE

I. Period of Reaction

IN ENGLAND the reaction to the French Revolution and its excesses had seemed to make impossible any opposition to the repressive acts of Pitt, Burke and the other Tories. For some years toward the end of the century, Fox and his followers absented themselves from Parliament entirely, either from disgust, laziness or the feeling that they could accomplish nothing. This was unfortunate, even though liberalism and reform were stone dead. The debates in the Houses were being reported in the newspapers, and the speeches which the absented members might have made might have been of considerable influence on public opinion at a time when it was sorely in need of liberal guidance.

The period we have been discussing, however, was not wholly discouraging, and we may turn from conditions in Britain and on the Continent to those in other parts of the Empire. If there were failures in some there were successes and the planting of seeds in others, which were eventually to result in a far more powerful aggregation of states than any over which Napoleon was to rule, and, more important than that, were to extend to many parts of the world that rule of law and freedom which may yet prove its salvation, and without which the present outlook would be almost hopeless.

Aside from the reactionary movement at home, England's chief failures were with Ireland, that eternal source of misgovernment and discord, and with the new nation which had developed out of the revolted American colonies.

Pitt before the French Revolution had dreamed of free trade with the Irish and a united nation though under separate Parliaments. Unfortunately under the existing laws, a Parliament as representative of the people was a cruel farce in the neighboring island. Not only were three-quarters of the population, because they were Catholics, excluded from sitting or even voting for members of that body, but private control of seats was even more scandalous than in England. Of the 300 members of the Irish Commons, 200 were actually returned by less than 100 persons who controlled the elections. By the system as it then existed, the Presbyterians of Ulster were as completely excluded from all political life and influence as were the Catholics themselves, and as a repercussion of the French Revolution the Society of United Irishmen was formed by the Presbyterian Wolfe Tone of Belfast.

Only minor concessions had been secured when Pitt badly bungled the situation by appointing Lord Fitzwilliam as Lord-Lieutenant to remedy conditions and then recalling him when he began to do so. Not only was the King opposed to any concessions to the Catholics or Dissenters but so were the English people generally under the reaction from events across the Channel. Grattan's eloquent speeches in favor of Catholic emancipation fell on deaf ears, and the recall of Fitzwilliam seemed to end all hope. Both the religious question and that of the land cried to heaven to be settled with some fairness to the Irish, and when it was obvious that nothing would be done, violence began to spread in the unhappy isle. The United Irishmen, although Presbyterian in origin, joined with the Catholics, and in 1796 invited the French to come over and help them establish an independent republic.

The failure of the expedition has already been noted, and a minor subsequent attempt was no more successful. Conditions, however, were so intolerable that rebellion against England as represented by the local government broke out. Much of the Irish violence was directed against the Protestants, as alien to Irish civilization, and the revolt against England developed into virtually a religious civil war. Hangings, burnings, shootings, the massacre of priests, and brutality of all sorts were the order of the day. The new Lord-Lieutenant, Lord Cornwallis, admitted himself powerless. The situation was intolerable, but the Irish Parliament, though it did not represent the Irish people, could be bought for cash. In 1799 the erstwhile reformer Pitt, through Lord Castlereagh, by the grant of peerages, the dispensing of patronage, and paying £1,-200,000 for the seats of rotten boroughs, secured control and took what he considered the easy way out of the difficulty by abolishing the Irish Parliament entirely, and by an Act of Union (1800) governing both countries through the one Parliament at Westminster.

From January 1, 1801, the "United Kingdom" included Wales, England, Scotland and Ireland, but although Wales, long since, and Scotland more recently, became united in feeling, Ireland was not and may never be. It remains even today England's great failure to govern and to conciliate. It is not possible to say how much of the failure is due to the faults of either nation. One thinks of Lord Cromer's remark that the kind of leadership which England can furnish is successful and magnificent for races of a low order of civilization but decreases as the governed rise in education and intellect. This seems to be borne out in India and elsewhere but is certainly not in Wales or Scotland.

England's complete, terrible and cruel failure in Ireland is an unique problem and could fill a lengthy study by itself. However that may be, the rising sun of a better day which Pitt had attempted to bring to full noon with his free trade between the two countries, had been completely obscured by the storm clouds which were to emit their thunders and lightnings until the very present.

II. ANGLO-AMERICAN RELATIONS

If it is hard to understand the continued misgovernment of Ireland century after century, it is perhaps easier to comprehend the mismanagement in these years of the problem opened by the successful revolt of the American colonies, unfortunate as its effects were for long to be. England at the end of the eighteenth century was not the England of the twentieth, but if she could have shown to the United States a larger degree of the generous spirit displayed toward the Boers in South Africa after the war against them, the friendliness of the two great English-speaking nations would have been less impaired for several generations. It was not so much that the Boers were conquered whereas the Americans, with foreign help, were the conquerors, as that the English had learned much in the intervening century and a quarter.

Not only were the Americans successful rebels, but they were "colonials" and it is a trait of the homekeeping Englishman to consider such as an inferior breed, "above the brute but lower than the angels," that is, somewhere between himself and a complete foreigner. As Nelson wrote after the failure properly to reward him for the Battle of the Nile, "it is a proof how much a battle fought near England is prized to one fought at a great distance." Moreover, for many years after the signing of peace in 1783 and even after the adoption of the American Constitution in 1787, the United States was a weak nation, and Britain knew it. The upperclass Englishman has always been a master of the art of making himself exceedingly irritating and disagreeable socially when he chooses to do so, and many of them chose to do so in personal intercourse in London with such American statesmen as John Adams and Thomas Jefferson, the former first Minister to England, and the latter first Secretary of State.

At the time of the negotiation of the treaty, Adams had wisely pointed out that if America did not carry out every point in it to the crossing of *t*'s and dotting of i's Britain would use the excuse not to carry out her part. In fact, neither nation lived up to the terms. America claimed that the British had carried off slaves and neither returned them nor made compensation. Britain claimed that the Americans were not living up to their obligations with regard to the confiscated property of Loyalists or the payment of private debts, and refused, in turn, to perform her obligation to evacuate the territory and army posts in the Northwest, even locating a new capital of Canada within the American boundary line. She also insisted on the right of search of American vessels to impress as seamen such men as she claimed might be British subjects,

38

a point to which we shall have to return later. And so the quarrel went on, year after year.

By winning independence, the United States had *ipso facto* become a foreign nation. In spite of Adam Smith, the old mercantile theory of empire still dominated most of the thought of the imperial powers. It could not be a matter of complaint that France and Spain soon annulled the special privileges which had been accorded the Americans during the latter phase of the Revolutionary War, or even that England cut off most of the American commerce with her West Indian islands. The Anglo-American situation, however, was peculiar. During the century and a half that the new United States had been part of the Empire, it had been required that most of the American commerce should be only with the Empire. Both the Empire and America had become adjusted to those economic relations. Trade with the West Indies, for example, had provided the merchants of New England with much of the exchange required to buy British manufactured goods. A number of sound thinkers in England, such as Pownall, advocated that free trade should be continued with America to the advantage of both nations. Unfortunately, few accepted his view, and Lord Sheffield triumphed with his doctrine of treating America with the utmost rigor as a foreign country.

It is interesting to speculate on what might have happened had such narrow views, combined with dislike of and resentment against America, yielded to Pownall's broader vision of the present and the future. In a world of competing empires, each striving to be self-sufficient in trade and resources, as existed then and has come about again today, it is impossible to calculate the change in history which might have been made if the two branches of the English-speaking race could have been formed into a friendly and free-trade bloc from the very beginning. To look forward only a few years from that time, Britain in her death struggle with Napoleon would have had the United States on her side, and there would not have been the second war of 1812 with the bitterness lasting for generations after.

There is another interesting aspect of the exclusion of the Americans from their accustomed trade with the West Indies. When, after an insulting delay of eight years England at last sent an utterly unimportant boy of twenty-seven to represent her in Washington, he took up with Jefferson, among other questions in dispute, that of the American debts. Some years ago, when, by request, I discussed the problem of the British World War debt to the United States with a former Chancellor of the Exchequer, he stated quite frankly that at the time the debt was incurred it was considered as one that would most certainly have to be paid when the war was over, but that various altered conditions, including world trade and the heightened American tariff, had made it impossible to fulfill the contract.

This subject will have to be noted again toward the end of this volume, but we may quote here in slight part the answer of the American Secretary of State to the youthful British Minister, George Hammond, in 1792 and which has considerable point today. Regarding the claim for payment of the debts, Jefferson wrote:

"To the necessities for some delay in the payment of debts may be added the British commercial regulations lessening our means of payment, by prohibiting us from carrying in our own bottoms our own produce to their dominions in our neighborhood, and excluding valuable branches of it from their home markets by prohibitory duties. The means of paiment [*sic*] constitute one of the motives to purchase, at the moment of purchasing. If these means are taken away by the creditor himself, he ought not in conscience to complain of a mere retardation of his debt, which is the effect of his own act."

However, the quarrels continued, and in 1794 Washington sent John Jay to London to settle matters in dispute. Jay was not a good negotiator, and Alexander Hamilton, who as Secretary of the Treasury had been the enemy of Jefferson in the State Department, had spiked Jay's guns in advance. Although Jay secured the promise of the turning over of the Northwest and its posts in 1796 and some other advantages, the treaty was considered so disadvantageous to the United States that Jay was hung in effigy in towns all along the Atlantic coast and even Washington's popularity was heavily impaired.

From the failure to grasp, as Pownall well saw, the possibility of a relationship with her lost empire in America, rich in possibilities, we may now turn to events in the developing empire in India.

III. INDIA

Warren Hastings almost single-handed had held the British possessions in India while struggling against not only Britain's enemies but also the local Council and the diabolic hatred of Philip Francis. The last had continued after the return of Francis to England, where he managed to win over such men as Fox, Burke and other leaders to his own view as to the complete iniquity of Hastings. Although probably honest in their opinions, they in reality lent themselves to the continuance of what had long been largely the mere personal feud of Francis against the Governor-General. Within a year after Hastings had returned from his duties he was impeached by the House of Commons (1786), on a long list of charges which would have been damnable if true. For nearly seven years, in session after session, the eloquence of Fox, Sheridan and other orators, as well as the now vitriolic violence of Burke, aroused the most intense feeling against Hastings both in Parliament and among the public, until as the years passed and it became evident that most of the charges could not be sustained, boredom took the place of hostility. Moreover, Burke's vindictiveness overreached itself. As it became ever greater while the proof of what he claimed became weaker, the real Hastings, the savior of the Indian empire, stood out more clearly in the public mind. Finally, in 1794, he was acquitted and was a free though a physically broken and financially ruined man, owing to the strain and expense of the long trial.

It is difficult to say just how much effect the persecution, rather than prosecution, had on public opinion as to the government of alien races in the Empire. In spite of many speeches which for his own reputation had best be forgotten, Burke at times had pleaded nobly for the responsibility of the British for the happiness and welfare of their overseas subjects. On the other hand, many of the reforms to come had already been initiated by Hastings himself and were not the direct result of the clamor against him.

Moreover, Pitt's India Act of 1784, passed ten years before the end of Hastings' trial, had already paved the way for better government by more clearly defining the powers of all concerned. It was no longer the East India Company which was responsible for government but the British Parliament, which in future was to control the Governor-General, who at the same time was made supreme in British India and no longer had to be subjected to quarrels with his Council or the jealousy of the Company's employees.

These advantages were increased by the character and position of the Governor-Generals who were sent out by Pitt, with Henry Dundas under him as Secretary of State. There is much to be said for placing overseas administration in the hands of a wealthy aristocrat, and Lord Cornwallis, the first Governor sent out after a brief interim, was not only sufficiently high in rank and wealth to be indifferent to money or sycophancy but was also a man of the highest character and courage. With the new régime there came an end for the most part to the former fortune-hunting personnel and the beginning of that Indian Civil Service which has been one of Britain's finest achievements. In general, instead of the old Company plan of small salaries and almost unlimited opportunities for private gain, which placed a huge premium on maladministration, reasonable salaries were paid, with prospects of advancement. The service soon came to have a large sprinkling of aristocrats and especially of the Scotchmen who have done so much for India. Dundas himself was Scotch, and it must be admitted that by a judicious use of the appointing power he helped to maintain a backing for Pitt in Scotland. Indeed, until Parliament itself was reformed, it was impossible wholly to ignore political considerations in patronage, any more than it is in the United States today.

In two respects the Act of 1784 did not work so well, and its failure in these points vindicated the judgment of Hastings against those of Francis and other critics. The first was the new settlement of the land question in Bengal. Hastings had been able to think in terms of Indian life and custom, whereas Francis, as well as some later Governors-General, thought of land and its economic problems in terms of the home system in England. In accordance with Pitt's Act, Cornwallis proceeded to turn the *zemindars*, who had formerly been mere tax collectors, into the owners of the property for a definite sum paid annually to government. By this blunder the *ryots*, or peasant proprietors, became subject to extortion from the *zemindars*, instead of by the Company as of old, and the government was deprived of any opportunity to secure increased revenue as the value and produce of land increased.

The second point was that Hastings had claimed that the British in India should act as an Indian power, make treaties, abide by them, and by means of alliances help to maintain peace. Pitt's Act, on the contrary, laid down the principle that there should be no treaties and no combinations or interferences with native states. Although well meant, it was an impossible policy and led straight to war instead of peace. The Indian monarch Tipu Sultan was intriguing with Napoleon and with others against the British power and certain Indian states who appealed to the British for protection. Tipu was an almost unique character, even in the East. He had abounding energy and in many respects was a reformer. His own subjects were well governed, but he was guilty of the most abominable cruelty to others and especially British prisoners taken in war. What an Indian potentate could inflict in the way of cruelty was exemplified by the Nizam of Hyderabad, who was an ally of the British, but who used the most shocking tortures to extort money from rich and poverty-stricken alike when taken in war.

Tipu's hatred of everything Western and especially his unrelenting hostility and cruelty toward the British made war sooner or later inevitable. Finally, Cornwallis, with the Marathas and the Nizam as allies, moved against him, and after the victory of Seringapatam, Tipu was deprived of half his territory and had to pay a huge indemnity.

Tipu's power, however, was only scotched and not killed, and when at the close of Cornwallis's term of office the Governor-General sailed for England, the situation in India was serious. Three of the great Indian powers were not only intriguing with France but French officers were at their courts training troops, and Napoleon had planned his Egyptian-Indian campaign.

The new Governor-General was the Earl of Mornington, better known as Richard Wellesley, elder brother of Arthur, who was to become the Duke of Wellington. He at once saw the danger and the impossibility of the policy of non-intervention and not only returned to that of Hastings but carried it far beyond anything which the earlier Governor had dreamed of. By a series of alliances and wars, British India became not merely a great Indian power but the paramount power in the whole peninsula. Seringapatam was captured by storm, Tipu killed, and the place given over to loot. "Scarcely a house in the town was left unplundered," wrote Arthur Wellesley, "and I understand that in camp jewels of the greatest value, bars of gold, &c., &c., have been offered for sale in the bazaars of the army by our soldiers, sepoys, and followers."

The Governor-General refused £100,000 offered to him, saying it belonged to the military, the leading officers of which were censured in England for their greed. It was characteristic of Wellesley, a man of great force and ability, that although he declined the great gift he was greedy of honors and demanded a much higher rank in the peerage than was allotted to him for his service, his victory being equal to that of Clive at Plassey. He accepted, however, an Irish Marquisate, an annuity of £5000 a year from the Company, and the Order of St. Patrick, the decoration being made of jewels from Tipu's hoard.

From this period of wars dates not only the emergence of British India as the controlling power but also the system of subsidies to rulers of other states which, although it allowed them to remain in control of their own governments locally, made them practically vassals of the British. Although this meant peace for India, and was the only means of achieving it, both the Company and Parliament were becoming alarmed over Wellesley's vigorous policy and the vast extension he was giving to British power and responsibility. Before his work was entirely complete he was recalled in 1805, though when he left, with the threat of impeachment hang-

44

ing over him, he had created the British Empire of India, rescued it from any French threat and molded it into much the form it has retained ever since.

He had proved a great administrator, and, dissatisfied with the type of many of the young men sent out for the Indian Service, he had established Fort William College, at which they were to remain for three years studying Indian languages and history and otherwise preparing themselves for their duties. Under him there grew up also a body of men, such as the Residents at the native courts, who formed a new type of civil servant of the highest sort. All this, however, beneficial as it was in many ways, definitely perpetuated the trend begun under Cornwallis of Europeanizing all the higher offices in the entire service, so that it was not long before there was no career of advancement open to the native who might be both able and ambitious. Such a system would in time be bound to be resented.

The position of the British was one of extraordinary difficulty. Starting as mere groups of traders, as had the Portuguese, Dutch and French, they had been led on, step by step, by each complication as it arose, until they became the paramount power over a population greater by far than all those conquered by Napoleon at the height of his career, and this with only a handful of white soldiers. The teeming millions, the poverty of the lower classes and the fabulous wealth of the native rulers, the inability of most of these to rule properly, the constant wars among them, the vast variety of peoples, religions, languages and customs, all offered temptations and opportunities to the lowest and best in men and raised problems that are still insoluble.

One of the most fantastic incidents of the days of the Company rule, the effects of which were felt for decades, may be briefly noted. In this instance it was a case of a ruler who lived on credit rather than wealth and who conspired with scheming Europeans, including Company servants, to ruin his own subjects. The Nawab of Arcot kept a splendid court and lived with lavish magnificence, but instead of administering his state well and living on its revenues, he preferred to borrow from Company servants, particu-

45

larly the notorious Benfield, who charged him from 36 per cent to 48 per cent interest and received assignments of the land revenues.

The result was the ruin of the Nawab's subjects and the creation of an unpayable amount of so-called debt which became to a large extent the basis of corruption in Parliament. The situation had lasted for more than a quarter of a century when Cornwallis in 1799 called the whole debt structure "fraudulent and infamous." An arrangement had been made that between 1784 and 1804 the debts should be paid off at the rate of £480,000 annually, but at the end of the period it was found that the Nawab had accumulated a new debt claimed to amount to £30,000,000. The matter was not finally settled until 1830, when all but £3,000,000 were declared to have no basis. Probably the same proportion of the first debt, which the Nawab's subjects had been forced to pay, was equally a fraud.

This had not been a case of a rich native ruler being plundered by military conquerors. The Nawab was not unintelligent, but he had conspired with criminal adventurers to ruin his own nation. The incident is illuminating as showing one aspect of the complex system of states and governments which made up the India of the time. The British did not overturn a settled and orderly civilization. When they came India was already a putrefying mass of decadent states. Left to itself after the break-up of the Mogul Empire, there is nothing to indicate that it would not have been a constant prey to the greed, misgovernment, and fighting between themselves of native rulers; or, if the British had retired, their place and role would merely have been occupied by the French. By the time the death grapple came with the latter, however, India had been secured and at least started on the path toward peace and improvement.

IV. Australia and New Zealand

Owing, nevertheless, to its climate and enormous native population, although it long might remain a part of the Empire, it could never be a British land, and, for significant beginning of the modern Commonwealth of Nations, we have to leave its glamor and romance, its wealth and sordidness, its heroism and avariciousness, and pass to empty and desolate wastes far across the oceans. Here, again, we find certain repercussions of the American Revolution in the building of empire.

During that war Captain Cook had been making his famous voyages and had explored, among other remote places, parts of New Zealand and Australia. In the eighteenth century the American colonies, until they won independence, had been used as a convenient dumping ground for English criminals. In a day when transported criminals might range all the way in their "crimes" from a starving man stealing a loaf of bread to a reputable and highly esteemed young Scotch lawyer such as Muir, who merely demanded the reform of Parliament, "criminal" had a very different meaning from that which it bears today.

The Americans had indeed resented the dumping on them of all sorts of persons from British jails, and Benjamin Franklin had suggested that America export rattlesnakes to England in exchange. Independence, however, settled the question, and in 1787 Pitt was looking for a new place for emigrants of this character. Botany Bay, Australia, was chosen without much thought being given to it when there were so many other pressing problems. If it is not quite true that the British Empire was built in a fit of absence of mind, certainly no great state has ever been so casually founded as Australia, and it is an example of the often fortuitous way in which the Empire has developed.

In January, 1788, the warship *Sirius* convoyed six transports with 750 convicts and the necessary goods and implements to start a colony, though Botany Bay was soon abandoned for the better location of Port Jackson, near the present Sydney. Sydney Cove was a beautiful and capacious harbor, and the hillside which sloped down to it was a perfect site for a great city. For a while the population was of a most picturesque and fascinating sort. With people of really exemplary life, but who had got caught in the toils of the law, were mixed such persons as George Barrington, the most celebrated of London pickpockets, who had stolen Count Orloff's $200,-

47

ooo diamond snuffbox in Covent Garden; a French forger of Bank of England notes; Margaret Catchpole of fact and fiction, who might have married a well-known botanist but remained true to the memory of a smuggler; and many others. Living in order and moderate comfort, it was as extraordinary a group of settlers as ever founded a great nation. The real founding of the modern state was in 1793, when the first shipload of free colonists went out. Unfortunately, owing to the character of many of the inhabitants and the fact that it had to be regarded as a penal settlement, Australia could not start with the self-governing institutions characteristic of British colonizing whenever possible, and the development belongs to a later period.

Meanwhile, another accident began to develop trade with New Zealand. The islands were already known, as were the whaling grounds off them, but these could not be utilized until 1798, as the East India Company claimed a monopoly of all trade in the South Seas. In that year, however, owing to the activity of Spanish war vessels off Cape Horn, the British Government ordered the whalers to proceed to the South Pacific by way of the Cape of Good Hope, then temporarily in possession of the British. The New Zealand whale fisheries thus began, with resultant landing parties trading with the native Maoris, although no permanent settlement was to be made until the next century. Another land, nevertheless, of extraordinary beauty and which, as is said, has become more British than Britain, was swinging into the orbit of empire. Thus, though neither was the result of conquest, the accident of wars presided over the beginnings of both New Zealand and Australia with no thought of their future.

Canada, on the other hand, had been won by war from the French in 1763. It was, moreover, affected by a later war, that with the United States, 1776–1783. The efflux from the revolted colonies, of the "Tories," in the American sense, carried perhaps 100,000 to Canada, of whom many tens of thousands remained permanently, to be known proudly today as the United Empire Loyalists. Their numbers in all the provinces were sufficient to bring the French and English populations nearer to a parity, but whereas the former remained concentrated chiefly in Quebec, most of the former Americans, who remained loyal to the Crown, went to what is now Ontario and to the Maritime Provinces.

Nova Scotia already had self-government, and as early as 1784 New Brunswick and Prince Edward Island, owing to the influx of American-British, also received it, though Newfoundland had still long to wait. It may here be noted to avoid confusion that self-government is not the same as responsible government, which latter is a technical term frequently not understood in the United States. We, for example, have self-government but not responsible government, which means an executive immediately dependent on the majority in the legislature. In Britain and such Dominions as have responsible government, a majority in the legislature, voting on a major question, can overthrow a Prime Minister and his government but Congress cannot turn out a President and his Cabinet however they may disagree on policies.

In the Canada Act of 1791, Canada proper was divided into Upper and Lower Canada, the former province including the present Ontario and a preponderantly British population, while the latter included Quebec with its French majority. Each was given self-government in the usual colonial form, which was designed as near as might be to be a replica of the government in Britain. The British North American provinces were now well started on their way, with free institutions and growing population, to becoming the leading Dominion in the British Commonwealth of the future.

Thus within twenty years or so of the disastrous end of the American War and the loss of a large part of the old Empire, a new one had been born. Britain was paramount in India and a genuine Indian Empire had been set up with Ceylon added though under separate government. Canada was on a firm foundation. Australia and New Zealand had begun their careers. The Mediterranean was guarded at the west entrance by British control of Gibraltar, and at the east end Malta was to remain in British possession in spite of the offer to give it up. The Cape of Good Hope, although temporarily abandoned, was very soon to be reconquered and to remain a permanent British colony on the route to India.

49

To the West Indian Islands were shortly to be added others and what is now British Guiana on the South American mainland. Here and there, all over the world, in an amazingly short time, the far-flung new overseas Empire was taking its lasting shape. But again the world was to be convulsed by France, and the centuries-long duel between that nation and the English was to recommence on a vaster scale than ever. What, at the end, might be left of Britain or the new Empire no man could tell.

CHAPTER IV

THE NAPOLEONIC STRUGGLE

I. The Renewal of the War

WHEN THE Treaty of Amiens was signed in March, 1802, it was thought the two nations could settle down in peace. In Britain dislike of the French had largely subsided as had also the emotions aroused by the Terror some years before. The rule of Napoleon appeared to promise order and stability, and the British for their part would gladly have turned their attention overseas and employed their energies in the development of trade.

The two nations were, it is true, profoundly different. The British, although willing to fight to the death for their existence and proud of their navy and its exploits, cared nothing whatever for military glory as an end in itself, and the little army was almost negligible as a factor in the life of the nation. There was no grand plan of imperial expansion, and the scattered Empire had been growing up almost by itself in a haphazard fashion. The government was clumsy and inefficient, while the reaction set up by the earlier excesses of the French Revolution had made any real reform impossible for a generation. On the other hand, there were an intense love of personal liberty and a deep pride on the part of all classes in the national belief that Britain was the freest nation in the world.

Across the Channel, France had become militaristic, and the only two factors that counted were the army and Napoleon. He was giving the people an example of perhaps the most efficient government since the best days of Rome, and it was this exhibition which was to count for almost as much as military genius in his overrunning of the Continent. But together with his transcendent ability as an administrator in peace he had the fatal ambition to be a great military conqueror. In 1804 he was to be crowned as Emperor and the dreams of a vast, perhaps a world, empire never left him. Even had it not been for this his position was that of a usurping despot and to maintain it he had to feed the army, and gradually the whole people, with ever new victories. He had risen by the sword and he would have to live or perish by it. Liberty had been replaced by despotism and glory, at home and abroad.

This became clear almost before the ink was dry on the treaty of peace. In Italy, Piedmont was annexed to France and two other Italian states were brought under French control, a French "Kingdom of Italy" soon following. A new constitution was forced on Holland. Switzerland was subjugated. The new states Napoleon had consolidated and built up out of the old Germany became mere French satellites. He had also sent troops to India, a mission to Egypt, and had taken over from Spain the vast American territory of Louisiana, which meant a large part of the Mississippi Valley west of that river. He had torn up the Treaty of Lunéville, which had guaranteed the independence of Holland and Switzerland but kept complaining during 1802 that Britain would not carry out her pledge to turn Malta over to a neutral power, which she refused to do in face of Napoleon's own acts and the growing menace of the situation.

It did not need the studied insult to the British Ambassador at one of Josephine's parties to show that Napoleon meant war or acceptance by Britain of a negligible position in world affairs. In the ports of France and Holland he was himself making preparations for war, and was in possession of the entire seacoast, including Belgium, facing England, when in March, 1803, just a year after signing the Treaty of Amiens, the British Government asked Parliament to take steps to prepare for the emergency. The following May, Great Britain, without a single ally, threw down the gauntlet to the dictator and delivered an ultimatum in Paris.

For the first few of the long additional dozen years of war which were now to ensue, France had the advantage of a concentrated command under an absolute dictator, whereas the British Government was weak and distracted by changes. Addington as Prime Minister did not have the confidence of the nation, which clamored for the return of Pitt, but he held on, refusing to resign for a year, and when Pitt himself returned he was seriously handicapped. He had wished to include in his Cabinet all the available talent from both parties, notably in the person of Fox, but the King would not consent to the inclusion of his old enemy, and although Fox willingly stepped aside, some of the leading Whigs declined to join unless he was in office. The result was a weak Ministry headed by a man overborne by ill health and pressure of work, who was to die at the beginning of 1806 at one of the gloomiest moments of the contest. At last the King agreed to a coalition government which would include Fox, and a new and completely Tory Ministry came into power which was to carry on for the remainder of the war.

It had been a misfortune for England that Fox and Pitt had been by force of circumstances brought into opposition to each other rather than collaboration. Both were born aristocrats though of very different types. Fox was of the heavy-drinking, gambling, sporting sort, loving the hearty country life of his day even more than his clubs in town, yet equally devoted, as so many were at the time, to love of literature and patronage of the arts. Pitt, extraordinarily austere, and cold for his age, when he headed the Cabinet at twenty-four, and with a will of steel, was in all ways a contrast to the stout and jovial Fox. Both men were disinterested patriots in spite of Pitt's inordinate ambition and Fox's easy-going laziness. Both were in favor of reform but Pitt in a cool, intellectual way as contrasted with the fervor of Fox's generous and warm-hearted nature. Pitt's great ability in organizing and finance, —perhaps his greatest achievements were his reorganization of governmental machinery and the re-establishment of the national credit,—combined with Fox's equally great abilities of such a different sort, could have accomplished much in the dangerous time

53

through which Britain was passing. Unfortunately it was not to be.

Yet, if in the struggle through which she now had to pass, Britain suffered like all self-governing powers as contrasted with the apparently greater efficiency of a dictatorship, she had certain advantages, which would turn the scales in the long run. The desire for personal liberty would prove better able to survive defeats than the desire for military glory or conquest. In fact, defeats would intensify the will to win and avoid submission to personal rule. In addition, the navy was at the height of its effectiveness with an incomparable leader in the person of Nelson, and in spite of the great armies and the land battles on the Continent, sea power would eventually prove the determining factor. Finally, although for two years Britain was to stand alone against Napoleon and his vassal states and allies, the nation was completely united in its determination not to be subjugated.

An insurrection in Ireland in 1803, under Robert Emmet, was quickly overcome and for the remainder of the long struggle even Ireland made no trouble and added many recruits to the armed forces. Nowhere in the Old World was Napoleon then opposed by a people with a strong sense of nationality save in Great Britain. For the most part his opponents on weak thrones were monarchs whose misrule had not given them even the strength which might have stemmed from the affection and loyalty of their subjects. Indeed, the strong and orderly government which Napoleon had established in France lured other Continental peoples to accept rather than to oppose his overlordship. No hot popular resentment or offended loyalties, personal or national, were aroused when he remodelled the states of Germany, deprived the Austrian ruler of his title of Roman Emperor, placed one of his own brothers on the throne of Naples and another on that of Holland.

Meanwhile, at the beginning of the war, Napoleon assembled his forces on the coast for an invasion of England. For months while the French lay encamped across the narrow channel there was deep anxiety but no panic in the island, where some 300,000 volunteers joined for its defense. Aside from their natural self-confidence, two facts encouraged the British. One was that there had been no successful invasion of England for nearly seven and a half centuries, as the landing of William in 1688 at the invitation of the nation itself cannot be considered as such. The other was the British fleet with Nelson in command.

This second fact had also to be taken into consideration by Napoleon, as he waited impatiently through the months to strike what he thought would be a sure blow at the despised "nation of shopkeepers" who occupied the richest island in the world almost at his door. From his own shore he could see the white cliffs of Dover in clear weather, but though he gathered one of the finest armies in the world for embarkation he came to realize that he would have to hold the Channel by a superior naval force for at least six days to get his troops across. The French navy was broken into detachments in its own harbors, chiefly Brest and Toulon, unable to get to sea because of watching detachments of the British who kept ceaseless guard over them. For two years the vigil went on with characteristic British doggedness, while the French ships and crews were deteriorating for lack of cruising at sea.

II. THE NAVAL WAR

Finally, in December, 1804, Napoleon forced Spain to enter the war and this seemed to open the way by giving him the use of Spanish harbors and the Spanish fleet. The plan was formed to have one or several of the French detachments slip past their blockaders when conditions were favorable and join their Spanish ally at Cadiz, the combined forces then to make straight for the British West Indies and capture them if possible but in any case to lure the British forces in pursuit. The French-Spanish combined fleet would then immediately return, give the British the slip, and be at the Channel before the British, who would be searching for them, could know what had happened.

The plan, though too complex, almost succeeded. The French admiral Villeneuve, utilizing a favorable moment, did get his ships out of Toulon, leaving Nelson uncertain of his destination, and in the days before radio or other swift communication Nelson spent a month trying to locate him, not knowing he had joined the Spanish at Cadiz and sailed for the West Indies. Based partly on further news and mainly on his own intuitive genius, Nelson sensed part of what was going on and set out in pursuit, reaching the islands in time to save them and send the enemy fleets across the Atlantic again, though nothing could be certain in the waste of waters. Suddenly, by a flash of insight, Nelson realized the whole of Napoleon's strategy and in spite of the islanders, who implored him to remain, made for Cadiz as fast as possible, reaching Europe almost as soon as the enemy. He reinforced the fleet guarding the Mediterranean and then sailed for the Channel. Napoleon was foiled. The French and Spanish after a short separation had joined forces at Cadiz, and Nelson sailed from England in the *Victory* to join Collingwood and the blockading squadron off that port.

Villeneuve, though he had thirty-three ships against the twenty-seven of Nelson, knew that he was no match for the latter. Nelson, on the other hand, felt confident of success if only he could get the enemy fleet out to sea. Fortunately, Napoleon ordered the reluctant commander to his doom, and on the very day planned by Nelson the great victory of Trafalgar was won, perhaps the most decisive naval event in history. On the morning of October 21, 1805, Nelson sent up the flags of the famous order for all the fleet to read: "England expects every man to do his duty." By afternoon the enemy had been completely overwhelmed. One of their ships had been blown up, and twenty-one captured then or soon after, while the rest were in full flight as a terrific storm was rising. England's control of the seas became, and was to remain, absolute.

The cost of victory, however, was incalculable, for Nelson had been killed, and so dazzling was his fame and so deep the love of the nation for him that the news of his passing, when the triumphant fleet returned to the island which he had made mistress of all the oceans, turned rejoicing into mourning. So transcendant was his genius that, had he been fatally struck at the Battle of the Nile instead of at Trafalgar, the history of the world would have been greatly changed. Fate so ordered, however, that when he did die for England he had saved her and set her on as high a pinnacle as that on which his own statue now stands in Trafalgar Square in the heart of the Empire.

It is difficult to write of his last moments without emotion. The greatest naval commander of all time, saving at her crisis the greatest maritime empire of all history, had himself much of the sentiment and even sentimentality which are English characteristics together with never-failing courage, professional as well as physical, supreme self-confidence and complete devotion to his country. As he lay dying, the battle won, his mind went to both his country and those he loved. His love affair with Lady Hamilton is known by all. When Hardy, captain of the ship, came to him, Nelson said, "Don't throw me overboard. You know what to do"; then, "Take care of my dear Lady Hamilton, Hardy: take care of poor Lady Hamilton. Kiss me, Hardy." Hardy bent and kissed his cheek, and as he was rapidly sinking, he said again to the doctor, "Remember that I leave Lady Hamilton and my daughter Horatia as a legacy to my country—never forget Horatia." His very last words were, "Thank God I have done my duty. God and my country." With that the soul of one of the greatest of the English passed to the unknown, after rendering England supreme service and making the supreme sacrifice for her.

His crowning achievement at Trafalgar was important as establishing the maritime primacy of England, with all that implied, rather than in saving her from invasion, for his action, on his reading of Napoleon's strategy, had already prevented that, and had had its effect. Earlier in the year Pitt had built up a third coalition against France by drawing in Russia and Austria with heavy subsidies. Britain might save herself by sea power, and sea power might in the end defeat the greatest Continental power, but so long as Napoleon was intent on conquering the Continent, rather than Britain, land power was also essential against him. So England, battling at sea, agreed to pay the Emperors of Russia and Austria $6,250,000 a year for every 100,000 men put in the field against the new Emperor of the French.

Napoleon, who had realized by this time the futility of his two years' effort to invade England, turned and struck at once far to the east, completely crushing Britain's new allies at Austerlitz. Unless Britain were content to see the entire Continent come under the control of one man, she evidently had to face a long war on land instead of on her natural element, the seas, which Nelson, latest and most glorious of a long line, had made her own. The common bond of a new memory in the fame of Nelson helped her to face the now inevitable ordeal, one so great that it sapped the failing strength of Pitt, who died murmuring, "My country. How I leave my country." Britain, though once more left alone and not a military nation, faced it unflinchingly, as she did the World War, and is now doing again rather than bowing, in the last resort, to a dictatorship.

If the handling of the war by Pitt had been far from brilliant, that by the "Ministry of all the Talents," including at last Fox, who, however, died in a few months, was worse. It lasted only about a year and refused to follow Pitt's plan of a coalition on the Continent while frittering away the military power of Britain in the Mediterranean and even the Argentine. Prussia, because of the pique of its King over Napoleon's duplicity in the matter of turning over to him the promised Hanover, suddenly turned on France without English aid and was completely crushed at the battle of Jena. Russia, which came to the help of the Prussians, would gladly have allied herself to Britain but it was only after the formation of a new Ministry, including Castlereagh and Canning, that the government turned once more to the policy of Pitt, and then it was too late. The Russians were completely defeated in the battle of Friedland, and the Czar, angry with the British, who he felt had failed him, made peace.

In June, 1807, Alexander and Napoleon met personally on a raft in the middle of the river Niemen and signed the famous Treaty of Tilsit. It was a dramatic moment when the Czar of all the Russias, the occupant of one of the greatest thrones of the old régime in Europe, agreed to divide the world with the upstart dictator whose dynasty was scarce three years old. Russia was to take Finland from Sweden and do as she would with Turkey while leaving all the rest of the Continent to Napoleon for him to rule and conquer at will. But there was more than that. Prussia was dismembered and the new Kingdom of Westphalia carved out of it for Napoleon's brother while another huge slice went to make the new Grand Duchy of Warsaw. All of the old Prussia, which had also to pay a huge indemnity, thus came under control of France and was forced to join her in war on England. Even all this did not complete the full measure of danger to the island Empire, for Russia not only recognized Napoleon's title to all he had won or claimed (which was a large part of the entire Continent), but also agreed to aid him against Britain and to force Sweden, Portugal and Denmark, practically the only independent states left, into the struggle. It was an unintentional compliment to the British that it was felt necessary to enlist nothing less than the power and resources of every state in Europe to crush them. Even so, the British navy sweeping proudly over the seas, with the spirit of Nelson in the breast of every officer and man, was believed to offer an almost insuperable obstacle to conquest, and the war was now to enter on a new phase with new weapons. Meanwhile England intended to make full use of those she had.

Napoleon was still to dream for some months of using sea power, which he never understood, to back his plans for commercial warfare. There was still some French naval force left, and this he intended to employ in connection with the Danish and Russian fleets, and the small one of Portugal, which accounted in part for his agreement with the Czar to force those two countries into the war against England. The terms and intentions of the Treaty of Tilsit, however, were no secret to Canning and the British Foreign Office. A British Ambassador, fleet and small army unexpectedly arrived at Copenhagen to offer the Danish Prince an alliance but on condition that his navy should be turned over to the British until the end of the war. The offer was immediately rejected, and even George III, when he heard of the proceedings, congratulated the Ambassador that he had had his interview with the Danish ruler on the ground floor of the palace. Otherwise, said the King, if the Dane "had half my spirit he would have kicked you downstairs." Many British felt as George did and were horrified when Copen-

hagen was bombarded and the Danish fleet was carried off to Eng
land, never to be returned. Like many other acts, its only justification, if it had any, was necessity. It was known that Napoleon
and the Czar had agreed to force Denmark to fight Britain, and
Napoleon's hand was stretched out to grab the fleet. Canning
grabbed it first. The punctilios of diplomacy or the drawing room
would have been wasted on the French dictator, and there was
no reason to believe, as far as the unfortunate Danish ruler was
concerned, that when faced by Napoleon's threats he would have
played the role of an Albert of Belgium a century later.

The unsavory Danish episode left the question of the Portuguese
fleet still open. When Napoleon demanded that Portugal declare
war on England, backing the demand with force as the British had
in Denmark, that state, although friendly to England, yielded at
once. Under protection of a British fleet, however, the Portuguese
navy got to sea, the Russian ships not having arrived in time to stop
it, and, convoyed by British, sailed to Brazil with the royal family,
who set up their throne in the New World. By 1809 new mishaps
had completely ended Napoleon's dream of conquering Britain by
any means except those commercial measures which together made
up what has been known as his "Continental System."

III. Forces against Dictatorship

Before speaking of that we may pause a moment to note that,
although his agreement with Alexander on the raft seemed to have
made him all-powerful and impregnable, and Britain was to go
through another eight years of terrible struggle, the dictator was
in truth not nearly as powerful as he seemed. The statue of the
iron conqueror had feet of clay, and many causes from now on
combined to bring about his inevitable downfall if only England
could hold out and take the bludgeonings still to come. For one
thing, we have spoken of how the fact that he had given good government to peoples who as yet had little or no national feeling had
made his conquests easy. This had been true up to the time when
he and Alexander discussed the division of Europe between them

for three hours in mid-stream while the King of Prussia kicked his heels in the rain on the shore waiting to hear his doom.

The terms meted out to the latter were so severe, considering not merely the reduction of his country to one-third of its former size, but also the indemnities and other penalties, that the Prussians instead of accepting Napoleon's rule became his bitter enemies.

The same hostility toward him developed in Spain. In 1808 Napoleon had deposed the old King and his son, and had placed his own brother, Joseph, King of Naples, on the throne, putting down a rising in Madrid with great cruelty. Within a few weeks the Spanish people throughout the country rose against the foreigner, and the French army had to retreat. This was another symptom that a new force was coming into being against him, the force not of unpopular monarchs but of aroused peoples to join, eventually, the British in his overthrow.

In view of the situation today the final failure of Napoleon, a far greater genius in both peace and war than any of the dictators who are now attempting to bestride the world, is of special interest. As time went on, his faults grew more obvious and the burdens he laid on the peoples, rousing themselves one after another, became greater. In the beginning he had brought order and conferred benefits, but gradually the peoples realized that that time had passed, and that, as long as he lived and ruled, there could be no peace or settled life for them. Human nature does not greatly alter, and although for some years emotions can be whipped up to the plane of war psychology, the time comes when people crave with insatiable longing the pleasures of peace,—home, children, love, business, safety, quiet, the simple happiness of everyday living. As the years passed, in spite of his great popularity and the "Napoleonic legend," peoples rose against him because they could not live as long as he ruled. Moreover, dictators must succeed, and as long as England stood firm and could not be forced to submit, it was blazed on the skies that Napoleon, who had made his war against her a sort of symbol, was not invincible. At long last the toast which Pitt had given at the Guildhall to celebrate the victory of Trafalgar was to have its justification. "England has saved herself by her exertions and will save Europe by her example."

IV. THE ECONOMIC WAR

At the end of 1806 Napoleon began his economic as contrasted with his military warfare against Britain. On November 21 he issued the so-called Berlin Decree, which closed all the ports under his influence or control, being practically all those on the Continent, to British commerce, and also declared all British ports blockaded. A year later, almost to the day, Britain issued the most drastic of a series of Orders in Council which announced that all French ports were in a state of blockade and that no vessel could enter any of them unless it had touched at a British port first. A few weeks later, Napoleon held any ship liable to capture if it had touched at a British port before unloading at any port under French control. These were merely among the more important measures and counter-measures taken by the two leaders in what was becoming a world struggle. All of them heavily infringed the rights of neutrals and international law as then agreed on. A minor contest of the same sort had been carried on from Napoleon's Decree of 1796 until his abandonment of the policy five years later, and had almost involved him in war with the United States and other neutrals. These early efforts at economic control, however, had been comparatively unimportant, but later, when he had extended his power over practically all the Continent, he could not refrain from again attempting to bring the one great Power which yet remained his unyielding foe to terms by trying to kill her commerce.

Britain was, indeed, forced to suffer fearful hardships and privations through the remaining years of the war, as we shall note more particularly in the next chapter. The stoppage of a large part of what had been the accustomed and growing trade of the world caused in the island not only a severe shortage of food, with attendant famine prices, but also unemployment, due to closing of markets for the goods produced by the rapidly increasing industrial population. On the other hand, Napoleon did not sufficiently count on the unbreakable stubbornness of his enemies nor the fact that his policy would raise up new ones against him. Canning, Castlereagh and the other Tories who were governing England in those years had none of the genius of the French Emperor, but they had their people behind them in an unshakable resolve not to submit to him, and in the end half the people of the Continent were to be forced to the same resolve.

If Britain, which controlled the seas, suffered hardships from the breakdown of trade, so also did the Continental populations which needed food, the productions of the tropics, and the new manufactured goods which Britain alone was making. Nor in their privations, caused by Napoleon primarily, were they buoyed up as the British people were by the knowledge that they were fighting for their freedom and independence. In fact, the British came to be considered the friends and saviors of those who were fast being alienated by the measures Napoleon felt it necessary to take if his Continental System were to remain a real weapon against Britain.

It is true that the British picked up a large remaining part of the tropics and other outlying regions of supplies, acquiring Cape Colony again and permanently in 1806, French islands in the Indian Ocean, the rich Dutch island of Java, and French and Dutch islands and mainland possessions in the West Indies and South America, including Dutch Guiana, Curaçao, Martinique, Guadeloupe, and the Danish islands. Many of these were returned at the end of the war, but Britain got their trade and her enemies saw their rich tropical empires disappearing. At this time, Britain also widened her markets, starting the profitable connection which still subsists with the Spanish colonies of South America, then already considering revolt from Spain.

On the other hand, there were along the whole northern, western and southern coast lines of the Continent innumerable small harbors and ports which the British used for contraband trade for the goods the people longed for, entrances which served increasingly as loopholes in the system which Napoleon vainly strove to make watertight. Because the Pope had refused to close his ports, Napoleon occupied the Papal States and finally drove the Pope into exile, with disastrous effects on his relations to the Catholic Church.

His efforts to close the ports of Spain had much to do with the rising of the people there and the later Peninsular Campaign which was one of the determining points in his downfall. The Dalmatian coast was annexed, as was Holland, and the rights of German Powers on the shore to the east disregarded. Sweden made no real effort to enforce the Decrees, and Russia broke with France gradually by practically restoring her foreign trade to normal. The critical year had been 1811, though the Orders in Council were not rescinded until 1812, too late to prevent the United States entering the war against Britain, for reasons we shall discuss presently. By that year, the bases of Napoleon's power were fast crumbling.

He had determined to put down the revolt in Spain and drive the English out of Portugal, and thither he sent one of his best aides, Massena, while the British were under command of Sir Arthur Wellesley, who had been recalled from India and who is better known under his later titles of Viscount and Duke of Wellington. We need not detail the vicissitudes of fortune in the campaigning until the final expulsion of the French from the entire peninsula in 1813, the main and immense importance of Wellington's work being the drain he had caused on the Emperor's military resources.

When Napoleon, having declared war on Russia, marched into that empire on his fatal expedition in 1812 with 600,000 men he had to leave the running sore of Spain behind him. Fighting only one battle with the Russians, who retreated before him, luring him ever deeper into the country, he reached Moscow in October to find it deserted and, the following day, in flames. Facing the terrors of a Russian winter on the plains without shelter or supplies, which he had not provided for, the seemingly invincible conqueror began the most disastrous retreat in history. The snow, the ice, the blizzard winds swept down, and of the 600,000 men he had led to their doom less than 20,000 on their way homeward staggered across the frontier of the empire they had entered to conquer.

Events moved swiftly. Napoleon raised a new and smaller army, of boys. His man power was drained to the dregs. Austria joined Russia against him. One more victory—that of Dresden—was to be his, but he was defeated at Leipzig, and early in 1814 the Russians, Prussians and Austrians entered Paris, exiling the fallen Emperor to the island of Elba. The Bourbons were replaced on the French throne.

V. THE PEACE AND THE "HUNDRED DAYS"

At last the long nightmare of twenty-two years of war seemed over, and the statesmen from practically every country in Europe gathered in Vienna to redraw the map of Europe, a task comparable only to that which faced those who assembled in Paris in 1918–19. New boundaries, new ambitions, new ideas, had to be taken into consideration, accepted, rejected, by men of the most conflicting beliefs and desires. The months dragged on as the glittering statesmen of the most aristocratic courts of the old régime spun their nets. In France there was relief that the agony of blood and the annual sacrifice of youth were over but there was also the feeling that glory had likewise passed. Louis XVIII seemed dull compared with the Emperor who had made France mistress of the entire Continent for a brief space and had taken his place with the greatest military heroes of all history. Meanwhile, he watched from his island exile. In March, 1815, while the diplomats talked, danced and dined in Vienna, he had escaped, crossed to France and swept to Paris like a hawk across the sky, to be wildly acclaimed again as Emperor of the French.

England, Prussia, Austria and Russia immediately went into action against him, but in the romantic "Hundred Days" which followed only the British under Wellington and the Prussians under Blücher were in time to fight him, though Wellington had a mixed army of several nationalities. After three months of campaigning the adventure ended at Waterloo where Wellington held the field all day waiting for Prussian reinforcements under Blücher, who arrived at last. The French army, crushed by the two, fled. Napoleon's dream was ended. The Powers decided to take no chances again, and the fallen Emperor who had drowned Europe in blood was carried, a prisoner, on the British ship *Bellerophon*, to the lonely isle of St. Helena to ponder on the past until his death in 1821. The diplomats in Vienna resumed their conference.

Forged in the fires and on the anvil of nearly a generation of war, anxiety and suffering, the ideas of nationality and liberalism had been wrought to a form and strength hitherto unknown in Old World civilization. They were to remain controlling forces down to our own day, perhaps the most important result of the French Revolution and Napoleonic imperialism. But these were ideas of the peoples rather than the rulers, the temporary idealism of the Russian Czar Alexander having little lasting influence. In spite of the wide representation at the Congress, the real remaking of Europe was done, as in Paris in 1919, by the "Big Four" of the day. In Vienna these were Britain, Austria, Prussia and Russia, with Castlereagh, Metternich and Alexander the leading figures. Alexander had the waywardness, the unreliability and the mysticism of the Slav. From an impossible idealism in international affairs he passed to his extreme reactionary attitude of a few years later. Metternich was always a reactionary and struggled only to re-establish the old order, which had passed in the cauldron of war. Castlereagh did not believe in democracy but was far the most genuine liberal of the three and had the English sense for compromise. He realized the world had changed, and a few years later, in 1821, made a public protest against the efforts of the Holy Alliance, of Alexander and Metternich, to put it back into the straitjacket of the past. At the Conference in Vienna, however, across the new ideas of nationalism and liberalism there cut the old ones of aggrandizement of territory and power. From the counterplay of all these there emerged the set-up and many of the problems which in time were to lead to the world catastrophe of our own century.

France, where the Bourbons were again restored, was treated liberally, receiving back her old boundaries, including Alsace and Lorraine, together with her more important colonies. A reasonable indemnity, paid off in a few years, was no heavy drain on her resources and no cause of lasting bitterness. Russia added to her territory Finland, about two-thirds of Poland (in the form of a temporarily vassal kingdom) and other possessions. Austria was reduced in power in the Germanic confederation but received compensation in Italy with cessions of Venetian and other territory and virtual control over a large part of the peninsula. The germ of the modern united Italian kingdom was planted in Piedmont, while Belgium was united to Holland, and that state and Denmark both were handed back their most valuable overseas possessions which Britain had conquered in the war. The change which was perhaps most pregnant with future consequences was the aggrandizement of Prussia. She was given a large part of Saxony and also smaller states which placed her boundaries west of the Rhine and contiguous with those of France. Nowhere had Napoleon unwittingly achieved greater results in the building up of a spirit of nationality than in this formerly humbled enemy and in the welter of small states surrounding it, henceforward to assume the role of chief Continental rival to his own country.

Britain emerged from the struggle the greatest power in the world and she alone had saved Europe and never bowed for a moment to the conqueror. Yet she alone returned most of her conquests, paid compensation of over £3,000,000 for others, and took no territory on the Continent, though Hanover was restored to the British Crown. The cash compensation was to the Dutch for the Cape in Africa and part of Guiana in South America. In addition Britain retained Heligoland, Ceylon, Malta, and the Ionian Islands. With these, however, and an India undisputedly hers, Gibraltar, her West Indian islands, Canada, Australia, New Zealand, innumerable trading ports, and above all her unconquerable navy and vast merchant marine, she was mistress of the seas and of their commerce. The Continent would perforce continue to occupy part of her attention and at times call for intervention, but in the century to come, which was to be notably one of the industrial revolution, of expanding world trade and of imperialism, she was to be, for a couple of generations or more, far in the lead of all other nations.

VI. The American War and the Empire

She had, indeed, in the preceding war, as we have seen, lost her original colonies in America, and at the climax of the Napoleonic struggle had had to count them, as the United States, among her enemies. Their intervention was in no way decisive or even, considering the immensity of the war, important, but it did have its influence from the standpoint of later Anglo-American relations, and so calls for at least brief attention.

When war first began between Britain and France in 1793 the sympathy of most Americans was with their former ally which had saved them in the Revolution and whose uprising now seemed to be leading her in their own path toward liberty and republicanism. Memories of the "tyranny" of Great Britain and of the eight years of war were still bitter, as were the disputes over the unfulfilled treaty and trade restrictions as already mentioned. Nevertheless, President Washington issued a proclamation of neutrality, and the interferences with American trade by France nearly led to war with that country from 1798 to 1801. Although parties were deeply divided, war was averted, and the sea-borne trade of the young republic advanced rapidly until the French Decrees and the British Orders in Council threatened its extinction. As a neutral, America lodged continuous protests with both parties but without avail.

As far as infringements of the laws of neutral trade went, there was theoretically little to choose between the two offenders, neither of whom, locked in a struggle to the death, paid much attention to law. If the United States was to go to war to defend neutral rights she would have had to defy both powers, and, in fact, America was divided by both party and sectional lines, the Federalist Northeast being pro-British while the more Democratic South was pro-French.

There were, however, special factors in the anti-British case besides trade. Not only could the British, owing to their naval supremacy, practically blockade the American coast, which they did, while the French could not, but the British also roused resentment by the impressment of American seamen on American vessels, claiming them as her own subjects. Some thousands were taken off American ships to serve in the British navy or be imprisoned, and it was said at one time that there were more seamen from the port of Salem, Massachusetts, together in prison on Dartmoor than could be found in their home town. Had Britain insisted on taking her bona-fide citizens off our vessels within three miles of her coasts no complaint could have been made, but she insisted on doing so anywhere on the high seas and often by most high-handed methods.

In 1807 the British frigate *Leopard* overhauled the United States frigate *Chesapeake*, which had just set sail from Norfolk, not fully prepared for sea, and fired a broadside into her, killing or wounding twenty Americans, subsequently taking four men off her. The country blazed with anger, and war was imminent, but President Jefferson, in spite of his being accused of being pro-French, averted it and negotiated with Canning. No change could be secured as to the general practice, however, or the British and French trade regulations. Jefferson then, as Napoleon had done, turned to economic pressure, although in his case to avert, and not to carry on, war, by declaring a general embargo of all goods from the United States. In view of the sanctions of the League and the failure of economic measures in our own day, it is interesting to note that they were tried and failed completely a century and more ago. Napoleon's effort led to his downfall, and Jefferson's almost to revolution in his own country, until the measures had to be withdrawn.

Meanwhile, in the American West a party was growing up among the younger statesmen known as the "War Hawks," who, because they saw a chance to gain Canada and remove British influence from the Indians of the Northwest, hounded Madison, who had succeeded Jefferson, to bring on war with England. The war, however, was rather due to a blunder of the President, who had announced that American trade would be open to all the world except with the belligerent who refused to withdraw the trade restrictions in case the other should do so. Britain refused while Napoleon fooled the administration into the belief that he had. Finally the United States declared war against Britain only five days before the latter actually did rescind the Orders in Council. Had there been a transatlantic cable in those days it is practically certain that the second and last war between British and Americans would never have been fought.

The unhappy affair dragged on for two and a half years, with land operations of no great importance, the two which have lived longest in American memory being the British burning of the city of Washington, with the Capitol, White House, and government documents, and the American victory by General Jackson over the British at New Orleans, after peace had been signed at Ghent in December, 1814, unknown to the combatants.

The Americans fared better at sea, in such fights as those between the *Guerrière* and the *Constitution,* the *Frolic* and *Wasp,* the *Macedonian* and *United States,* and the *Java* and *Constitution,* in all of which the Americans were victorious. Weight of the British navy was bound to tell, however, and in spite of some brilliant actions between individual vessels, there was scant glory in the war as a whole for either side.

At the end, both wanted peace, and were glad to sign a treaty which ignored all the original causes of the quarrel. The United States, which had nearly been disrupted by the divided party feelings of the previous thirty years, was glad to turn its united strength to the development of its vast West, and its back on Europe, if possible, for good and all. This fact was one of the important by-products of the Napoleonic struggle in both its military and commercial phases, as was the tradition, long maintained, that Britain was the chief enemy. In spite of deep grievances, the United States had tried to keep at peace with Britain, and had the sequence of events been altered by only a few weeks, she would either have not gone to war in 1812 or if she had it would have been on the side of the British instead of the French, with great influence on the public sentiment of the next two generations.

For one section of the Empire—Canada—this minor war had a considerable and lasting significance. Not only did the heavy inflow of American immigration cease but the fighting between the Canadians (with the help of 10,000 of Wellington's Spanish veterans) and the Americans gave the colony, as it was then, a greater sense of unity within itself and with Great Britain. Even the large American population had to discard Republicanism and other American ideas, and become definitely British. The Canadians had both invaded the United States and been invaded, and from the experiences of the war there grew up the first Canadian tradition of a single people, made up of British, Americans and French. The future development of government and life in Canada would now definitely be British and not American.

If it did nothing else, the War of 1812 thus helped to a great extent to settle the center of gravity for the Empire's greatest Dominion in the future at a critical time. Otherwise American penetration by migration, and similar conditions in many respects,—vast area and unexploited riches, frontier existence, an increasingly heterogeneous population, remoteness from the Old World,—might have swung her way of thought and life more in the direction of her more populous and powerful neighbor to the south.

Another result of the war was the Rush-Bagot Convention between the United States and Great Britain, consummated in 1817, by which both agreed not to maintain war vessels on the lakes between the former and Canada. From this Convention has grown the present unique situation of the two nations having nearly 5000 miles of common boundary without any defenses of any sort on either side throughout its entire length, yet with mutual sense of absolute security.

If Canada had been cemented by the American War of 1812, Australia had, as we have already seen, been born of the American Revolution. Except for that there would have been no settlement in the great oceanic continent in 1788, and even at that time Britain laid claim to only half of it, a claim disputed by others. The minor fighting between Americans and British in Australian waters in the later war was of slight importance but the greater struggle was to have profound influence. Remote from the war itself, local development continued and especially exploration. The possibilities of the vast interior came to be better understood, but it was only the dominant position achieved on the seas which allowed Britain later to claim the entire continent and to maintain that claim. As the star of Napoleon waned, the sun of Australia rose, and the home government began to take more interest in its distant possession. Some of the former convicts had become prominent citizens, earning as much as £3000 a year, and the difficulty between them and the free immigrants continued, Governor Macquarie (1809–21) taking the side of the former. In 1812 a committee of the House of Commons in a Report sustained him in his "liberal views," and men like Jeremy Bentham and Sir Samuel Romilly were attacking the whole penal system.

It is interesting to note that even while engaged in the death struggle with Napoleon, groups of British were still keenly interested in promoting humanitarianism and good government overseas. In 1807 Parliament put an end to any British participation in the slave trade, and in 1812, the same year in which Parliament inquired into conditions in Australia, it was also busy with India, issuing the fifth of its Reports, which a select committee had been compiling for the previous five years. As a result, the Act of 1813 abolished the monopoly of trade (except with China) which the East India Company had formerly enjoyed, and, with judicial and other reforms, introduced more modern and satisfactory relations between the home government and its great Oriental dependency in which the nation was beginning to take pride. In India itself minor wars continued, and there was oscillation between the policies of forward advance and non-intervention, depending chiefly on the Governor-General in office, but the period was notable for the emergence of great administrators, such as Elphinstone, Malcolm, Metcalfe and Munro.

The roll of Scotch names is indicative of the great part the Scots have played in the sound development of the Indian Empire, and to these and others we can add again that of Dundas, who was responsible for the five years' careful examination into Indian affairs by Parliament just referred to.

It may also be noted here that another effect of the long Napoleonic wars, besides those we have already mentioned, had been the genuine welding into one nation of Scotland and England. Not only had the valor of Scottish troops on the battlefields, including that of Waterloo, won admiration, but the poems of Burns and Scott, and the founding of the *Edinburgh* and *Quarterly Reviews*, were adding a new element to the intellectual life of the united kingdoms which had been hostile and almost foreign to each other for so many centuries. Of Scott's novels only one, *Waverley*, was published before 1815, but when Napoleon sailed to his permanent exile—he left behind him a Scotland which no longer looked toward France but, instead, a "Great Britain" in which the slow process of combining the complementary qualities of the peoples north and south of the Tweed had been accomplished. There was at long last a union of hearts in sympathy and understanding, looking forward to a great common future in which each would play its part, no longer divided by contentions and bitter memories.

CHAPTER V

AFTER NAPOLEON

I. The Economic Aftermath

Hisтоry does not repeat itself in precise detail but certain historical movements and epochs do bear a remarkable resemblance to one another in their main outlines. Among these are revolutions and post-war periods. During the long Napoleonic struggle, lasting almost a generation, there had been intense distress among the poor and working classes. We have already noted some of the factors at work, such as the introduction of machinery, the breakdown of the old systems of agriculture and village handicrafts, the increase and shifts of population, and what we would now call technological unemployment, as well as the different relation between the working class and their employers.

This situation would have been serious enough in itself and would have raised problems calling for the ablest statesmanship and a reforming zeal to solve. The revolutions and wars on the Continent, however, rendered it yet more desperate. As a result of the atrocities of "the Terror" in France we have seen how reform was halted. Then the long wars dislocated trade, raised prices to famine levels without raising wages, and there chanced to be poor harvests from 1792 to 1813. But if the poor suffered, the rich grew richer. The well-to-do classes had perhaps never been more prosperous or content. Armies were still small and professional. Britain itself was not invaded and death took only a slight toll. Property was still chiefly in land, and as food prices rose so

74

did the rent rolls. If markets for those who were investing in the new manufactures were being altered rapidly, speculative prices added to the wealth of the shrewd or lucky, who could also use the general uncertainty as an excuse to keep down wages.

Labor, without the right to organize, was helpless and ground down. In the Tudor period the government had tried to maintain some sort of balance between prices and wages, but at the end of the eighteenth century had been rapidly drifting toward the *laissez-faire* doctrine of the Adam Smith school of economists which was to reach its highest point in the generation after the fall of Napoleon. Without being able to help itself by the organization of trades-unions and without help from the government, labor was forced to revolt.

In 1811 came the so-called Luddite movement among the weavers, headed by an unknown leader who went by the name of Ned or King Ludd, and who became a sort of new Robin Hood to the poor. Without representation in Parliament and governed locally by justices of the peace who represented ultra-conservatism, the workers had no means of securing their rights but by organized revolution. That, however, is not the English method as a rule, and was not adopted in spite of great suffering. Labor neither threatened armed revolt nor, as contrasted with the situation during and after the World War, a century later, did it receive any concessions from government.

When the final victory over Napoleon was won at Waterloo men looked forward to a period of prosperity at once, in the normal post-war belief that because peace has come all other good things will also. It is the mood that almost invariably creates the deceptive first boom. The British did not realize, however, that the greatest war in modern history, up to then, was coinciding with the greatest social and economic change which the world has known. The expected boom did not last, and instead there ensued the deepest gloom and distress. The impoverished world could not buy the manufactured goods which had been produced in too great quantity. Due to more abundant harvests and cessation of war-time demand, the price of corn (which, it may be noted, means in Eng-

75

land all cereals, especially wheat, and not American maize) fell by about 40 per cent, and landowners faced the sudden ruin of their hopes. For the working class the decrease in food cost was more than offset by unemployment. The low "real" wages of the war had at least been better than the no wages of peace.

All classes now began to suffer, the landlords from reduced rentals, the farmers from decreased profits, the factory owners from shut-down plants, and the laboring class and workers from unemployment. The general distress combined with the fact that all felt that peace should bring good times and that sacrifices should not be called for, now the war was over, brought about a period of unrest and repression. Although historical movements always pass through stages covering considerable periods, we may conveniently take the year 1815 as marking a real change in English life. From it we may date not only the rise of modern socialism but the beginning of an ominous cleavage between classes, the comparative absence of which we have noted as having previously been one of the soundest elements in English life. The economic problems, resulting from both the war and the industrial revolution, were colossal. We of our generation can scarcely blame those in power in 1815 because they could not solve them. The difference between the two periods, however, is that in the earlier one the problems were not even sensed. The only two considered after Waterloo were the maintenance of social order, which caused cruel repression, and the safeguarding of property, which caused the enactment of unwise laws.

Parliament was dominated almost wholly by the landed magnates and in 1815, in the hope of salvaging their war-time incomes, they secured the passage of a Corn Law which prohibited the import of foreign grains unless the price went above 80 shillings a quarter (eight bushels), and the following year they succeeded in having the Income Tax repealed. As a tax on food the Corn Law was not only bitterly resented by all consumers but also by the unenfranchised factory owners who considered it an unwarranted interference with their cheap labor. The law thus destroyed the former harmony between the upper landed class and the rising moneyed middle class. The laboring class, now rapidly developing into a proletariat, was not considered by either except as a menace.

It is impossible to generalize about different years, types of employment, and geographical sections, but it may be said that the British poor and laboring people were now entering upon their darkest period in modern times. In England actual paupers might vary from a tenth to a quarter of the population, and when in that condition were almost slaves, as they could be hired out by the Poor Law Authorities, and even families separated forever. But conditions were also extremely bad for vast numbers of those who managed to keep above the level of complete destitution. Efforts to limit the working hours of children were blocked by the House of Lords, and it was only in 1819 that a very inadequate measure was passed, applying to cotton mills alone and without adequate provision for enforcement, forbidding the employment of children under nine, and limiting the working hours to twelve a day, exclusive of meals, for those between nine and sixteen. In other kinds of work children might be taken from their parents, and set to labor at even five years of age, for longer hours in fields, factories, the mines or elsewhere.

We cannot entirely blame either the stupid conservatism or callous selfishness of the Lords. As late as 1830 in the textile mills of Massachusetts in free America, children were worked thirteen hours a day, six days a week, which, a contemporary Report noted, "leaves little time for daily instruction." Long hours in industry were taken over from the "sunrise to sunset" of agriculture, and the growing humanitarianism of the age was slow in disentangling itself from evil economic doctrines and ingrained social attitudes. Without leisure and with practically no opportunity for healthy physical or intellectual recreation, the lives of even the adult workers tended to become drab and hopeless.

Housing conditions were bad, perhaps worst in the rising jerry-built towns whose ugliness has left permanent stains on England. Proper sanitation, including water closets, had to wait the coming of pipes and mains, the cheap glazed earthenware ones not being made until 1846. In the general dislocation of the old order of life, innumerable workmen had to sink into drunken idleness while they watched their cheaper-paid wives and children wear out their lives in mills or mines. What the latter meant was shown by a Report almost a generation later in which it was testified that children of five were forced to work alone all day in the dark underground, while even pregnant women had to pull coal cars on their hands and knees by a chain round their waist.

If the upper classes did not realize the problems they were facing, the exploited ones did not know what to strive for, except that to a considerable extent they did come to understand that the one thing without which nothing else could be done was the reform of Parliamentary representation. Until they could have a voice in the making of laws their grievances were not likely to be driven home to the consciousness of those in power.

In spite of the welter of human misery which marked particularly the decade following the peace, there was surprisingly little violence, and much of what there was was deliberately provoked by the fears and stupid measures of the government, which employed spies and even *agents provocateurs* to discover non-existent plots. The sporadic riots in 1816 and 1817 were put down without difficulty, and in the latter year workmen began to organize some secret societies. The government, fearing another French Revolution, which had been the nightmare of the upper classes, suspended the Habeas Corpus Act, for the last time in British history, and the following year it was allowed to come into force again. Meanwhile, a large body of suffering workmen in Manchester had started to march on London for the simple and sole purpose of presenting a petition to the Prince Regent, old King George III having long been incapacitated by his now incurable insanity. Unarmed and each man carrying a blanket, which gave them the name of the "Blanketeers," they travelled on foot, gathering recruits as they went. The government broke up the march easily with troops and Yeomanry, sending many of the workers to jail for months, though they had been guilty of no crime. In the general distress there had been a revival of the doctrines of Spence, mentioned in our first chapter, and a Spencean Society had been formed which the government pretended to believe threatened revolution, although it was the government's own spy, the notorious Oliver, who had stirred up the local insurrections.

One of the leaders of the time in stirring thought on economic problems was Robert Owen, an interesting character who had made a fortune in manufacturing cotton. Becoming disturbed by the conditions of the working class, he had developed a model factory and village for his work people at New Lanark, and had gradually come to the belief that fair conditions for all could be brought about only by the government's controlling both production and distribution. His ideas were vague and never wrought into a definite and practical system but attracted much attention, all the more because he had shown that he could be financially successful while being far in advance of the age in his treatment of his employees. His later career does not concern us here, but between Owen and his disciples and successors, such as Thomas Hodgskin, William Thompson and others, most of the ideas of later British Socialism were worked out at this time, though the term itself had not yet come into use.

More important were the Radicals, who demanded manhood suffrage and annual Parliaments, though they had no constructive social program beyond that. The leader of this group was William Cobbett, who published a paper, *The Political Register*, which he turned from a news sheet to one carrying only his views, and by thus escaping the heavy tax he was able to reduce the price from about a shilling to twopence, with the result that its circulation and influence among the working class were correspondingly increased. A Major Cartwright founded "Hampden Clubs" through the country, Sir Francis Burdett spoke to deaf ears in the Commons, and "Orator" Hunt harangued mobs from platforms. Though nothing immediate came of all this oratory and writing, workingmen were being taught to think in terms of a possible future instead of merely a return to a now irrevocably lost past.

There was a short period of prosperity, 1818-19, but distress deepened again, and with increasing unemployment the Radical ideas of Parliamentary reform became widespread. In August,

1819, a crowd estimated to have been about 50,000, unarmed and entirely peaceful citizens, gathered to make a demonstration. The crowd, meeting in St. Peter's Fields, Manchester, was attacked by a troop of Hussars who came to the help of the Yeomanry, who were hustled when attempting to arrest "Orator" Hunt. Nine men and two women were killed and about four hundred wounded. Although those in charge of the troops had lost their heads, they were heartily applauded by the government, but "Peterloo," as the massacre came to be called, was widely condemned throughout the country by sober people, and the Common Council of London sent a protest to the Regent.

The answer of government was to congratulate the magistrates responsible and to pass the notorious Six Acts through Parliament. Three of these were not unreasonable but others struck at the right of assembly and free speech. One limited practically all public meetings to members of the parish in which the meeting was held. Another hit at the right of free discussion in print by permitting magistrates to seize whatever literature they might consider blasphemous or seditious, and extending the heavy stamp duty to all papers and pamphlets of a certain size. The press was thus partially muzzled and the circulation of reading matter enormously restricted among the poorer classes.

It must be recalled, however, that if stupid repression seemed to be the government's only way of dealing with popular grievances, it did feel genuine alarm. Also there was then no police system. Today the British police, from long experience in handling crowds, and from the mutual good feeling which subsists between them and the people, have become not merely maintainers of law and order but a remarkable lubricant in the social machinery. In this earlier period there was nothing to represent order as opposed to a mob except small forces of the army or untrained and high-strung Yeomanry. The danger of bloodshed in any collision was vastly greater then than now. Any one who has watched the London "Bobbies" "protect" marchers and demonstrators, with the mutual chaffing between them, will realize the vast difference between such situations in the two periods.

After five years, in 1820, there occurred two events which appeared to give some color to the fears which the government, through its spies and in other ways, had tried to inculcate in the nation. The Cato Street conspiracy was the work of a group of only some thirty desperadoes who planned to assassinate the entire Cabinet when present at a dinner. Discovered in time, the leaders were executed. In Glasgow a small group of Radicals resisted the troops sent to disperse them, but sound opinion was shifting from the government, and turning to the view that some amount of reform was due.

The Cabinet itself, Tory in name, under the leadership of Lord Liverpool, had not been a unit as to policy. Canning, Huskisson and the rising Peel were in favor of gradual reforms, and even if all reform were opposed by men like Lord Eldon, the public was becoming reassured. In 1821 the Bank of England had been able, by a measure sponsored by Peel, to resume gold payments, a sign of returning stability which probably had a considerable psychological effect politically and socially. On the Continent revolutionary movements continued but British sympathy was growing for the peoples struggling for liberty against the autocrats of the Holy Alliance. As the years passed after the end of the war excitement, these movements could be viewed in proper perspective. Castlereagh during his long term as Foreign Secretary had not been wholly opposed to them, but feeling it necessary for his policy to keep on good terms with the leading Powers, he had limited himself chiefly to protests in secret dispatches, and had not only become extremely unpopular but had made the government appear more reactionary in some directions than it really was. In 1822, in a fit of insanity, he committed suicide, to the delight of the populace and not a few in high places, and was succeeded in office by Canning, who had never hesitated to show openly his dislike of Metternich and the other leaders of the Alliance and his sympathy for the struggling peoples. Peel had also become Home Secretary with plans for reforms.

It was high time that a change of attitude should be expressed. We have already spoken of the cleavage beginning between the different classes, and perhaps at no time had the poor been so estranged from those above them. They might not indulge in violent rebellion in spite of refusals to consider their condition, but many of the old ties of respect and loyalty had been snapped in the course of the war and the changing industrial situation, and the highest loyalty of all, that to the Crown and ruling House, were under severe strain.

II. THE CROWN

That House was still largely foreign and the first two Georges did not even speak English. In fact, German continued the language of the royal household until Edward VII, and George V, in our own day, was the first of the line to speak English without an accent.

George III, perhaps unfortunately, spoke the tongue of those he ruled, to the detriment of constitutional development and of risk to English liberty. The mad old monarch died in 1820, and the Regent, George IV, came to the throne. He was a vulgar, vain old profligate without a quality to command the respect of the nation. He had long been estranged from his wife, who had been living, it was said, a dissolute life on the Continent. His only legitimate child had died in 1817, and, at the time, none of his six younger brothers had legitimate offspring. The outlook for the succession appeared hopeless. Never had the monarchy ranked lower in the esteem of all classes, though there had been more hated monarchs. Into this Augean sty there was born a legitimate child in 1819 to the Duke of Kent, a daughter named Victoria, who was to have a profound influence on the nation and to prove the most popular monarch since the days of the great Elizabeth. Her influence was to be enormous. She was not only to restore in her day respect for the Crown but to do so just in the period of imperial development when the Crown was to become the one link holding the Empire together. If she had done nothing else in all her long life her service to the Empire would have been transcendent.

But that could not be known in 1820, when the silly fop, George

82

IV, with a touch of his father's insanity, mounted the throne. Almost immediately his cast-off wife, Caroline, returned from the Continent, demanding to be crowned Queen. The King not only denied her claims but brought suit for divorce. No one knew then or knows now whether the charges against her were true or not, but the degrading vices of the King were public. He was not only living openly with his mistresses but had committed bigamy, and even the House of Lords could scarcely swallow the noxious dose when asked to bring in a bill to dissolve the marriage and deprive the Queen of her title. The ordinary people, without other means of showing their resentment against the existing order, took up the cause of Caroline with wild enthusiasm, and the proceedings had to be dropped, though a "trial" had been held in which testimony against her had broken down. Her coarseness and vulgarity, as well as her husband's, had, however, long been obvious, and when she was forcibly restrained from entering the Abbey for the Coronation, respect for royalty ebbed to zero. After accepting a pension she died in 1821, and it was perhaps fortunate that Castlereagh cut his throat the year after, for his death opened the way, as did also some revival of prosperity, to the alleviation of feeling against both Crown and government. It had become so intense that it might possibly have brought on one of the great constitutional crises in English history.

III. LABOR AND REFORM

The Tory oligarchy in the country was still in control of Parliament but the Ministry as reorganized began at last to heed the demands for reform. Sir Robert Peel, as Home Secretary, ended the whole system of government spies and agents which had done so much harm without accomplishing the slightest good. Another great advance was made by amending the penal codes. The reforms, originating with Jeremy Bentham, had long been advocated in the Commons by Sir Samuel Romilly and Sir James Mackintosh but had always been blocked by the Lords. Under the old laws over two hundred offenses, even such minor ones as stealing fish from a pond or in any way injuring Westminster Bridge, had

83

been punishable with death. Although in many cases juries had refused to convict because of the utter disproportion of the punishment to the crimes, nevertheless the laws stood as a constant menace and were enforced in many cases. Even after Peel secured the abolition of more than half of these capital offenses the law remained harsh, but the advance was considerable and at least indicated a changing spirit.

The influence of Bentham's mind was felt in another reform, largely brought about by his disciple, Francis Place, with the aid of Huskisson in the Cabinet and Joseph Hume in the House. This was the repeal of the Combination Acts which had made trades-unions illegal and greatly hampered the workers in improving their position. The Acts were repealed in 1824 and unions have been legal ever since, though owing to the great number of strikes which occurred in the following year the sphere of trade-union activity was limited for a while to the fixing of wages only. The fact that workmen could now again form associations free from fear of legal action against them greatly fostered the machinery of the reform movement. It showed also that panic was passing, and with it the repression which had done so much to create the new and dangerous bitterness between the classes. As the Exchequer had an annual surplus at last, there was even a step made toward free trade in the reduction of duties on a number of imports. Britain seemed to be settling down after the storm, though there were yet active forces at work to bring about the crisis which we shall note in the next chapter.

IV. Foreign Policy

A fresh breeze of liberalism also appeared to be blowing through the Foreign Office. There had been revolts in Spain, Italy, Greece, and Portugal, all condemned by the great Powers with which Castlereagh had felt obliged to act. Canning's open denunciation of the attitude and actions of Austria, France and Russia in their efforts to suppress the rebellions made him popular in Britain and the hero of the Continental liberals. It is true that except in the case of Greece and Portugal Britain did nothing to assist by arms any of the struggling peoples on the Continent, but they had, as they were frequently to have in this century, a powerful voice speaking for their cause from across the Channel. The Greek revolt against Turkish misrule gained much sympathy in France as well as England, and Byron was merely the most celebrated of the volunteers who went to aid the Greek people, in whom the upper classes in England had a romantic interest because their education was so thoroughly imbued with the art and literature of the classic age. The bringing to London of the Elgin marbles from Greece in 1806–12, the death of Byron at Missilonghi, and the working-class struggle for a reformed Parliament, were all bits of the same mosaic. In 1826 Britain joined with France and Russia in a demand on Turkey to grant autonomous government to Greece. The Sultan, who for six years had been unable to subdue the rebels, had called for help from Egypt, but in the battle of Navarino, 1827, the three allied powers completely defeated the Egyptian fleet, and Greece became independent.

Meanwhile, the Holy Alliance, with which Britain had broken, had made France its agent to bring the Spaniards to the heel of their abominable King Ferdinand VII, which the French army did with ease. English emotions—anti-French, anti-Catholic, and love of freedom—were all deeply aroused. Canning made a strong protest to France and warned the reactionary government of Spain to keep its hands off Portugal, and when it refused he sent 4000 troops to the defense of that country.

There was also talk of the combined Bourbon kingdoms attempting to reconquer the revolted Spanish colonies in South America. British public opinion and governmental policy were clearly moving rapidly away from the despotic powers which they had had to use as allies in the struggle to overthrow Napoleon, and in favor of the peoples rising for their liberties against the despots. Economic interest was also heavily involved in the former Spanish-American colonies, which had become important customers for British goods after their commerce had been thrown open to the world. Canning therefore warned the powers that the British fleet would stand between them and any effort to bring the young nations rising from the ruins of the Spanish Empire under control.

Meanwhile, the United States was also watching the situation closely, not only in South America but also in the Oregon country concerning which the American Secretary of State, John Quincy Adams, was having a heated dispute with the British Minister in Washington. On the Pacific coast, still farther north, Russia, one of the most reactionary of the European powers, was colonizing and threatening southern extension. The Monroe Doctrine was already hatching in the minds of American statesmen, when Canning suddenly proposed to the United States Government that the two nations should unite in a joint declaration which in part would deny that either of them would take for itself any part of the South American colonies, and that neither of them "could see any portion of them transferred to any other power with indifference."

The two English-speaking nations might have stood before the world in a united New World policy except for the fact that the United States had recognized the independence of the new Spanish nations to the south whereas Canning refused to do so for a year and more, when it was too late. President Monroe in his message to Congress, December 2, 1823, embodied his famous Doctrine, which was rather that of Adams, as to the relations to subsist between Europe and the Americas, closing the latter to any further efforts at appropriation or colonization by European powers. This Doctrine has been maintained and observed ever since. It was far more sweeping than the British suggestion, and Canning was none too well pleased. An opportunity had also been missed for Anglo-American co-operation which might have done much to wipe out old memories and alter the relations of the two peoples in the several generations to come.

In October, however, in a several days' conference with the French Minister, Polignac, Canning had definitely warned France to keep her hands off Spain's colonies and declined to consider any general European conference on the subject unless the United States was represented at it. Although he disliked many of the implications of the Monroe Doctrine he saw that, for the immediate occasion at least, it placed another card in his 'hand. As a result Britain in Europe was able to override the pressure of Russia, Prussia, Austria and France. Although the part played by the United States, now rising to the position of a ranking nation in world affairs, must not be overlooked, the deciding factor in keeping the members of the old Alliance out of South America was the British fleet, and to that extent Canning was justified in his famous remark that he had called "a new world into existence to redress the balance of the old." France, with her temporary control of Spain, could, at least, not obtain the resources of the old Spanish American Empire.

Canning also took the occasion to warn the powers on the Continent. "Let it not be said," were his words in a public speech, "that we cultivate peace, either because we fear, or because we are unprepared for, war.... [England] while apparently passive concentrates the power to be put forth on an adequate occasion." If England had been largely reactionary for the period since the war, she was evidently, both at home and abroad, entering on a new phase.

The extreme Tories, notably Eldon and the Duke of Wellington, however, had been restive under the various moves toward reform and liberalism. The Prime Minister, Liverpool, though not a great statesman, had had the ability to hold the Cabinet together but, struck down by paralysis, he had to resign, and Canning, himself, ill and to die in four months, became head of the government. Neither the reactionaries Eldon nor Wellington, nor the liberal Peel would join him, though some of the Whigs did. The Tory party, indeed, was disintegrating, and was split into the Old Tories and the Canningites. After Canning's death, and an abortive effort to form a government under "Goody Goderich," Wellington became Prime Minister, carrying some of the Canningites with him. These, however, soon resigned and practically joined the Whigs.

Although the Old Tories were in control, two reform measures were carried out by the Wellington-Peel Ministry. By the repeal of the Test Acts in 1828 the Dissenters were freed from the political disabilities with which they had been burdened for nearly a hundred and seventy years, though Catholic Emancipation was still opposed. The other, which has been of inestimable benefit and added two words to the language, was the creation of our modern metropolitan police force. Inaugurated by Sir Robert Peel, the men have, because of his own name, since been known as "Peelers" or more commonly and affectionately as "Bobbies." The humor, kindliness and efficiency of the London "Bobby" is known the world over. He has not only become one of the most typical of British institutions but has rendered incalculable service to government and society. With these two measures the reforms ended temporarily, for the uneasy unity of the Old Tories was soon to be split wide by the problem of Ireland and the Catholics, which will be better considered in the next chapter, along with Parliamentary Reform.

V. Art and Literature

Intellectually the period we have been discussing was one of the most brilliant in British history, but socially and artistically it was dull and mediocre. The royal court, as we have seen, was at its lowest ebb. It was neither regal, moral, intelligent nor in any way interesting. Even its scandals were cheap and vulgar. As for statesmen, although a Canning would have stood out in any age, most of the Tory leaders had grown to be rather "dull dogs." The new manufacturing rich, largely Dissenters who had come from limited backgrounds, whatever else they might be were not socially brilliant. Even among the older aristocracy the long war had interrupted the habit of the grand tour which had earlier led young noblemen to spend several years travelling on the Continent, having their minds opened to a certain extent by its art, scenery and social life.

The collecting of art from foreign countries had largely ceased for the time, the Elgin marbles, already mentioned, being a most notable exception. The building of great houses had also gone out of fashion and Wellington, for example, after Waterloo undertook no such ambitious project as the Blenheim Palace of Marlborough a century earlier. The smaller houses, the factories and squalid new towns would not then have interested great architects even had they existed. In painting, the great school of Gainsborough and others had no successors in this period. Lawrence was merely academic. A local group of landscape artists, notably John Crome, flourished chiefly around the little town of Norwich, but on the whole painting became insignificant and trivial.

Among the working classes the two great means of escape were drink on the one hand and religion on the other. If many unhappily chose the former, vast numbers also chose the latter. In high society Deism and an easy-going infidelity were still fashionable, but the increasing wealth of the Dissenters and the turning of masses of the poor to the Evangelical sects brought about increased power and a rivalry of creeds. This was evidenced not only in the repeal of the Test Acts but in the increase of the facilities for education, particularly primary. The established Church saw to it that no government money should be spent on schools for those outside its own fold, but private contributions gathered themselves together into a great stream, and in mere self-defense the Church had to bestir itself. Professor G. M. Trevelyan is authority for the statement that, by 1818, 600,000 English children out of 2,000,000 were attending a school of some sort. Without this tendency toward a vastly increased literacy the orderly working-class movement and Parliamentary reform would not have been possible, poor and scattered as the education received may have been. It would seem to be unquestionable that it was the rivalry and conflict between the various religious sects which had tended to delay even such educational improvement as was now at last beginning.

The literature of the period, so different from that of the Age of Reason of the eighteenth century, reflects the new spirit of the times and presages that of the generations about to come on the scene.

The chief note struck by the intellectual and æsthetic literary life of the period was that of individualism. With the exception of a few leading writers this was closely linked to deep interest in social problems. There were, in general, four groups. We have already spoken of the beginnings of Socialism in the writings and activities of such men as Spence and Owen. There were also the Economists, such as Ricardo, who were preaching the doctrines of both individualism and the need of social reconstruction. There was also the group who came to be called Benthamites, as followers of Jeremy Bentham. Bentham's philosophy was superficial, with his best-known sayings that the end of society was "the greatest good of the greatest number" and that "every man is the best judge of his own happiness," yet he had a profound and salutary influence. The first of the phrases mentioned was so simple, apparently, and yet so new that it was a powerful slogan with which to combat the abuses of the earlier nineteenth century. The second was an antidote to the nascent theory that the individual exists for the good of society instead of the reverse.

The theory was not, indeed, being preached in the crude and brutal form adopted by the totalitarian dictators of today, but there was nevertheless a subtle and dangerous belief growing up that if the *national* wealth and power increased all would be well regardless of effects on the lives and happiness of individual citizens. Attention was too much concentrated on the statistics of national wealth produced by the factory system and not on the well-being of the operatives. English economy and government were threatening to become one vast and soulless machine instead of means to create a land of happy homes. If during the nineteenth century the doctrines of *laissez faire* had their evil influence, the above doctrines of the Economists and the Benthamites did an untold amount to keep Britain from drifting toward the German idea of the state.

Bentham's influence was also permanent in another form. It is true that he was dry and limited in vision, looking, for example, in his great work of law reform to procedure rather than to spirit. But the careful examination of facts and detail which the Benthamites made of problems before they suggested measures may be considered as laying the foundation for the later Royal Commissions and their Reports which have been, to our own day, such an extraordinary help in British government and legislation.

90

In pure literature any age should be called great which includes such names as Scott, Byron, Wordsworth, Keats, Shelley, Lamb, Jane Austen, De Quincey, Landor, Coleridge and Blake, with other lesser ones. If Scott, whose Waverley novels appeared annually to help him pay off what he considered a debt of honor of £100,000 incurred by the failure of his publishing house, sought refuge from the present in the romance of the past; if Miss Austen's ever-delightful stories reflect little of the stress of the times; if Keats felt that all he needed to know was that "Beauty is truth, truth beauty"; and if there is nothing revolutionary in "St. Charles" Lamb's quiet and whimsical essays, yet the whole literature of the period is marked by a new spirit toward the simple, the poor and the downtrodden.

The fiery verses of Byron and Shelley breathe genuine revolt, but though the calm verse of Wordsworth is in utter contrast there is no less implicit in its preoccupation with all humble things, the revolution in thought which was to characterize the century to come. Perhaps, also, at no other period than this in English life was the literature that flowered more characteristically English in its wide gamut from the inflated egoism of Byron to the self-effacing whimsies of Lamb; in its love of the past history of the race and of the beauties of the countryside; in its preoccupation, pragmatically rather than theoretically, with the problems of government, and in its soaring imagination and glorious rhetoric.

Different as the many authors are from one another there is not one who could not be recognized at once as British not only in the material with which he dealt but even more in his treatment of it. The literature also offers strong contrast to those of the earlier two great periods. There is a vast change from the buoyancy and optimistic patriotism of the Elizabethan era, and an abandonment of the classicism of the Age of Johnson. The kings and queens who strutted in the Elizabethan theatres have gone, as has the complacency of the Age of Reason. The common man has taken the stage surrounded by a winged host of problems.

The conditions of literature were also changing. Not only were authors influenced by the currents of the time, but publishing houses and magazines were enabling authors to be printed without the aid of the aristocratic "patron" of earlier days. There was also a new public. The whole generation before the Reform Bill of 1832 was stirred by deep emotions, hopeful or fearsome and hardly realizable to us today, by the increase in the numbers of those who could or were reading. We have spoken of the great increase in primary education but among the working class adult education, also, was beginning to make progress. Bookshops multiplied, although England was far behind America in public libraries, which did not come until 1850. Reading, with its influence on reading matter, increased not only among the workers but also in the middle class. It was said, soon after this period, that in the Mechanics' Institutes which were found in almost every town, there were far more "merchants, manufacturers, clerks, shopkeepers, tradesmen, artists" than mechanics, and that their libraries were almost wholly taken over by the middle class. Reading was no longer a privilege of merely the aristocratic and rich, nor were authors any longer dependent on them only, or on political parties, as in the days of Swift and Defoe. The great improvement of the roads, thanks to Macadam and Telford, whose names still persist in road-making, and the consequent increase in amount and rapidity of travel stirred the minds of the nation and made the dissemination of news and literature more easy.

The smooth, hard surfaces of the network of new roads enabled both merchandise and passengers to travel with a speed which seemed as great an advance then as later in the 1830's was that made by the railways, and in our own day by the motor car and plane. It was the great period of the stagecoaches, which sped at ten miles an hour and transformed the life of the country. So deep was the impress made by the new life of the road and the coaching inns that, with all the changes in the following century, Christmas cards and tradition still bear witness to the fact that we think of coaching days and ways as being peculiarly England. Some years after the first steamboats had been tried in America, one was launched on the Clyde in 1812, and they gradually came into use for coasting service. The canal system was practically completed after two generations of work, and all parts of the United Kingdom were, in one way and another, closely bound together. Ease of transport increased domestic travel for both business and pleasure, and this meant better understanding and enlarged minds. Thus it was a nation increasingly alert intellectually and with a shifting center of gravity of intellectual and political interests that approached the great crisis of the reform of Parliament.

VI. The Empire Overseas

The Empire had also been developing, although owing to the collapse of empires in the preceding half century, including the British loss of the United States, imperial possessions were regarded lightly or as possible liabilities by most people. If the Empire grew it was chiefly because of trade and the now increasing pressure of population and of unemployment at home. The acquisition of Malta, Mauritius and the Cape had rounded out Britain's already strong control of the sea routes for the defense of her colonies and India. Yet when Castlereagh paid some £3,000,000 for the Cape the argument was that it would be a needed market for manufactures, a trading depot and a means of preventing the extension, by other powers, of the slave trade, rather than an integral part of a deliberately planned world empire. In fact there was much opposition, in the hard times following the war, to the expenditure of the money necessary for the defense of the various possessions which, it was argued, were not worth the cost.

In South Africa the reduction in the garrison led to some difficulties with both Dutch and natives, for the Cape was scarcely regarded as a colony, and English immigration was slight until after 1820. The first going out of settlers in considerable numbers was due to a movement assisted by Parliament, and in a few years the English ascendancy was marked by their language becoming the only official one. Most of the local Dutch were not able to speak any language save their own, but it was also impossible to carry on the work of administration and the courts in one the English did not understand. The bilingual problem is always a difficult one, and the change, together with certain economic restrictions, undoubtedly did much to give the rural Dutch a sense of inferiority and resentment, and even tended to reduce them to the status of "poor whites." Britain had treated Holland generously in the peace treaties and paid a good round sum for her South African possessions, but her citizens in the transferred territory naturally did not take kindly to the cession. The very fact of change of control and the problems it inevitably raised were the seeds of future strife.

The Cape, however, was not only a market but it occupied for the route to India, before the days of the Suez Canal, somewhat the position of Gibraltar for the Mediterranean. In India itself the period was marked by the complete and final subjugation of the Marathas and the annihilation of the Pindaris. With these events came the pacification of all the central part of the peninsula. In 1826 British rule was also extended to Burma, the Burmese having foolishly attacked India, pushing in their boats even up to Calcutta. The tattooing of their bodies with pictures of ferocious beasts to frighten the British failed of its object and was poor defense against the firearms of the enemy they had wantonly attacked. Yet, although no match for their opponents, they could fight well under certain conditions, but, as they gave no quarter and executed all prisoners taken, the two years' war developed into a cruel one on both sides.

Exaggerated accounts became current both as to the ferocity of the Burmese and as to British defeats, which, together with certain real and alleged grievances connected with military service, resulted in a mutiny by Sepoy troops at Barrackpur, in India, an ominous forerunner of the great mutiny a generation later. The trouble centered chiefly in the 47th Native Infantry, which refused to obey orders, and which, after ample warning had been given, were fired on on the parade ground. Many were killed, five ringleaders were executed, and hundreds were sentenced to fourteen years' hard labor.

In 1828 Lord Cavendish-Bentinck arrived as Governor-General to find disordered finances and much to reform. In spite of the fact that one of his economy measures involved the licensing of the direct passage of opium from Central India to Bombay, instead of its former route through Sind, so that the British Government acquired an income from the demoralization of the Chinese smokers, his general reforms and attitude toward the natives were such as probably saved the charter of the Company in Parliament in 1833 when England was bent on reform and humanitarianism and had grown tired of mere conquests and additions to Indian territory.

Although there had been much that had been noble and ideal in Indian thought, Hinduism had become corrupted by a mass of revolting customs, including that of *suttee* or the enforced immolating of a widow on the funeral pyre of her husband. Cruel and degrading as this practice of burning alive would have been even if acquiesced in, it was frequently enforced against the extreme unwillingness of the widows, often mere children. In 1829 Bentinck abolished it in Bengal and the next year extended the abolition to other provinces. A Bengalese, Ram Mohun Roy, a highly cultivated man who knew Sanskrit, Persian, Arabic, English, Greek and Hebrew, had long been writing against the custom, incurring complete ostracism among his own people, but he served his race well when, a few years after Bentinck had made himself unpopular by forbidding the rite, Roy appeared in London before Parliament to speak against a petition of 500 high-caste Hindus who demanded that Bentinck's action be rescinded.

The Governor also succeeded in suppressing *thagi*, the thags, or thugs, forming a powerful hereditary caste of criminals. With these and other reforms, such as the abolition of female infanticide, the seven years' service of Bentinck marked a peaceful and highly beneficial period between two long series of wars. He had gone to India imbued with the best reforming zeal of the time in England. At home, India, which in its early days had afforded a conspicuous hunting ground for self-seeking adventurers, was closely connected with the establishment of the modern British Civil Service. Government posts had always gone by favor, and the situation was much like that which is prevalent in the United States today. Speaking of members of Parliament, even the Duke of Wellington, who was no reformer, had said, "In fact the only question about local patronage is whether it shall be given to the disposal of one gentleman or another." We have already seen how his brother had established a college in India for the training of men for the service, and in 1806 a college at Hertford in England, later moved to Haileybury, had been established for the same purpose. Toward the end of the Napoleonic war the East India Company had agreed that all candidates for administrative posts should have spent at least four years at Haileybury, and although another generation was to pass before there were any such sweeping rules for Civil Servants in the home government, this may be taken as the beginning, in Britain, of the idea that those in higher permanent government positions must be trained and not be mere political appointees.

In the Pacific colonies progress was not rapid. In New Zealand, there was more or less anarchy among the group of traders, colonists, and escaped convicts, of many nationalities, and in 1823 the Colonial Office even declared that the islands were not a British possession. In spite of the fear of the Maoris as fierce cannibals, a fear fostered so as to deter criminals from New South Wales from escaping thither, various companies were formed to assist immigration, but these proved mostly abortive and real settlement belongs to our next period.

In Australia exploration had continued rapidly and the full value of the continent had begun to be realized. Sturt, who was tracing the river systems, was so overwhelmed with joy when he found that the Darling was a tributary of the Murray that he ordered the Union Jack to be hoisted and the men to give three cheers. His comment must be added as an example of British reticence. "It was an English feeling," he wrote, "an ebullition, an overflow, which I am ready to admit that our circumstances and situation will alone excuse." Victoria was settled and the foundations laid of West Australia. By 1826 there was even talk of local self-government. Population was increasing quite rapidly but there was still the difficulty of the large proportion of convicts and ex-convicts before self-government of the type that had existed in the earlier North American and other colonies could be inaugurated.

In Canada there was something of the same difficulty, owing to the large French population in Lower Canada. The Act of 1791 had established a representative government, but in practice the Colonial Office control and the patronage that went with it largely nullified the intentions of the Act, and there was little common ground between the governing clique and the electorate. A leader, Louis Papineau, came to represent all the French stood for, whereas the Governor, Lord Dalhousie, represented English ideas. In London, Lord Bathurst had long held sway in the Colonial Office, but after his retirement in 1827 his successors were to prove more friendly to a genuinely popular government and expressions of opinion. The time seemed ripe to send a delegation to England to lay the whole situation before Parliament, a move which was to eventuate in the famous Report by Lord Durham some years after, in 1839, which is now a landmark in the history of British imperial policy and which will be considered later.

Thus in the post-war period, one always to be dreaded, Britain in spite of many ills and acute distress had not only avoided revolution and armed strife but had continued to build up her power abroad and to set her course at home in the direction of reform and a wider extension of liberty for all classes. The period of stupid repression had passed, and the years of her greatest power and prestige lay just ahead, in spite of problems yet to be solved.

CHAPTER VI

THE REVOLUTION IN IDEAS

I. The Sense of Law and Order

THE FEW YEARS covered in this chapter, 1830–1837, were among the most fateful and characteristically British in the long history of empire. Amid revolution elsewhere England succeeded in transferring power peacefully and by Parliamentary action from one class to another. Also the accession of Victoria completely altered the moral atmosphere of the Court, enabling the Crown to gain the affection and respect of the British peoples at home and overseas, and to become the mystic symbol of unity. Both these events, the transfer of political power largely to the middle class, and the position which the Queen and the Crown assumed in the consciousness of the race, were of profound influence upon the destinies not only of Britain but of the whole Empire.

George IV had died in 1830 and been succeeded by his brother, the fourth William, who was eccentric and whom many thought likely to become insane like his father. In any case, the change of monarch had done nothing to restore the position of the royal family in popular regard, though William adopted an ultra-democratic manner in public which tended to lower rather than to raise him in the esteem of the people. The question of "the people" was looming very large everywhere in 1830. In France, that year, a popular revolution deposed the King, Charles X, and enthroned a distant kinsman, Louis Philippe, in his stead with the new and significant title of "King of the French" instead of "of France." The movement was largely of the middle class, who objected to Charles chiefly because he had ignored them and used his autocratic power solely on behalf of himself and the aristocracy. In that respect his overthrow exerted a considerable influence on the English situation where the middle class was also to demand transfer of power from the great landed magnates to themselves.

The situation on the Continent was, however, in reality very different from that in Britain. The repressive system of Metternich and the other rulers had suppressed freedom of speech from Waterloo to the overthrow of Charles. Without liberal institutions and the habit of peaceful discussion, the peoples resorted to violent revolution, upheavals in Germany, Italy, Poland and Belgium following immediately upon that in France. No permanent gains, however, were made, and eighteen years later in the vast revolutionary wave of 1848 practically every government was to be engulfed except the despotic one of Russia and the free one of Great Britain. It was typical of the British, as contrasted with their Continental neighbors, that their revolution, if we may call it so, of 1830–32 was comparatively peaceful, as well as constitutional, and lasting.

The long English history of give and take, with compromise at the last and often critical moment, might have indicated that such would be the case, but many were by no means sure it would be so in 1830. In Birmingham Thomas Attwood had organized his Political Union with thousands of members, demanding the reform of Parliament. In the counties south of London occurred a revolt of the agricultural poor with much burning of hayricks and destruction of farming machinery. It was wholly non-political but it terrified farmers and the large landowners and was put down with merciless severity by the government. In London itself there were large meetings of radicals who did nothing worse than make threatening speeches, but so great was the alarm that it was judged better not to allow the new King to drive through the streets for the opening of Parliament. In the industrial North there were many strikes with wild talk of overthrow of the existing order and a march on London, which did not materialize. Nowhere was there any genuine revolutionary propaganda, leader or party. The scattered and uncoördinated mutterings, threats, and even burnings were the more or less simultaneous expression of men driven desperate by their economic condition, low wages, the burden of tithes to the clergy and the unsatisfactory Poor Laws. Even among the farm laborers, who were the most violent, although many threats were used there were many cases of talking the situation over with the clergyman or landowner, and settlements peaceably reached, as with Lord Gage of Sussex. In reading some of the papers presenting the grievances of the poor, one is impressed equally by their reality and by the clear and moderate way in which they are set forth. Nevertheless, the well-to-do were in a panic, and this fact, contrasted with the actual amount of violence, allows us to infer how deeply rooted the sense of law and order had become in the nation.

II. Ireland Aflame

There had also been trouble in Ireland. There, racial, economic and religious problems were inextricably entwined. To a large extent the great landowners were Protestants, and many were absentee English. The Irish land system was always worse than that in England, the Irish landlord refusing to make the improvements which were customary on English estates, and even charging higher rents when the impoverished tenant made any himself. As elsewhere in this period, population was rapidly increasing, and may have been 7,500,000 by 1830, much too large for the rack-rent farming without the industries which it had been hoped might be established after the Union in 1800.

That Union, from which so much good might have flowed, had been disliked by the Irish, and with just cause. Catholic Emancipation, which it had been believed would follow, was denied, and if the Irish Parliament in Dublin had been inefficient that at Westminster proved to be more so. It did nothing whatever to relieve the desperate economic situation which even before the serious famine of 1822 had been reducing the peasantry to almost incredible pov-

erty and which was the cause of most of the constant agrarian outrages. For these repression was the only policy adopted. Parliament acted much like a doctor who in treating a seriously ill patient refuses to consider the disease and merely knocks the patient
on the head when he has an attack of delirium. Even the Irish reformers gave most of their attention to the religious problem.

Grattan, who had realized he could do nothing as a member of
the Parliament in London, died in 1820, and the new Irish leader,
Daniel O'Connell, was a man of different type. In Ireland, there
was no middle class to mediate between the downtrodden peasantry, almost wholly Catholic, and the Protestant landlords who
controlled their votes under threat of eviction, a threat almost universally effective, for, bad as was the English Poor Law at this
time, the Irish peasant thrown off his bit of land had not even that
slight protection against beggary and starvation. For a dozen years
before the famine, Catholic Emancipation, which among other
things would have permitted Irish Catholics to hold public office,
might have passed the Commons several times, but was always
blocked by the Lords. In Ireland O'Connell built up his organization of the Catholic Association to snatch political power from
the landlord class, mixing racialism, economics and religion in the
stew he offered to the starving Irish, and in 1828, in County Clare,
he won election to Parliament for himself against one of the most
popular landlords in the country. It was a momentous event.
O'Connell, who had become the recognized leader of the Irish
people, had been elected but because he was a Catholic he was not
allowed to take the seat he had won. Ireland was aflame, and the
question which had simmered so long now threatened civil war.

The Duke of Wellington, who was Prime Minister and who,
like the recent sovereigns, had been strongly opposed to Catholic
Emancipation, now realized that such an Act must be passed to
avoid revolution or civil war, and in 1829 it was carried through
Parliament against the wishes of George IV, the University of
Oxford and almost all of the Tory elements, who were furious.
Though the Act was passed the British showed themselves as little
magnanimous in carrying it out as they had to the American col-

onies after their successful revolt. A number of important results, however, ensued. O'Connell, who was required to be re-elected, was able to gather about him a group of Irish members in Parliament who were in the future often to hold the balance of power between the English parties, and Wellington's Tory government had to resign.

III. The Great Reform Bill

The Duke had lost practically the support of all the factions in his party, and the way was open for the reinstatement of the Whigs, a most fortunate event pregnant with vast consequences for the Kingdom and Empire. The Tory party had been shipwrecked on the rock of Catholic Emancipation. The Irish question had ceased to have repercussions merely in Ireland. It had broken up a great historic party in England, and O'Connell had also prepared the way for the coming Reform Bill by showing how effective mass action by the people could prove. These were the Irish contributions to reform in Britain, where an added impetus was to be given by the acute depression in 1831.

The times were fast changing, and everywhere the peoples were demanding a larger share of self-government, which meant a reorganization of the old order. This, in the shape of Parliamentary reform, had been bitterly opposed by the Duke and the Tories. Catholic Emancipation and the seating of Irish members in Parliament and on the bench formed the first breach in the walls of entrenched privilege, but the whole system had to go. The problem for the men of that day was whether the system would be overthrown by revolution or transformed by constitutional methods. Had the Duke, with his narrow military mind, and his reactionary party followers remained in power, the first alternative might unhappily have been the one which would have had to be chosen. Fortunately the accession of the Whigs enabled the people to follow the path of peace though not without excitement and danger.

The new government, headed by Lord Grey and including such men as Lord John Russell, Lord Palmerston and Viscount Melbourne, brought in a Reform Bill on March 1, 1831. Lord Grey and a few other reformers had believed since 1820 that a wide-sweeping change was essential. This seems clearly obvious to us, to whom the then existing system of election to the House of Commons appears utterly absurd. The qualifications of electors and the basis of representation of towns, boroughs and counties varied all over the United Kingdom and Ireland. To mention only a few of the glaring anomalies we may note that in Scotland less than 4000 electors returned all the 45 members for that country, there being only 34 voters in the entire county of Sutherland and 33 who elected the member for Edinburgh. The counties and boroughs of Catholic Ireland were for the most part under the control of the Protestant landlords. In England there were a few boroughs in which there was genuine representation and the county members were fairly representative of the smaller gentry and larger farmers. These members, however, were swamped in the House by the 403 members from boroughs which were almost wholly owned or controlled by certain magnates or small oligarchies. It was estimated in 1827 that 276 of the borough members out of the total number of seats in the House of 658 were owned by large landlords. Of these 203 belonged to Tories.

These seats could be bought and sold like any other personal property and sometimes almost the entire value of a country estate would lie in the ownership of a seat in Parliament. Seats were sometimes sold for as high as twenty or thirty thousand pounds, and a general election might thus bring a handsome fortune to the lucky owner of a seat. In some places a mere handful of electors, who could be easily bought for small sums, elected two members. The most notorious case was that of the borough of Old Sarum which sent two representatives to Westminster, though it had no inhabitants at all, the members being appointed by the owner of the vacant land! On the other hand such large new cities as Sheffield, Leeds, Birmingham and Manchester had no representation whatever, though the last had a population of 180,000. To cite other figures, it was stated in the *Black Book* of 1820 that 144 peers nominated 300 members of Parliament and that the government with

123 other persons could nominate 187 more, a heavy majority entirely under control of the landed aristocracy and the government with its hangers-on.

Thus the working class was practically wholly disfranchised, the middle class mostly so, as were also the rapidly rising business and industrial magnate groups, unless here and there a few of the latter might buy landed estates with a seat attached or combine to buy a borough. Absurd as this system may seem, it had been many centuries in developing and involved vested interests in the private ownership of seats and in the control of government by a class. Not only does no class ever give up its privileges without a struggle but it is human nature to regard one's own privileges as somehow the basis of a sound and orderly society. Moreover, any situation, whether it be that of the American revolutionists in 1776 or the Tories struggling to maintain themselves in 1830, is always rationalized. It was claimed that the Parliamentary system, odd as it was, had made Britain great; that all classes were "virtually" if not directly represented; that it enabled brilliant young men to enter public life and developed a governing class made up of the most substantial ranks in the country; and that the liberties of England, from Magna Carta down, had been won without any such dangerous broadening of the franchise as the reformers proposed.

Some of these statements could not be gainsaid, but nevertheless both the middle and working classes were insistent, and properly so, when Lord Grey introduced his bill. In considering any historical crisis we have to allow for the atmosphere, the conditions and prejudices of the time,—and not of our own,—if we are to be fair. To do otherwise is to be unjust to those who were opposed to the course history was to take and to detract from the vision and ability of those who aligned themselves with the future.

The old system was fast breaking down. During the nineteenth century the House of Lords, including both peers and bishops, was to remain an almost steady drag on social progress of every sort. In the last years before the Reform Bill the level of intelligence and public spirit had also fallen low in the Commons, and the "spoils system," which still plagues the United States, was at its height in England. Members of Parliament, stubbornly resisting reform of their own body, were inclined to resist change or reform in any other department of the national life lest the flood once let loose should carry away their own privileged position. In spite of all, however, and with all its faults, the form of Parliamentary government in Britain was the most democratic in Europe, and the anti-reformers could justifiably point to this fact, as well as to the excesses of "reform" or revolutionary movements on the Continent. Such was the situation when Lord Grey introduced his measure.

He had been placed in power not merely by the Whigs but by the ultra-Tories as well, who had helped to force the resignation of Wellington. All parties believed that whatever measure of reform might be introduced would be very moderate and, while throwing a sop to the reformers, would not in reality change matters much. When it was proposed that sixty boroughs should be totally disfranchised, one member taken from forty-seven more each, and other drastic changes be made, including a uniform £10 householder qualification in all boroughs, the cry went up at once that the Constitution was in danger. The £10 clause, that is, the occupying of premises renting for 4s. a week, would have given the vote to small shopkeepers and higher-grade workmen, and although the old supposed balance between King, Lords and Commons had long been upset in favor of the first two, it was now claimed that it would be upset wholly in favor of the last. The way seemed opening for manhood suffrage and mob rule, with government by whim and passion without the steadying influence of property. The French Revolution and the Reign of Terror, only a generation back, came forcibly to men's minds. Many believed that not only was all property endangered but the very stability of society and the state which had been built up through many centuries.

On the other hand the Whig leaders had undoubtedly spoken for the bulk of the nation and a part at least of the governing class had taken the popular side. The fight, however, was to be terrific. Not only the 150 members of Parliament who were told that their seats were to be abolished, but the governing class in general felt that the whole life they had known was to be ruined, while excitement among the general populace was intense. The debates in Parliament, which were by this time being published, filled the news sheets, and discussion was universal throughout the country. On the second reading of the bill (the first on which a vote is taken), it passed by a majority of only one vote in the Commons, and a general election was called for. To the new Parliament came a large majority pledged in favor of the bill, and this time the Commons passed it by over one hundred. In the Lords it was heavily defeated, and the aroused people expressed the vehemence of their resentment not only in huge mass meetings but in some places by mob violence. Public buildings were sacked, jails burned, and the great Birmingham Political Union pledged its members to pay no taxes until the bill was passed. The whole nation was in a turmoil, and, after the measure was passed for a third time in the Commons, the now frightened Lords passed it in March, 1832, by a majority of nine, but shortly after undid their work by altering it so that the pocket-boroughs should not be abolished. The government at once asked the King to create new peers, as Queen Anne had done to overcome the opposition of the Lords on a previous occasion, but he refused and the government resigned. The storm was now at its height. So strong was the public feeling that Wellington was unable to form a ministry and Grey had to be recalled.

A run started on the Bank of England and plans were made for open revolt. Finally the King consented to create the necessary number of peers to force "the Bill, the whole Bill, and nothing but the Bill" through the Upper House. He was most reluctant to do so, but the threat was to suffice. At his suggestion Wellington and enough peers refrained from voting to allow the bill to be passed by its supporters, and on June 7 it was signed by the King. Even in the unreformed Parliament it had been shown that the Lords could not permanently hold out against the expressed will of the people, and with the reformed Commons a new era began.

The moment had been one of the most critical in English history and England had probably never been nearer to a serious class war. Fear of revolution had had its influence on the moneyed men among the Tories as well as the Whigs, but fortunately sound leadership on the part of such men as Grey, Russell and others, as well as the English sense for discussion and compromise, had saved the day.

It must be recalled that democracy at this time was considered almost as Communism is today, and it was thought by many that the Reform Bill would immediately usher in democracy full-fledged with overthrow of the monarchy, the aristocracy and probably vast impairment or confiscation of private property. Opposed to the change had been a large part of the great families and the Church almost as a solid unit. It had been wrought in English fashion by a combination of aristocratic leadership and the more sober elements in the classes below them, with the rest of the nation consenting to "play the game" when the choice lay inevitably between compromise and ruin. It did not, however, have the immediate effects feared by its opponents. Power was indeed largely transferred from the former ruling oligarchy to the rising middle class. The poorer working classes were still almost wholly unenfranchised and had to wait another generation for their turn, but King and Lords remained parts of the Constitution and there were none of the dire results anticipated as to property.

It is true that there had been radical changes of principle. The old type of government had gone for good: government, as the Federalists in the early United States called it, by "the rich, the wise and the good" (as though they were synonymous), for the benefit of the many. The Lords had had to bow to the national will, and William's threat of creating peers, following on Anne's actually having done so, established a precedent of controlling that House which became permanent and of which we shall hear again later in our story. But if the Lords had learned that in the last resort they would have to yield to the popular will, so did the Crown, and William was the last monarch who tried to control the formation of a ministry, which hereafter was to be solely the prerogative of the majority in Parliament.

Nevertheless if the workers were for the time left voteless, they had done much to help the middle class to attain to power, and a cleavage occurred in consequence between the two lower classes of English society. Having got power, the middle class became steadily more conservative, as was natural, whereas the working class, who had largely fought the fight and then lost the prize, turned to more violent methods in the industrial field. The new middle-class government, however, because it was broader-based, proved more difficult to fight than had been the power of the great nobles and magnates. Even after the Reform Bill five out of every six adult males were still without the franchise, and an era of more radical agitation for universal manhood suffrage, under the leadership of such men as Cobbett and Henry Hunt, was to be the natural result of the disappointment of the laboring class.

It may be noticed here that, although Pitt's Reform proposals, which had been accepted by Lord John Russell less than a decade before the passing of the great bill in 1832, had called for compensation to owners of seats, compensation was not even mentioned in the later debates. People may have asked themselves, as they did a generation later, at the time of doing away with ownership of officers' commissions in the armed forces, whether the nation had to buy back its own government. Life in the eighteenth century, however, had been honeycombed with private ownership of public offices, and many an owner of a seat which, as we have seen, might bring him in a windfall of twenty to thirty thousand pounds in a general election, may well have felt that the protecting walls around the Jericho of property were falling at the blast of the trumpet of Demos.

The effects of the passage of the great Reform Bill may be regarded from two other aspects also. England as yet cared little about empire. The period of later nineteenth-century imperalism was yet far ahead. The Empire was still to grow in haphazard fashion, but it was of inestimable benefit that it was to grow and be governed by an increasingly free and democratic Britain at its center. If, as has been said, manhood suffrage was implicit in the £10 qualification, it may also be said that the twentieth-century British Commonwealth of self-governing nations was likewise implicit in the Reform Bill of 1832. This was not due to any extraordinary vision of the future on the part of those who had passed the bill. They had saved England from possible revolution but they did not envisage the growth of democracy. The point is that the step they took inevitably led to later steps and developments.

IV. EFFECTS OF THE BILL

The effect outside of England in the Empire was felt first and immediately in Scotland, where the people had before possessed no real representation or any opportunity to make themselves heard politically. As soon as they had genuine representation in the British Parliament they secured the passage of an Act, 1833, to enlarge their municipal electorates and reform their local governments. The Reform Bill had in fact, as Gladstone said long after, been the "political birth" of the Scottish nation.

In England, also, there was to be reform of the local administrations which was second in importance only to that of the national system. English municipal governments had been run almost entirely by petty oligarchies, and few indeed had anything like a democratic franchise. Most citizens, including almost all Dissenters, Whigs and what we would now call radicals, were totally excluded from any voice in their own local affairs. At a time when towns and cities were growing rapidly local administration was a mass of venality and confusion without the citizens being able to do anything about it. This system was closely bound to the old national political system which we may call that of the rotten boroughs, which had its roots in local control as the American party system now has in city and ward politics. Unless the Reform Bill had swept away the old national system there would have been no possibility of improving local conditions. In 1835 everywhere, except in London, the old corporations of the larger municipalities were abolished and new forms of local government were substituted in which the franchise was extended to include all who paid taxes. This involved an even greater revolution in ideas than the Reform Bill itself. County government, however, which meant all the rural life of England, remained unchanged and in the hands of the justices of the peace for more than a half century longer so that the countryside remained aristocratic long after the towns had become even more democratic than the nation itself.

V. Further Reforms

In the early 1830's reform was in the air and we can sense a new England taking shape. Parliamentary representation, if not yet including all classes, had changed its basis and it was obvious that including a large part of the middle class in the governing one was but a step toward the inclusion of all at some later day, as the £10 qualification was likewise a step toward manhood suffrage. The complete ascendency of the House of Commons and its electorate had also been achieved. From 1832 may be dated, moreover, the rise of the modern parties. The name Whig was still used for the party which had achieved reform without revolution but now included so many groups that Liberal became the better and accepted designation of it. In the same way Tory, which had come to mean the die-hards and opponents of all change, was replaced by Conservative, and under these titles the leading two parties were to continue for more than a century and thus the modern political alignment, except for the Labor Party, had come into being. The Liberals were to remain in almost undisputed control for ten years after the Reform Bill, and the important developments in the Empire at large will be spoken of in the next chapter, but we may here speak of other reforms and changes in Britain itself which helped to shape life to the form in which we know it.

The Penal Code, which had still been marked by excessive and self-defeating severity, was greatly modified and only the gravest crimes, after the reforms of 1837 and 1841, remained punishable by death. The self-respect and morale of seamen in the Royal Navy were also greatly increased by the abolition of the dreaded and degrading method of securing men for service by means of the press gangs of the eighteenth century.

In 1833 came the first workable factory legislation, including the "Children's Charter," by which the ages and hours of labor for children working in factories were limited, although the limits placed seem cruel to us today. Except in silk mills no children under nine were allowed to work, and the hours were limited to eight a day for children under thirteen, and twelve for those between that age and eighteen. Slight as the reform was it marked a significant change from the popular doctrine of *laissez faire* and the beginning again of a policy of national responsibility for the condition of all citizens. Perhaps the greatest advance made by the Act was the establishment of a government-paid body of inspectors whose duty was to see that the law was enforced. It was in such changes in legislation, involving both centralization and enforcement, that the influence of the Benthamites achieved most both for the poor and the workers in factories.

Closely connected with this new sense of responsibility was the abolition of slavery in the West Indies, which, although it was an imperial rather than a British problem, may be mentioned here, as it stemmed from the same reforming and humanitarian spirit which produced the beginning of the long series of factory Acts. As we have seen, the slave trade had been abolished a generation earlier, but, as in the South of the United States, slavery still flourished as an institution and seemingly as the only form of labor on the great plantations. Slavery, both in America and the Islands, had in the past been fostered by the British Government, but in the general reform wave of the 1830's British feeling against it had grown too strong to be longer stayed.

The problem was simpler than the American one, both from the standpoint of numbers and of economics and politics. In America one great section of the nation was arrayed against the other section, but there could be no question of civil war between a few small islands and the rest of the British Empire. It was characteristic, however, of British respect for property and vested rights, that when slavery was abolished in 1833 the slave-owners received £20,000,000 in compensation. Had the population and resources of the island plantation owners been sufficiently comparable to those of Britain, which was believed to be ruining their prosperity, as the American South believed theirs to be in comparison with the North, compensation would have been refused and civil war would have ensued.

In 1833 also began the system of national education, although, like other beginnings, it was wholly inadequate. The established Church had practical control of all education. Dissenters were excluded from Oxford and Cambridge, and therefore established the non-residential University College in London, which later became a model for many of the newer provincial universities in the latter part of the century. It was an event of great importance, but even more so was the grant in 1833 of the sum of £20,000 by the government to two private societies, one supported by the Church and the other by Dissenters, which had been founding schools based on new ideas. This public aid, which has been steadily and enormously increased ever since, followed in a half dozen years by the formation of what developed into the present Department of Education, was the beginning of real public education in England in the American sense as contrasted with what the English call "public schools" but which are in reality private and frequently, as in the case of Eton, Harrow and other notable institutions, very exclusive and costly. For the smaller private boarding schools of the worst type we have to turn to Dickens, as for so much else relating to the evil aspects of English life in the next few decades.

Another sign of advancing ideas was the new Poor Law of 1834. The old system of poor relief in homes had done much to keep wages down and to pauperize the population. Even more than some forms of relief today in both England and America, it undoubtedly had a most demoralizing effect on the poorer classes and emphatically called for alteration. Moreover, taxes in many instances had become unbearable for the industrious and even wealthy who saw an ever greater proportion of taxation going into poor relief without affording any solution of the problem. Poor relief, under the new law, was centralized in a national committee of three, the Whigs, or Liberal, government thus marking another departure from the theory of *laissez faire* which had prevailed in the preceding generation. Outdoor relief was stopped entirely and those receiving aid were forced to live in "workhouses" supervised by local Guardians.

The measure was a drastic one and frequently conditions in the new workhouses were intolerably bad, but harsh as the change seemed to the poor, the dread of the workhouse became so great that large numbers, if driven into the Chartist movement of revolt, of which we shall speak later, were also driven to work instead of idling in their own homes on public charity and a bare subsistence level. In the absence of government regulation as to wages and of strong trades-unions, wages did not rise and for a time there was unquestionably much genuine distress caused by the change of system, but in another respect it marked, in the closely connected local Boards and central control, a new feature of government which carries us back to Tudor days and forward to our own.

Britain was also being rapidly bound more closely together in other ways. The railway age was beginning with its swifter transportation for both persons and goods, and its social and business effects. The age of "the road" and the stagecoach was passing, not to come back for nearly a century until in the motor age the old life was to return in a different form and reinvigorate many an old coaching inn and village which had been left one side by the new rail lines of travel which did not always follow the old main roads. The intellectual effect of railroads has often been neglected, as has that of motors, but with faster, cheaper and more comfortable means of travel Britons came to know their island better, in both its good and bad aspects, and reform owed not a little to railways.

Another movement of similar import was the inauguration of the modern post-office. If Stephenson, with his locomotive, influenced the life of England as much as any statesman so also did Sir Rowland Hill, who invented the postage stamp and by 1839 had secured the adoption of penny postage throughout the Kingdom. The postage stamp, which now seems such an ordinary and commonplace thing, is a good example of what forces may mold the history of nations. Before its invention the cost of postage had to be paid by the recipient of a letter and in England this cost varied from 4d. to 1s. 8d. All sorts of devices for communication were resorted to, but the chief point is that communication was costly and difficult. Hill estimated the total number of letters handled before his changes at 126,000,000. Within thirty years after, it had attained to over 1,000,000,000. When we think of what that means in human terms, of the increase of intelligence and knowledge by the rapid and easy exchange of facts and ideas, of the increase in ties of family, friendships and groups, and of the effect on business, we can realize to some extent the part which a mere postage stamp has played in developing our complex civilization. We do not think of Rowland Hill as of Clive or Cecil Rhodes, but he was, like them, a genuine builder of the Empire.

In the contrasted political lives of England and the United States three points in particular strike an American, however patriotic he may be and however understanding of the necessary differences due to environment, history and age. For example, England, with two thousand years of training and increasing natural political aptitude, can have a so-called "unwritten constitution" (though many of its important features are in writing), whereas a new Federal State must have a written one just as any newly formed organization has to have a written set of rules and bylaws. But in the maturity of the British state there have developed perhaps the best civil-service system in the world, least cumbered with the faults of bureaucracy, the abolition of the spoils system, and the wide and constant use of Royal Commissions to study all aspects of a problem before legislation is initiated in Parliament. This last is a most useful part of the machinery of modern government, and it developed in this period of reform in the 1830's. It came into being because of the great number of complicated problems arising from the reforms suggested and the seriousness and sense of responsibility which were characteristic of the period. Royal Commissions have continued ever since and have been, perhaps, one of the richest of the legacies left from the days of Lord Grey and the Reform Bill.

The statesmen who had emerged in this period and some of whom were to last into the next were in many ways what we think of as typically English. There was, for example, Lord John Russell, considered a radical by many of his own social class and who introduced the Reform Bill in the Commons. Headstrong, and democratic and aristocratic at once, one of his famous remarks was "Let us first be Englishmen and then economists," though he was, in fact, a most orthodox economist of the then reigning school of that pseudo-science.

There was Lord Grey, an aristocrat of the aristocrats, and yet he was always for the reform of the old Parliamentary system, and with his resources and prejudices bode his time for a generation until he could carry his plans through with the great Bill of 1832. It is an interesting sidelight both on this great peer, who in his day was considered rather aloof, and on the Victorian period, that the habit, which is now considered ultra-modern, of children calling their parents by their first names, was constant in the household of Lord and Lady Grey. One point of Lord Grey's tenure of office has a special and coincidental interest, aside from his great service with respect to the Reform Bill. As we have said, 1830 onward was a revolutionary period on the Continent. Among other changes consequent on this, Belgium had won her freedom from Holland, and it was to a considerable extent owing to Lord Grey's activity and foreign policy that Belgium was finally recognized in 1831 as an independent state and in 1839 for seventy-five years neutralized, like Switzerland, under the guarantee of the Great Powers.

In the Cabinet of the first Lord Grey sat one of the most picturesque and British characters of the nineteenth century, Lord Palmerston, almost continuously in office from 1808 to 1865. As Trevelyan has well said, he was "a national institution on his own account." He did not, perhaps, accomplish much for the cause of liberty abroad, but he had a way of appearing to stand up against injustice and for the smaller nations, as well as making the British Lion roar, which was immensely popular with many at a time when British democracy and imperialism were both growing to maturity. Thoroughly English in his faults and virtues, nicknamed "Lord Pumicestone," he is still a tradition and a living force. I have watched, not long ago, an Englishman beat his fists on the dinner table, amid the nuts and port, and roundly assert, "If we had old Palmerston today, this fellow Mussolini would not dare call the Mediterranean an Italian Lake!" Whether "Pam" was threatening Greece with the bombardment of Athens if it did not at once release a worthless Gibraltar Jew of British citizenship; or the United States with a war "immediate and bloody"; or other nations with similar dire threats, there was always something about him that caught the British imagination with the ideas that Britain was all-powerful and always on the side of the oppressed.

Sir Robert Peel, although not in the Cabinet, had been steadily growing out of a rather narrow Toryism to perhaps the position of the ablest statesman of his day in either party. In the Opposition in 1832 he gave assistance to the work of reform, and was always honest and upright in opinion. His shifts were due not to muddled views or to mere expediency but to his characteristic British cautiousness. He regarded each situation as it arose as a separate one, involved in all the circumstances of the moment, and not as an *a priori* proposition in a political and social vacuum. This is essentially a quality of British development, and Peel was one of the most British of all the long line who have taken leading parts in the history of the nation. When in 1834 the Grey Ministry, having accomplished its reforms, was, for the last time in English history, dismissed merely at the wish of the sovereign, William IV, Peel was called to head the new government.

For the wider history of empire it is unnecessary to speak of the politics of the next three years, for something far more important was to occur. On June 20, 1837, William died and, owing to a succession of prior deaths in the royal family, the young Princess Victoria, a girl just over eighteen, came to the throne. It was one of the most fortunate in the endless skein of tangled events of the life of men and nations which we call history. One of the minor, but important, changes was that Hanover passed to the male line of succession, and the British Crown was freed from its last Continental possession and connection, if we omit Gibraltar. More than that, the despicable, dissolute, disliked and even hated line of monarchs had given place to a simple, virtuous and beautiful girl whom the nation could idolize and idealize. At that moment when reform was in the air at home and the Empire could be linked together only through the Crown, the wearer of that Crown had become an innocent but well-trained girl, who won all hearts and could portray all the qualities most revered by the middle class, newly come into power in Britain, and could also symbolize in the growing and increasingly self-governing Empire the glory of a common link and destiny.

CHAPTER VII

THE BREATH OF NEW LIFE

I. Victoria

ON THE June day, when at six in the morning the young Princess was called from her bedroom in her dressing gown with her Victorian night-cap almost falling off, to be told by the Archbishop of Canterbury and Lord Conyngham that she was now Queen, a glorious summer was opening in the history of empire. No one could foresee the vast changes and expansion which were to occur in the long reign of well over sixty years lasting into our own century, and that the Victorian Age would constitute the greatest perhaps in all British history. But after the winter of the eighteenth century, the seemingly endless reigns of George III and his worthless sons, and the long agony of the Napoleonic struggle and its post-war effects, there was now a sense of freshness and rejuvenation. Nations are not like individuals who must progress steadily through all the stages from birth to death. England had been old when under Elizabeth she again became young, and now, more than two centuries older, the nation was again feeling the stirrings of new life.

The wonders of applied science seemed to open endless vistas of increasing wealth and comfort which, although they might terrify the ultra-conservatives with their possible social results, brought to most that facile optimism which was one of the characteristics of the latter two-thirds of the past century in the Empire as in the United States. The middle class, which was largely to direct the practical energies of the new age, had received a new incentive in the vast change in their favor which had been secured by the alteration in government. The romantics, Scott, Shelley, Wordsworth, Byron and others, had had their effect in stirring people out of the easy acquiescence of the eighteenth century. Their influence had, perhaps, also not a little to do with the joyous acceptance of the young Queen.

Little was known about her by the public. During her earlier childhood some half dozen lives had stood between her and the throne, and even of late, after a series of deaths had made her the heir apparent, she had lived a quiet and sequestered life in the old red palace in Kensington Gardens to which her mother had been rushed from Germany so that her child might be born in England. There, except for occasional visits from German boy cousins, she had lived a singularly feminine life after the death of her father. She had been rigorously brought up by her mother, the Duchess of Kent, and the child's greatest friend, the German Baroness Lehzen. The far from admirable Duchess had trained her daughter for the position which she always firmly believed she would occupy, and had so far succeeded and failed to succeed, that her own influence ceased on that June morning when she assured Victoria that she was really Queen. She had never allowed the girl to be alone, even forcing her to sleep up to that night in the same room with herself. The new Queen, whose girlish dignity of manner and composure deeply impressed the statesmen, including the Prime Minister, Lord Melbourne, who called officially that fateful morning, at once asserted herself. She commanded her mother to leave her for an hour, and after that hour of meditation she arranged for a separate suite, which, when they soon moved from Kensington to Buckingham Palace, was far from the Duchess's.

The young woman who was from now to preside for so long a life over the destinies of the Empire had many of the simple qualities of the average middle class. Perhaps, in view of much that her subjects would have to forgive, it was her more commonplace characteristics which caused her to win their affection and in later years a veneration granted to few monarchs. She was not a brilliant woman, and, not alone during her overlong period of mourning and retirement after her husband's death, the life of the court was dull. Her poor taste in literature and the arts became a byword. She had nothing of the almost masculine robustness of the great Queen Bess. But she was to win her subjects, long after the first burst of enthusiasm, by her domestic virtues and qualities, her simple dignity, her devotion to duty and her limiting herself to the constitutional role she had to play. It appears true that in the later years of her reign, especially after 1861, there were occasions when she showed a tendency to overstep the bounds of her strict constitutional position, but any open clash was avoided by the tact of her Ministers, particularly Gladstone, and the public learned nothing of the difficulties she was creating. The result was that by the time of her death in 1901 she had become such a symbol of British life, character and Empire as might not have been the lot of a more brilliant mind.

But if she had many commonplace traits, she was far from being a commonplace woman. Even allowing for British sentimentality, only a great woman could have come to be the symbol she became. At the close of that exciting day when her life had been so suddenly altered, as head of the most powerful Empire in the world, she wrote in her Journal: "I am very young, and perhaps in many, though not in all things, inexperienced, but I am sure, that very few have more real good will and more real desire to do what is fit and right than I have," and "I shall do my utmost to fulfil my duty towards my country." It is perhaps ludicrous to link Victoria with Nelson, but in that word "duty" we have the common factor which has bound both the leaders and the ordinary folk of the Empire together down through the ages, which has made it what it is, and enabled it to bear the buffetings of all the seas and ages. She was right, and this she did, and this was chiefly the reason that on her Diamond Jubilee after sixty years of reigning the celebration was almost a deification.

On the morning when she unexpectedly had the responsibilities of empire thrust upon her, she had informed Melbourne that she would continue with the present Cabinet, which was then satisfactory to the Commons, and it may be noted here that throughout her reign, although not seldom having to accept Ministers who were personally repugnant to her, she never attempted to revive the claim of William IV to appoint Ministers other than those who represented the will of Parliament, establishing a usage of the Constitution beyond any future possibility of infringement.

Melbourne's government, however, was so hampered by attacks in the Lords against proposed reforms that it was weakened to such an extent as to lose popularity in the country and in 1839 the Cabinet resigned. Obviously the man to be called to form a new government was Peel, but fearing the influence over the young Queen of the Ladies of the Bedchamber, who were chiefly members of the families of the previous government, he declined to try to form a new one unless they were dismissed. The Queen refused to cast off her old friends on what she considered a non-political issue. Peel was equally firm. So Melbourne was recalled, remaining in power until 1841. By that time the Ministry was heavily defeated in the Commons, and the Queen, having been happily married to Prince Albert of Saxe-Coburg, one of the German cousins who had visited her as a boy, the question of what women she had about her had become unimportant. Peel then had no difficulty in forming a new Ministry to represent the large majority of Conservatives who had been returned in the general election. From the time of his marriage, the Prince Consort was, until his death, to be largely the mind and a happily tempering influence behind the Queen, who, although she accepted the Ministers demanded by the majority in Parliament, nevertheless had a womanly inclination to have her own way and deal only with her own friends. Her friendliness with Melbourne, leading to her correspondence with him on political affairs after Peel became Prime Minister, as well as other matters in which she allowed her personal likes and dislikes to obtrude themselves into the constitutional machinery, were smoothed over as long as Albert lived, and his influence both on the Queen and on constitutional development has been too much underrated in the past.

If Melbourne, however, was perhaps unwise in continuing to

be the political confidant of the Queen after the change of government he had rendered great service to the country. If not a great statesman, he was courtly, kindly and witty, devoted to both the country and its Constitution. The young Queen had a mind and will of her own but needed guidance. This Melbourne gave during the critical period, and he gave it in the direction of a strict constitutionalism. If in her sixty years' reign Victoria, on the whole, respected the more important constitutional conventions and hardened them into unbreakable usages, it was due in no small measure to the man who first won her confidence and treated it and his country's interests with selfless fidelity.

Meanwhile, Palmerston, as Melbourne's Foreign Secretary, had been altering somewhat his policy of rapprochement to France into an antagonizing of that nation. In the civil war in Spain England and France had united in supporting the constitutionalist government of Queen Christina against the absolutist monarchial claims of Don Carlos, the English sending a force of 10,000 men to take part in the conflict. Civil wars in Spain, down to our own day, seem to have always afforded an excuse for the interference in both the wars and politics of that country by outside nations. The Carlists were completely defeated by 1839 with the help of France and Britain, but those countries were by no means agreed as to Spanish political questions, and the bad feeling engendered between them was increased further by events in the Near East. As a result of wars between the Turks and Egyptians, the question of the freedom of the Dardanelles had been raised in acute form. Russia, Prussia, Britain and Austria had formed a quadruple alliance to enforce terms on the contestants, to the excessive annoyance of France, who felt she had been snubbed, and she at once made preparations for war. Although all the powers agreed in 1841 that the straits should be closed to all warships unless Turkey herself was at war, the wound to the pride of France rankled and the arrangement was far from pleasing Russia, which felt herself bottled in the Black Sea.

II. LABOR AND THE POOR

Of more importance than foreign affairs at this time were those at home and in the growing Empire. At home the reforms which we have already noted, some before and some after the accession of Victoria, were to have far-reaching and beneficent effects, but for the moment the artisan and working classes were bitterly disappointed. It appeared to them that although they had played a large part in securing Parliamentary Reform they had been completely ignored and that the middle class, which had gained all the benefit, refused to do anything to help the poorer citizens now that it had come into power.

Not only did the middle class seem to do nothing to ameliorate conditions but there was intense bitterness over the new Poor Law which the workers considered as having placed an almost criminal taint on mere poverty and unemployment. A cycle of bad business and agricultural years which began in 1837 increased the distress and resentment. There was much talk of what we would now call Socialism, direct action and Syndicalism. These movements failed, however, and their leaders became discredited among the workers themselves. Looking back it would seem that the failure must in considerable part be ascribed to the inherent moderation with which they were conducted. In a sense they were revolutionary but the vast mass of the working class wished to gain the results aimed at by constitutional means. The sobriety with which they acted, combined with the sensible decision of the government not to resort to the repressive measures which had been applied earlier, avoided what in a race of different temperament might easily have developed into a social war.

Gradually the workers turned away from other forms of exerting pressure to the political method, which meant gaining influence in Parliament and effecting their ends through legislation and not force. Out of this change of policy emerged the Chartist movement which began in this period but was to reach its acme in the next. In its first phase it may be considered to have begun in 1837 and collapsed two years later, to rise again. The episode is of great interest for the light it sheds on British character and development. The movement was extremely radical for that day, and spread, especially in the North, with alarming rapidity.

Its organ, a paper called the *Northern Star*, preached doctrines which to all conservative minds spelled the ruin of the economic and political life of the country, while huge mass meetings, including one almost under the shadow of the Houses of Parliament, were held at which there was much wild oratory. Troops were massed in certain places in the North and in Wales, where the worst trouble was expected, but the government did everything possible to allow the storm to blow itself out without interference or bloodshed. Its attitude, very different from that of thirty years earlier, was well expressed by Lord John Russell when he declared in the midst of the excitement that "The people have a right to meet. If they had no grievances, common sense would put an end to their meetings. It is not from free discussion that governments have anything to fear," and that there was cause for real fear only when men were "driven by force to secret combinations."

They were, however, driven to do something by their miserable condition. The system of paying wages in goods instead of cash was still largely in force in industry and sometimes resulted in a real cut in wages of a half to almost two-thirds. The cost of living was high, wheat having risen in price by nearly 80 per cent from the average prices of 1836–39 to those of 1840-43. Housing conditions were atrocious from overcrowding and were ruinous to family life, self-respect and morality.

The most popular remedies for these ills were embodied in what was called the People's Charter, which called for annual Parliaments, abolition of a property qualification for membership, pay for members, manhood suffrage, vote by ballot, and equal election districts. A monster petition was presented to Parliament, which was said to contain a million and a quarter signatures but was rejected by a vote of about seven to one.

After this there was a little sporadic rioting, easily put down, and the movement collapsed for the moment. Both in its early and later phases, however, it exemplified the rise of the common man to political self-consciousness. It marked the growth of genuine democracy at home and provided the background for the political development of the overseas Empire. The various events of the 1830's indeed form a watershed in the national life, a range of mountains in which the Reform Bill and the accession of Victoria rise like peaks, and on the hither side of which that life takes on quite a different form from that on the side from which we have crossed.

III. Changes in Early Victorian Period

The change is notable in many departments and not least in literature. We shall speak in a later chapter of the stagnation in most of the arts,—painting, music, architecture and the minor household ones,—but in letters the Victorian Age was to prove second to none, save possibly the Elizabethan, in all British history. It is noteworthy that both were periods of rapid change, and of great increase in trade and expansion in far parts of the world.

Detailed consideration of the authors will best be left until we discuss Victorian life in general in the mid-century when the Great Exhibition and Crystal Palace in 1851 marked its apotheosis. But it is important here to note the sharp cleavage between old and new which we can now see occurred with the accession of Victoria.

When she came to the throne all the great luminaries of the previous period had passed, with the exception of Wordsworth, who lingered on, though doing no more of his best work, until 1850. Keats had died in 1821, Shelley 1822, Byron 1824, Scott 1832, and Coleridge 1834. A whole generation of genius had been swept from the stage but the new was just coming on. Tennyson and Macaulay first published in 1830, Browning, Carlyle and Dickens in 1833, Ruskin 1834, and Carlyle in 1837. The elder generation had been romantics, egoists, singers of the common man in the abstract or lovers of nature and sheer beauty. The new was to be chiefly preoccupied with the social scene and especially its evils and abuses, with men as part of an organized society, with the new ideas of science, and with the reorganization of institutions. Naturally these are generalities but there was a marked break between the two generations. It is seldom that we find so complete a shift in the intellectual climate so sharply defined.

There was another great change, in the field of religion, which, added to the Evangelical movement spoken of earlier, was to have marked effects on life throughout the Empire. In 1833 a quite different movement, the Oxford or Tractarian, was inaugurated by a sermon preached by Keble. The Evangelicals and Nonconformists had broken from the Church and laid great stress on personal religion and salvation. The Oxford movement, on the other hand, minimized the importance of the individual and laid chief stress on the Church as a continuing body, a living organism in itself, the existence of which was more important than the personal views or life of any mere single member. For this reason its adherents strongly objected to the Church being subject to lay or government control, and so deeply did some of the leaders like Newman and Manning, both later Cardinals, feel that they left the Church altogether to go over to that of Rome. The secession of such leading figures in the High Church Party tended to weaken it in the Anglican Church and so gave a certain impetus to the Broad Church or Modernist movement within it. This was emphasized by the influence of such men as Doctor Thomas Arnold, who were inculcating a new spirit of moral earnestness.

Almost coincident with the beginning of the Oxford movement in England there was a renaissance of religious feeling and interest in Scotland accompanied by a demand for separation of Church and state. When compromise was found impossible in 1843 practically half the clergy left their churches and livings, but so great was the popular support and religious fervor of the day that in less than a year 500 new churches had been built for them by private subscription, and the Free Church of Scotland had been established.

Not only these two movements, with the Evangelical, but a renewed spirit of devotion within the Church of England itself all testified to a great religious revival throughout the United Kingdom, made up of diverse currents. This must be taken heavily into account when considering other aspects of the national life, such as the recrudescence of Puritanism, the improvement in the Civil Service and political life generally, the new attitude toward social questions, the preoccupation of literature with reforms of many sorts, the missionary movement, and the new sense of responsibility toward the backward races within the Empire.

If there was much hypocrisy in the early Victorian period there was also an immense body of genuine religion, of various shadings, which had an all-pervasive influence.

We must now turn to the growth of the overseas Empire, remembering all these currents at home,—reform, the rise to power of the largely business middle class, the demands by the workers for greater democracy, the religious fervor, the optimism and energy, as well as all the conservatism and selfishness constantly inherent in all classes. The result is confused, and many interpretations may be made of almost any event. We must recall that nations even more than individuals are not always motivated by a single set of emotions, ideas and ideals. In both cases we have to take the life, the work accomplished and the results in the large. It is the total of these which make up the final account and not any particular lapse or flaw.

IV. New Theory of Empire

The cleavage between the old and new Britain which we have noted as occurring in the period covered by this chapter was nowhere more marked than in the sphere of imperial relations and the theory of empire. In general, that theory was still based on the old Mercantilist doctrines. Roughly, the colonies were supposed to supply the raw materials and in part the markets for the goods manufactured in the mother country. Theoretically, an empire should be a complicated but self-sufficing unit in which there was division of labor and products, the whole regulated from the Parliament in London. Theoretically again, regulations would be made for the benefit of all, but practically, as the colonies were not, and could not be, effectively represented in Parliament, the entire machine would be run principally for the benefit of those who were. Colonies were valued wholly for the advantage which the mother country might derive from them in one way or another.

The various streams of thought and emotion, however, which we have described as converging more or less in the decade of the 1830's brought about a revolution in imperial theory. Among them we may cite the free-trade doctrines of Adam Smith, which were to triumph a few years later; the revival of religion and the sense of responsibility for others which led to missionary enterprise; the swelling tide of democracy and the demand by the individual for a voice in the management of his own affairs, and what we would now call self-determination. The change in attitude was due in large measure to a general change in national outlook, but there was a group of notable leaders who did much to canalize the new ideas, such as Charles Buller, Edward Gibbon Wakefield, Lord Durham, John Stuart Mill, Lord John Russell and the third Lord Grey.

The old theory which had persisted down to this time, in spite of its having lost Britain its continental American empire, except Canada, now gave place to the new one which was to develop the Empire as it is today. Britain had rejected the suggestions for such an empire when made in America, and had learned nothing from the American Revolution. A half century of intellectual and moral changes at home had been required to bring the new theory into being and make it practical politics. It was fortunate, not only for the Empire but for the world, that the change occurred before the vast extension of empire in the latter part of the century. The scramble for the outlying portions of the globe would have come in any case, but if the British attitude toward colonies and subject races had not altered it is unlikely that the Empire would have held together. In spite of manifold faults and errors it cannot be denied, I believe, that owing to the new theory the lands and peoples under British rule have had a larger degree of freedom and good government than they would have had under any other rule, and the great block of the British Commonwealth of Nations remains today, with its offspring, the United States, the chief hope of freedom in the troubled future.

The new imperial theory, springing from the three streams of political, economic and religious thought, had two chief points. One was that the colonies, instead of being wholly managed from the mother country and primarily in its interest, should as soon as possible be given a far wider scope for local self-government and economic growth in accordance with local desires. The other was that Britain should not merely exploit native and undeveloped races but act as guardian and trustee for them. It is all too easy to point to innumerable instances in which the theory has not been carried out in practice, and in consequence to suggest the hypocrisy of the British. Nevertheless the ideas have been of incalculable benefit to the world.

To estimate their novelty and importance we have, on the one hand, to compare them with all previous ideas in history as to the relations between an imperial power and its subjects; and, on the other, to consider the Empire as it exists today in that absolutely unique political structure, the British Commonwealth of Nations. Human nature is both imperfect and fallible, but I do not know of any other race—French, German, Italian, Russian, Japanese—which would have brought so great a measure of freedom and justice to a quarter of the whole world as has the British, and it has been largely because it conceived and worked the two main ideas mentioned above. Naturally many were opposed to them, outside the Liberal and progressive group which struggled for them, and it is an example of how manifold are the forces working to make what we call history that one reason why the ideas could be put into action was the belief that largely because of them the colonies were ceasing to be of value to the mother country. If trade were not to be regulated and natives used for her benefit, then, argued many, were not colonies a drag, danger and expense instead of an asset? For some decades the nation was to take little interest in empire even when not opposed to extension, and this mood of indifference gave a freer hand to those who were trying to mold imperial relations in accord with the new ideas. This mood of indifference, we shall note again, was one of the important currents of thought during the decades preceding the revival of imperialism in a new form toward the end of the century.

It was indeed time that something was done. Trouble and discontent were rife. The West Indies, where the planters felt that the abolition of slavery, even with compensation, had ruined their prospects, formed a problem of their own, but the general difficulties and dangers of the imperial situation are best shown in Canada. Canada as yet was a mere geographical expression, and the six colonies—Newfoundland, Prince Edward Island, New Brunswick, Nova Scotia, Lower Canada (Quebec) and Upper Canada (Ontario) were all separate and each had a government of the type which had been general in the revolted colonies which now formed the United States. With an unchanged colonial theory and policy and the same faults in local government, the Canadian colonies were on the verge of revolting in turn as their neighbors to the south had done a half century earlier.

V. The Successful Experiment in Canada

In each colony there was a royal governor, a Council appointed by him and a popularly elected Assembly. There were all the old difficulties between the last and two former which were practically inevitable under the circumstances. These were greatly accentuated by two factors. In Lower Canada the race problem had become acute and there was intense bitterness between the enormous French majority and the British minority. Nor was there any prospect of an increase in the British population, for immigrants were not attracted and usually went south to the United States or on to Upper Canada. Government and justice were both breaking down. Owing to the racial feud it was impossible to do anything with a British Governor and Council and a French Assembly, nor would French juries give just verdicts when British were involved. The *habitants* were ignorant, intensely devoted to the idea of keeping their colony French, and were easily swayed by the priests and French local lawyers, the chief agitator among the latter being Louis Papineau. He aspired to a role similar to that of Samuel Adams in earlier Massachusetts, though his mind was more of the type of the French revolutionists. Independence of Britain was openly preached. In 1832 there was a cholera epidemic in the British Isles and in spite of quarantine it entered Canada with the immigrants, and the French actually believed that the British Government had sent the infection over to destroy the French population. There were disturbances and in one unfortunate affair three citizens were killed under circumstances very similar to those of the so-called "Boston Massacre" of 1770. This was likewise dubbed a "massacre" and used, as the earlier incident had been, to stir up the anger of the people.

By 1836 government had come to a stand and a commission was sent out from England to report but could make no suggestions. The British Government then announced that if the Assembly would not provide the money necessary for local public purposes it would be overruled from London. Clearly, the form of government was not adapted to the colony and some change would have to be made. There was not time at the moment, and the unconstitutional, although necessary, decision of Lord John Russell created a storm in both Lower and Upper Canada leading to rebellions. Upper Canada (Ontario) was strongly loyalist in sentiment and steadier in opinion than its French neighbor. After some minor fighting between the loyalists and the rebels, in which the casualties were few, the rebel leader, W. L. Mackenzie, fled across the border to the United States. Although the rebellion was really crushed, Mackenzie, together with other refugees and border ruffians over the American line, continued raids which were nearly to involve Britain and America in war. Mackenzie used the American vessel, the *Caroline,* to transport men and munitions, and finally the British authorities destroyed her in American waters. American feeling in any case at that time was hostile to England and this breach of international law created a furore in the United States. The British Government would not admit that the incident was official until in 1840 a drunken Canadian in New York boasted that he had been one of the party which had destroyed the *Caroline* and that he himself had killed an American in the affair.

He was put on trial for murder and only then did Palmerston assert that the attack was an official military operation, threatening that if McLeod, the Canadian in question, was found guilty and hanged, Britain would declare war immediately. Owing to the federal form of government in the United States, Washington could not intervene, and the Governor of New York was as prickly as Palmerston himself. The question of a third war between the two English-speaking peoples hung on the verdict of an ordinary jury in a local criminal case in New York, but fortunately it found that McLeod was merely a drunken and boastful liar and had in reality not been in the *Caroline* affair at all. The disorders in Canada, however, were evidently extremely dangerous to Anglo-American relations, especially with Palmerston in the Foreign Office.

In Lower Canada, the rebellion, although also on a small scale, was more important, but was put down with British troops, Papineau and his chief colleague, O'Callaghan, escaping over the border to the United States. It was clear, however, that some sort of governmental reorganization of the colonies was absolutely essential. In 1838 Lord Durham, with Wakefield and Buller, was sent to North America to investigate and make a report. Of all English statesmen of his day, Durham, with all his peculiarities of character and his ability for making enemies, understood what would have to become the basic principles of imperial relations better than any one else. His famous *Report* was to become a classic and may be considered the cornerstone of the Empire in its modern form. Unfortunately, on his arrival, Durham exceeded his authority by condemning to death the leaders of the revolt who had fled Canada, and transporting eight others to Bermuda. This arbitrary act opened him to legitimate attack at home by his personal enemies and those who were opposed to his views of imperial policy. He was recalled in disgrace, even the government which had sent him out deserting him.

His ideas, however, were happily destined to be carried out and to help to establish the Commonwealth of Nations. The important point in the *Report* was the recommendation to establish full responsible government in Canada, following the British model of choosing the executive in accordance with the wishes of the majority in the Assembly or Lower House. Owing to the race problem this would have been impracticable in Quebec, as the British would not have consented to be ruled perpetually by a majority of French peasants. Durham therefore recommended the union of Upper and Lower Canada in one colony, and although the French objected strenuously this was done by Parliament in 1840. The grant of responsible government, however, had to wait a few years longer, owing to strong opposition among leading British statesmen, such as the Duke of Wellington, until Lord Grey, as Colonial Secretary in the Liberal government, established the new régime in 1847 by instructing the Governor of Nova Scotia to choose his Ministers in accordance with the majority wish of the Assembly and assume no political responsibility himself.

In other words, the Governor sent out from England was to occupy practically the same position with respect to the local legislature and parties as did the sovereign at home to the British ones. Lord Elgin, Governor of United Canada (Quebec and Ontario), received the same instructions when commissioned, and he carried them out in spite of great unpopularity on occasion because of the fact that the colonists had not yet learned how to manage the political responsibility they had been granted. Parties, cutting across religious and racial lines, began to develop, however, and the people began to understand the new system.

Thanks to both Durham and Elgin the seed of free responsible self-government took firm root in the greatest of the future Dominions, though many at home believed that such a system must be utterly incompatible with imperial unity. In 1852 Disraeli declared that the colonies must all become independent within a few years, and others believed the same. Later in our story we shall find other colonies receiving the same right to self-government, gradually broadening into the relations which subsist between the members of the Commonwealth today. Those Liberals who first started the experiment in Canada were performing not only an act of consummate statesmanship, essentially British in character, but were also exhibiting a great faith in the belief that permanent and happy union could be based only on freedom, and not restraint or

133

force. The following century proved that that faith was amply justified.

In Canada the experiment was a great success. The racial wound was healed, talk of secession from the Empire ceased, and the dangerous drift toward annexation to the United States, based largely on economics, was halted by the new economic self-government and the abolition of the Imperial Navigation Laws. In this period, also, two serious disputes which had occasionally threatened war with Canada's great neighbor on the south were settled, though not altogether to the satisfaction of either party, which may be an indication of the fairness of the decisions.

The Maine boundary in the east had long been in question, but was finally defined in the Ashburton Treaty of 1842, and four years later the boundary to the Pacific through the disputed Oregon country was also agreed upon. Extravagant claims as to the latter had been made on both sides, and in America the popular cry was "fifty-four forty or fight," meaning insistence on carrying the American northern bounds up to that line of latitude. Finally, however, helped by the fact that the United States was facing war with Mexico, the line of the forty-ninth parallel from the Great Lakes to the Rockies was extended to the ocean, except that the island of Vancouver went to Canada entire. That country was now, to a degree hitherto unprecedented in the world's history of empire, mistress in her own house and the bounds of her vast lands were definitely fixed. There was no fear of invasion from any quarter and her future seemed unlimited.

VI. THE AMAZING DEVELOPMENT OF AUSTRALIA

The very greatness of opportunity in Canada and the United States, both English-speaking nations for the most part and with English institutions, militated against the development of the second most important British colony, Australia. Population there had grown slowly and, owing to the nature of the mostly unexplored interior, in only three widely scattered colonies on the coast, New South Wales, Tasmania and Western Australia. The chief hindrances had been the distance—12,000 miles from England—and the stigma of the penal settlements. According to a census of 1828 of the something over 36,000 population of New South Wales, about 24,000 were convicts or ex-convicts, and 4673 had come to the colony free. The remainder were children of these several classes, and the same was roughly true of Tasmania. Taking the drawbacks into consideration,—distance, cost and the overwhelming proportion of convicts,—it seemed impossible that Australia should grow. The marvellous progress of the next twenty years was wholly due to the group of Liberals and colonial reformers who were fast laying the foundations of the future Empire.

Wakefield had developed his theory of assisted emigration, the money to be raised in part from the sale of lands, instead of giving them away, and partly by straight government grant. He had also a theory for the early institution of democratic self-government which was not adopted, but within a few years 16,000 settlers had been moved out to the new colonies, Victoria and South Australia, established so that they would not suffer from the convict taint, and annually the numbers swelled so rapidly that the free settlers began to outnumber the convicts. The reformers at home also realized that the penal system would have to be abolished entirely if Australia were to develop to the greatness which her size and resources warranted. Nothing more clearly demonstrates the influence on the growth of the Empire of the various currents of thought which we have described in England than the events of these years in Canada and the great island continent. By 1840 the reformers had succeeded in passing through Parliament a bill ending transportation to New South Wales, and in another decade, of the 265,000 population the convict element had dropped to under 1 per cent. The old system was likewise ended for Tasmania in 1853.

With the change and increase in population came also a striking economic alteration. At the beginning of the century England had obtained practically all her best wool from Spain, the Spanish merino being alone considered good enough for fine cloth. Then the source gradually shifted to Germany, and German imports into England were between four and five times those from Spain. But, as one of the consequences of the Napoleonic wars, supplies were largely cut off from the Continent and by 1850 Spanish wool had disappeared and England was importing 137,000 bales a year from Australia as against 30,000 from Germany. It is one of the most fantastic stories of sudden changes in commerce, and what had been a neglected and forlorn penal colony was now making princely contributions to the strength and wealth of England. It is an interesting example of what the colonies, though scorned by Disraeli and others, meant at the very time when he was calling them millstones around the neck of the mother country.

The change in the character of the Australian population, combined with the work of the reformers at home, made the political development of the Australian colonies one of the most amazing episodes in imperial history. Under the altered circumstances self-government could be introduced, and by 1850 a bill brought in by Lord John Russell, and passed by Parliament, gave the Councils of each of the Australian colonies the power to draft a constitution for itself, as also the right to levy duties on all goods, British and foreign alike, entering Australian ports. The constitutions, as drawn up, closely followed the British and were confirmed by Parliament, now indeed becoming the mother of Parliaments, in 1855. One hardly knows which to marvel at most, the incredible change in Australia in twenty-five years or that in British imperial theory. As one considers the latter one is struck by the overwhelming results of a time-lag of thought in one country as compared with another. A half century earlier the political thinkers in the American colonies had moved forward to the position of the British colonial reformers of the period we have just been discussing. Had it not been for the time-lag in Britain, there would have been no American Revolution or Declaration of Independence, at least in 1776, and it is one of the most fascinating "ifs" in history as to what would have happened in that case.

VII. Government Established in New Zealand

Apparently close on the ordinary map but in reality 1200 miles distant from Australia lies the present Dominion of New Zealand,

which has been described as "more English than England itself."
Unlike Australia, in which the native population was one of
the lowest types in the world and has had practically no influence
in peace or war on the white settlers, the native Maoris of New
Zealand, with possibly a Caucasian strain in their Polynesian
blood, were one of the finest savage races in the world, though
cannibals. Early in the century, when the few white settlers were
of a low sort, missionary enterprise was particularly active among
the natives, and the ideas of the missionary groups were to clash
with those of the colonial reformers, complicating the problem of
large-scale settlement of the right sort. Nevertheless Wakefield,
with Durham and others, formed a £1,000,000 company to buy
land and send out emigrants on the general lines of Wakefield's
theory of colonization. It was intended honestly to protect the
interests of the Maoris, but as so frequently happens in the clash of
cultures the different concepts of land titles made serious trouble.
Just as in early North America some 500,000 barbarians claimed
tribal ownership of 3,000,000 square miles of the present United
States, so in the islands of New Zealand 100,000 Maoris claimed
about 65,000,000 acres though even in their savage way of life
they actually occupied less than a tenth of the whole. The islands
had never been formally annexed to the Crown but this was done
in 1840 after the early settlers, the Wakefield colonists, the missionaries and the Maoris, among them all, had brought about such
a confused situation as to demand strong action by Britain. In the
Treaty of Waitonga the natives surrendered all rights of sovereignty and became British subjects guaranteed in possession of
their lands, a clause which obviously would make trouble later.

The difficulties were, for the time at least, adjusted by Sir
George Grey, who, after fine similar service in Australia, had been
appointed Governor in 1845. Meanwhile the New Zealand Company of Wakefield, Durham and others, had succeeded in planting
30,000 British in the two great islands of the group, and when the
Company, which carried on the tradition of the colonizing companies of the seventeenth century combined with the humanitarianism of the nineteenth, surrendered its charter in 1852, each of the

six provinces which had grown up was given a local self-government with a large degree of responsibility. In spite of the fact
that the Crown reserved the right to make all land purchases from
the natives and maintain their tribal rights, there was to be war
and difficulty, but in a few years the government had established
another future Dominion and started it on the same lines of political independence as Canada and Australia.

VIII. THE SHIFTING POLICY IN SOUTH AFRICA

Unfortunately the story in South Africa is a very different one,
and the mishandling of the situation there is more like the long
and unhappy story of Ireland, though the trouble largely began
through a misguided humanitarianism and not from any desire
for annexation or oppression. We have already seen how the Cape
Colony was acquired and paid for after the Napoleonic wars, much
as Porto Rico was by the United States after the Spanish War. The
white population consisted almost entirely of Boer farmers who
had all the stubbornness of the Dutch race and who in their isolation
had lagged far behind the newer intellectual outlook of Europe.
Even by the 1830's they greatly outnumbered the comparatively
few English settlers. Had it been merely a race problem similar
to that in Canada, where a nucleus of foreign whites had to be
absorbed or gradually outnumbered by British, the difficulty might
have been peaceably settled in time. But there was a far more
serious race problem which was to destroy hope of adjustment of
the mere dual British-Dutch one. This was the problem of the
African Negroes.

It was clear that the vast majority of the white population, being
Boers who were primitively religious but had had no training in
self-government on British lines, would preclude subjecting the
British to them in any such form of local democratic, responsible
ways as were then about to be adopted in the next few years in the
colonies we have just discussed. The Governor of Cape Colony
had frankly despotic powers, though under the close control of the
Colonial Office, which, in turn, in this period of reform, religious
fervor and humanitarianism, was controlled by Evangelicals. Un-

happily they saw everything in Africa through the eyes of the missionaries, who as in New Zealand objected to any one having anything to do with the natives except themselves. The natives in and immediately near the colony were Kaffirs, but beyond them were other savages of various races, the Zulus, Matabeles and others. All were fierce, and like waves of the sea in a storm the teeming millions of blacks were constantly in upheaval in their intertribal wars. It was estimated that a million had been slaughtered in such conflicts in a quarter of a century. The Boers had maintained themselves against attacks, and if not high in civilization themselves were far higher than the savages who took their chief delight in torture, murder and rapine. Nevertheless, the missionaries, in excess of zeal and sentimentalism, sided with the savages and misrepresented in England and especially in the Colonial Office their real nature as well as that of the Boers. In missionary eyes the Boers were always wrong and the savages always right.

The situation was complicated by another effect of the reform movement when in 1834 slavery was outlawed in the colony. If the abolition of slavery was considered an unwarranted hardship by the British in the West Indies, who received handsome compensation and who might be expected to have shared to a considerable extent in the British currents of thought of the day, it could not fail to be considered an act of oppression by the Boers. These took the Old Testament view of slavery. Moreover, although their slaves outnumbered themselves, they received in compensation only a little over a third of the market value of their property, besides having thrust on them the problem of what to do with the emancipated savages surrounded as they were by millions of free blacks bent on war.

Almost at the moment of emancipation, thousands of Kaffirs raided over the Boer frontier, burning and killing. The British Governor drove them back, and annexed an additional strip of territory, in which the Kaffirs were to be left alone if they kept the peace. However, under missionary influence, the Colonial Secretary, Lord Glenelg, an ardent Evangelical, recalled the Governor and revoked the settlement. The Boers felt that they had first been

139

robbed and then left unprotected. The result was the Great Trek of the 1830's. Some Boers had earlier crossed the Orange River but now they swarmed, mostly in unorganized bands, first into the High Veldt of what is now the Orange Free State, and then into Natal. The fights with the Kaffirs in the latter territory threatened to drive the natives over into Cape Colony and in 1842 the British Government in self-defense annexed the new section, which lay partly along the seacoast. The Boers were incapable of governing themselves or of maintaining peace with the Kaffirs, and it was a question of abandoning Cape Colony or of creating a new colony under the Crown in Natal.

The Boers, after some show of fight, abandoned their new-won land, and the Trek now entered a new phase. Moving from Natal to the number of some 12,000 persons, and from Cape Colony and the High Veldt, great swarms moved still farther north, fighting the Zulus, and having broken the resistance of two of the most powerful savage tribes, by 1854 had established the independence of the Orange Free State and the Transvaal.

Meanwhile the British Government, genuinely anxious not to extend its responsibilities and at the same time, under missionary influence, wishing to protect the natives and induce them to lead a peaceful and orderly life, had pursued a constantly shifting policy. It had tried the plan of the erection of barrier-protected native states, and of annexation again of part of the territory claimed by the Boers, but the confusion merely deepened, and in the Sand River Convention of 1852 and the Bloemfontein Convention two years later, the independence of the Transvaal and of the Orange Free State was respectively recognized. The native problem, however, had not been settled to the satisfaction of either the advanced humanitarian-minded English at home or of the more primitive-minded Boers, and although large numbers of the latter in the Free State would have preferred to remain under the ordered government of the British at the Cape instead of the semi-anarchy of Boer rule, intensely bitter feeling had been aroused between the greater part of the now independent Boer Trekkers and the British.

The two conventions were clearly but a temporary and half-settlement of questions which would some day be raised again in more aggravated form. By the end of the century they were to divide opinion bitterly even in England itself but the final solution, after long blundering, was eventually to become one of the most shining examples of British statesmanship and character, though the muddling through for three generations was even more typically British. It must be admitted, however, that the problems involved were among the most difficult of the many in the developing Empire. Naturally under the conditions there could be no opportunity for the bestowal of that responsible self-government which was being established elsewhere.

IX. NEW TRENDS IN INDIA

The same was obviously true of India, where a mere handful of British were maintaining control over several hundred millions of varied and alien races. Nevertheless, roughly the decade under review in this chapter was pregnant with great events in the Indian portion of the Empire, whose effects are felt in our own day. They were the resultants of all the forces of the time, including those of European politics and fears, and so give that mixed effect which so often in the life of nations enables critics to class them as advancing morally or as being hypocritical. The forces of reform, educational ideals, humanitarianism and the new sense of responsibility for native races were all to bear fruit in a new Indian policy, but European politics and international rivalries were also to bring about ten years of war in the East.

We have already mentioned the fact that the charter of the East India Company was to expire in 1833, just when many of the new forces in Britain were coming to a head. The result was to be of immense importance to British India. As in so many other cases in the acquisition of colonies or possessions, the period of usefulness of the trading company under which they had originally been brought within the imperial sphere had passed. In this case, however, it was convenient to keep the Company alive as a link in the chain of administration, but it was almost completely altered and the new charter reflected the new ideals of empire. The Company, which now became purely a political and governmental organ, had to give up all trading rights and all ideas of dividends. Not only was the welfare of the Indians to be substituted for what we call today the "profit motive," but the Report of the Parliamentary Committee whose recommendations were followed also declared that whenever the interests of Europeans and the natives might come into conflict those of the latter were to have precedence.

The new charter also established a single unified government over all British India for the first time, and thus paved the way for better administration. (A large part of India was still under the rule of independent native princes.) The point of view of the native Indian was also adopted to a remarkable extent, though the new ideas were to create in time problems incomparably greater than those they developed in South Africa. The new code of laws for all British India was to be based on Indian, and not on British law and custom, and Macaulay's work in revising the Penal Code was one of his most constructive contributions to the development of India. Moreover, it was provided that no Indian could be refused office under the Company on account of creed, birth or color, a principle comparable to the XIVth Amendment to the American Constitution with reference to Negroes after the Civil War. But other changes were even more important for the future. As the Company was no longer a trade monopoly the old licensing system became an anachronism and all Europeans were allowed free access to the country. Moreover, the change in attitude toward Indian education still further altered the outlook and aspirations of the natives. Macaulay had been sent out to study the educational problem, and in his famous Report of 1835, which was accepted and followed, European learning was not only brought to India and taught in Indian institutions, but in view of the fact that there were nearly 150 different languages in the peninsula, English was used as the common vehicle of instruction.

From all these various changes it came about that the victory of the newer trends of thought over the old roused the ambitions of the natives, brought them increasingly into contact with Europeans and European culture, and gave to the more educated classes of all races a means which they had not possessed before by which they could communicate their ambitions and discontents. The seeds were thus being sown which in the course of some generations would grow up into the Indian movements of our present time. Gandhi and others of today are the natural successors of the reformers and humanitarians of the 1830's. Had the population been British, the process would naturally have led to a self-governing Dominion of the general type, but the results of the different conditions will be considered later in our story.

Bentinck was Governor in India when the new regime and new title of Governor-General were inaugurated and he continued until 1836. We have already spoken of his social reforms in the abolition of suttee and the efforts to uproot the practice of thuggism. For the dozen years from his return until 1848, under his successors, Auckland, Ellenborough, and Hardinge, we have to turn from reform to war, conquest, blundering, and heroism. In European foreign policy, Palmerston and not the missionaries or reformers was now in control in Britain, and Palmerston had constantly before him in this period the bogey of a Russian conquest of India. North of British India lay border states and tribes, the most important being the Afghans, with whom the English had tried to cultivate and maintain friendly relations as a barrier against Russian aggression. When Palmerston found that Russians had penetrated to the Afghan capital of Kabul he at once jumped to the conclusion that the dreaded attack might be imminent.

The Afghan situation had been complicated by the overthrow of the ruler, Shah Shuja (who subsequently took refuge in British India), by Dost Mohammed, who, however, had not been able to control much of the country outside of the capital, but who had grievances against the British. Briefly, in view of the real or supposed Russian menace, the Governor-General, Lord Auckland, finally sent a force to reinstate a friendly prince in the person of the elderly Shah Shuja. Although he was placed on the throne the Afghans resented outside interference, and the small isolated force in Kabul was forced to retreat after the British Resident had been assassinated, and was wholly destroyed in trying to make its way through the gloomy Khyber Pass. Caught in its defile, the annihilation of the little British army was the worst disaster which British military force had yet encountered in India, and the loss of prestige was felt to be so great that unfortunately the next Governor, Ellenborough, felt it necessary not only to recapture Kabul but, as soon as that was evacuated for the second time, to make war on Sind. It was conquered but there was practically nothing to justify the proceeding.

Meanwhile the Sikhs in the Punjab, with a highly trained army of some 90,000, had, during Lord Hardinge's administration, attacked the British and been driven back only after the most bloody and furious fighting the British had ever had to suffer. It was not until the battle of Gujerat in 1849, after Hardinge had been recalled and Dalhousie had taken his place, that the Sikhs finally submitted, and the Punjab province was annexed. British India, now increased by the entire Indus Valley, stretched over the peninsula up to the Himalayas and the waste lands of the Northwest frontier. Although these formed the natural northern boundaries of the Raj, the extension had taken place at enormous cost, and had occurred not from a desire to expand in India but owing to a natural sequence of events following the effort by Palmerston to block Russia in Afghanistan. A new Burmese war entered into on account of Burmese attacks on British trade resulted in further annexations in that small peninsula, the acquisition of what was to become the important port of Rangoon, and control of both coasts of the Bay of Bengal, much as the recent Italian conquest of Albania has given that nation control of the Adriatic.

X. CHINA AND THE OPIUM WAR

Owing to a series of unforeseen and fortuitous circumstances, not only had the bounds of British India been vastly extended but the Empire had advanced farther into the East and now included Oriental races who had nothing in common with its subjects in India. Still farther beyond lay China, and British relations with that country in this period form a sordid ending to the story of the reform and other forces which we have described as at work.

The great Reform Bill had, as we have seen, enthroned the middle class in power at home, and to a great extent the interest of the middle class was in trade. From it, however, also came largely the nobler motives and movements we have noted, but in far-away China, where Britain had no territorial foothold, the trade motive was dominant without a sense of responsibility for a people not under British control. The Chinese had steadily attempted to keep foreigners out for nearly two centuries, but a considerable and lucrative trade had been carried on under the monopoly of the East India Company because there were plenty of Chinese, from Mandarins down, who were personally interested in its profits.

When the Company's new charter was issued in 1833, outsiders flocked into the Chinese trade as they had into that with India in 1813. The Company had been making a profit of about £1,000,000 a year by exporting opium from India in exchange for Chinese tea, silk, and chinaware, although the importing of opium had been prohibited, since 1796 by the Chinese Government, if we can use that term for this period. With the connivance of Chinese officials the trade had been a smuggling one, and it was largely this business which the outside traders went after when the Company ceased to have trade privileges. There can be no question that the prohibition of the trade was for the good of the miserable Chinese addicts to the drug and there can be no excuse for the insistence of the Company on its continuance. Its representatives, however, had at least known how to deal with the humiliating exactions of the Chinese officials, and there had been no serious difficulty until the new swarm of traders refused to comply with the exactions enforced. The Chinese still wished, theoretically, to exclude all foreigners and all foreign trade, but the immediate cause of the miserable war of 1840 to 1842 was ostensibly, and to a large extent really, due to the opium question, and consequently has been known as the "Opium War."

Not match for Western arms, the Chinese were finally obliged to consent to trade through five Treaty Ports, and Britain annexed the splendid port of Hong Kong. It has been said that the stoppage of the opium trade would have laid a heavy burden on the tax-payers in India, but clearly the object was British profits rather than any tenderheartedness for an alien race. In view of the harm opium was doing to the Chinese the answer to the tax problem would have been a revision of Indian taxation rather than a lucra-tive debauching of another race. The British treaty of 1842, like the American opening of relations with Japan in the next decade, was among the most important events in world history, and the present Sino-Japanese conflict, with all the deadly weapons and methods of so-called Western civilization in the twentieth century as well as the menace of the Oriental situation today, may be consid-ered to stem directly back to the increasing trade demands of the Western nations a century ago. No one could then foresee the re-sults, and perhaps the chief interest of many of the episodes in this chapter lies in showing the inability to forecast the results of acts whether deriving from the highest motives of missionaries and re-formers or the baser ones of unidealistic businessmen bent only on a profit. All start threads in the tapestried picture we call history, woven by fate and in which human foresight plays a negligible part.

CHAPTER VIII

EARLY VICTORIAN

I. Peel and the Corn Laws

IN FOLLOWING the story of the long Victorian reign which will continue for several chapters we must bear in mind that there is a very distinct difference between the earlier and later portions of it. The former was one of genuine idealism even if strongly tinged with materialism, whereas the latter, with more sophistication and modernity, was a period of high-finance and rampant imperialism. We have already spoken of the religious revival, but the results of applied science created much of the shallow optimism of the American Emerson on both sides of the water. People believed, in Emerson's phrase, that somehow "the railroad, the insurance office, the joint-stock company" and the other new inventions would be raised to "a divine use," and also that "in a free and just commonwealth, property rushes from the idle and imbecile, to the industrious, brave, and persevering." These beliefs were genuinely and honestly held by great numbers of those in England toward whom the new wealth was "rushing," and they had undoubtedly much to do with that energy which brought Britain to perhaps the apex of her economic career about midway in the Victorian era, even though the poor might question, if they ever heard of it, the soundness of the doctrine, during the hard years of "the hungry forties."

But even in the period including these, great things had been happening and were to happen. We have seen the overthrow of the old oligarchy and the regaining to a great extent of public control of governmental machinery by the Reform Bill. There had also been increasing emphasis laid upon the simple Biblical doctrine of being one's brother's keeper, that is the duty of the State to see that the dice of fate should not be loaded too heavily against the merely unfortunate, even though, as in the Poor Law already noted, the insistence on individual initiative might have seemed harsh. In addition, Britain made one of her greatest contributions to a sane world by giving up the old idea of a self-sufficing empire, which is again ruining the world today, and embarked on the experiment of free markets for herself and others. In the period under review she was the greatest power and controlled the sea routes of all commerce, but it is notable she reached her own zenith while she left them free and open, and that the century of world peace, disturbed by only minor and local wars, between the Napoleonic struggle and the World War, was a period in which nations were not striving for self-sufficiency but were trading with one another and were willingly dependent on one another. The change was to come with the rank imperialism of the later part of the century when colonies began to spell prestige even more than materials and markets.

When Sir Robert Peel became Prime Minister in 1841 the country had been suffering from a severe business and agricultural depression for several years. Moreover the Liberals, in spite of their reforms, had proved extremely inefficient in the daily routine of governmental business. The handling of such business, and especially the development of the Cabinet as a team with collective responsibility, was one of Peel's strongest points, and Peel proved his strength where his predecessors had been weakest. With such men as Durham, of the *Report on Canada,* as Grey and Russell of the Reform Bill, and others, Peel is one of the great men of the 30's and 40's to be reckoned with in the history not only of Britain but of the Empire, and, owing to the preponderant influence of that Empire, it may well be said the world.

His career holds a special interest also as showing the good as well as the evil which might come out of the now rapidly passing system of the old governing class with all its corruption. His father had been a self-made manufacturer, created a Baronet, who had been interested in the new ideas of such men as Owen, and who was determined that some day his son should be Prime Minister. His wealth secured the boy the expensive and career-opening education of Harrow and Oxford, and a purchased seat in Parliament at twenty-one with a Cabinet office as Secretary for Ireland a year later. This sounds like the worst of the eighteenth century, but there is this to be said. A privileged governing class made up of leaders who do not have to worry about money and who are genuine in their desire to lead in a noble and independent fashion may fall below their privileges and opportunities and get out of touch with the needs of the people at large. Yet, on the other hand, a democracy, as is evident today, may show itself unable to produce capable leaders of both party and country.

Peel proved himself an example of the best that could be produced by the aristocratic system of privileged men trained in the art of government, and the debt which Britain owes him far outweighs what modern Laborites might regard as his iniquitous privileges, and the inherent injustice of a whole system of society. We have already spoken of the reforms he secured when in the Home Office, such as the repeal of the death sentence for more than a hundred offenses, and of his establishment of the "Peelers," or Metropolitan Police, with its far-reaching beneficial effects on all classes. Although he continued to regard himself as a Tory, his mind remained opened to the needs of the poor as well as to those of rich but short-sighted landlords. In his budget of 1842 he not only for the first time since Pitt imposed an income tax so as to place the government finances on a sound basis but also lowered many of the protective duties on home-manufactured and farm products. The budget which produced a surplus instead of the deficits of the Liberals, was bitterly opposed by the Tories, but in 1845 Peel used the surplus to abolish a great number of other import and all export duties. Helped by nature's bestowal of bountiful harvests, except in Ireland, as well as Peel's establishing of sound government finance, prosperity had returned. The temporary income tax was retained and has been from that day to this, but even more striking was Peel's conversion to the repeal of the Corn Laws. In 1842 he had made some reduction in the sliding scale of duties which satisfied neither those in favor of total abolition nor those favoring retention.

Meanwhile, the work of the Anti-Corn Law League had been actively carried on under such leaders as Richard Cobden and John Bright, who with lesser followers came to be known as "the Manchester School." Both were men of untiring zeal, of magnificent public spirit, and both believed in Free Trade as a holy cause and not a mere economic dogma. Peel, as we have seen, had been moving in their direction, and by 1845 his conversion was complete, probably largely helped by the disastrous potato famine of that and the following years.

Peel had come to realize that Britain could not at once be the workshop of the world and raise enough food for her increasing population engaged in manufacturing. In view of that, and almost within sight of the starving millions in Ireland, it seemed to him impossible any longer to continue the system which made food artificially scarce and high-priced for the benefit of the landlord and agricultural interest alone. The Corn Laws, by placing a duty on imported cereals, including wheat, tended to raise or keep high the price of bread, and Peel was undoubtedly right in abolishing them. His party, however, furious at what they felt their betrayal, refused to follow him, and he was forced to resign in December, only to be called back to office next month in 1846, when Russell, who had been unable to form a Ministry, pledged him support. By June the Corn Laws had been practically repealed in entirety, though not totally so until three years later. The popular demand was so great that the measure passed the Lords, as the Reform finally had, for fear of a revolutionary crisis. On the day the bill passed, however, Peel was defeated in the Commons on his Irish Bill and his administration was followed by six years of Liberalism under Lord John Russell, supported by Peel and his more devoted followers.

II. UNREST

The new Ministry had to serve through stormy times, at home and abroad. Peel had done what he could to aid the stricken Irish but owing to the same old troubles in that unhappy island between tenants and landlords there was much disorder and the bill on which the Prime Minister had been defeated by Disraeli and his group had been one for the protection of life. The famine was even worse in 1847 and it has been said that there was room in the poorhouses for less than three per cent of those dying from starvation. With the ever-present Irish difficulties and hatreds, the slow movement of Parliamentary reforms, and the lack of organized relief for such a vast mass of misery suddenly needing it, people died and emigrated on a colossal scale, the Irish population falling from eight to perhaps six millions. Most of the emigrants went to the United States and carried with them an abiding resentment against England, whom they blamed for all their troubles, a feeling which unhappily has to be taken into consideration even to the present. The Irish landlords were many of them sunk heavily in debt, and Russell got through Parliament a bill to allow them to sell their estates in the hope that new owners, with cash resources, would be able to improve the estates for the tenants. Unfortunately this did not prove to be the case, many of the new "moneyed" men being harder on their tenants than the former easygoing ones. Other bills designed to save the tenants the improvements they had made and to avoid some of the worst evils of eviction failed of passage. Armed resistance flared up again in 1848 and any settlement of the Irish question appeared farther off than ever.

In England itself in the same year there was a renewal of the Chartist movement, which as we have seen demanded the secret ballot, manhood suffrage, pay for members of Parliament, equal electoral districts, abolition of property qualification for the suffrage, and annual Parliaments. At first the movement seemed alarming and a petition said to be signed by over 5,000,000 was to be delivered to Parliament. A huge illegal mass meeting was scheduled to be held on Kennington Common but was attended by only about 25,000. Fortunately the government did not get in a panic. The meeting was kept in order by the civil authorities without the calling in of the military, and the petition was received by Parliament, when it was found to contain only 2500 genuine signatures. It was a year of revolutions and everywhere on the Continent revolutionists were in motion, with civil war between Austria and Hungary, and Italian risings against the Austrians. Most of the movements were promptly crushed, though not without fierce fighting, and in an effort to obtain internal tranquillity France elected Louis Napoleon, a nephew of the great Bonaparte, president of the newly created "republic," for ten years. All of this was but the prologue for events of the same generation which were to change the map of Europe and establish those nations which are the protagonists today in the latest act of our drama.

III. Optimism and the Great Exhibition

Indeed the world was changing fast, though few realized how fateful the changes were to prove. In fact, in 1851 men were saying that the days of wars were past owing to the victory of free trade and the opening of the world to peaceful commerce. The Russell Ministry had fallen on the question of the Catholic Church in Ireland, and the new government, with Lord Derby as Prime Minister and Disraeli at the head of the Exchequer, had pronounced the final doom of Protection. But before Disraeli was to leave office an event pregnant with fatal consequences occurred. Louis Napoleon had had himself proclaimed Emperor of the French. Men's minds, however, were more on trade than on war, and in 1851 London was thinking infinitely more of the wonders of the Great Exhibition, just opened in the Crystal Palace in Hyde Park, than of imperial or Continental dangers.

The optimism and self-satisfaction of the English were boundless as they sauntered around the impressive if gaudy building in which were housed the inventions and other things which were deemed to spell the then "World of the Future." A few months before, Tennyson had published his *In Memoriam* with its prophecy of

> "One God, one law, one element,
> And one divine far-off event,
> To which the whole creation moves,"

and Browning's *Pippa Passes* was still comparatively new, with its

> "God's in His Heaven—
> All's right with the world!"

If too many felt that the one divine event was the future culmination of British greatness, there was some foundation for that comforting belief.

There were, it is true, dark spots. There was Ireland, but Englishmen had come, through centuries, to consider Irish misery and discontent so much the order of things (which was one of the reasons that they were so) that Irish conditions were not taken seriously. There was to be India in a few years, but that was not realized. There were many evils at home, which we shall note presently, to be worked out in time, but the fiasco of the last flash of the Chartist movement seemed to indicate that even the working classes had no wish to disturb matters. And meanwhile were not things all working out for good?

First of all, there were the Crown and Court. There was the adored young Queen, deeply devoted to her husband, against whose married life not a whisper of scandal could survive for a moment the obvious truth of their unblemished lives. Not only that but the Crown had become a symbol for the greatness and traditions of the people, while the Sovereign maintained publicly her constitutional position, and almost worship had taken the place of disgust or fear. Moreover, although owing to the Reform Bill the middle class had gained great additional power, enough to satisfy them, there was little or no class feeling, and the new governing class as well as many of the old aristocracy made moves toward still further broadening of the franchise. Parliament was becoming more representative than ever before, and the free institutions on which the British so prided themselves were in course of being bestowed on New British nations overseas. As Britain contrasted herself with other nations which had once been great—France, Spain, Italy, and others—she might well be complacent over her peculiar ability to govern herself and maintain liberty, and in addition to bestowing it on others in far parts of the world.

The Exhibition, which included foreign countries as well as Britain, with a generous allowance of space for the colonies, was divided into the four classes of raw materials, mechanical inventions, manufactures and art. Except for the last section it was frankly materialistic and afforded a view of what was then considered the amazing advance of applied science in the previous generation or two. The next great invention, that of Armstrong's guns, lay some years ahead, and as yet science seemed to promise better communications, cheaper production, a wider range of goods for all with none of the terrors with which our own age has become familiar. Science seemed wholly on the side of a richer civilization for all than the world had ever dreamed of before, and Britain was leading in its application to all sorts of goods and their distribution throughout the world. Over 6,000,000 visitors, many of them travelling to town for the first time in their lives by the new railways and reported as consuming (an English touch) 2,000,000 buns, saw the 19,000 exhibits. For many of the sight-seers it was a vision of a marvellous world to be in which the Empire would take the lead. In addition, the quiet and friendly crowds from all parts of the nation seemed to symbolize the termination of the anxieties and disturbances which had racked society since the end of the Napoleonic wars and to be ushering in a settled period of harmony and social calm.

The Exhibition, due almost wholly to the Prince Consort, was, unlike some smaller ones already held on the Continent, not a mere show. It was an event with its influence on the mind and history of the nation. It was a turning point, as was also the fall of the Russell Ministry. The "Victorian Age," as it is called without considering its two contrasted periods, was to last for nearly a half century more, but it was entering on a new phase, in which the dreams of pacifism, of a world made peaceful and happy by free trade and inventive industry were to be rudely shattered. The culture of materialism was to be attacked by Matthew Arnold, the economics of an industrial society excoriated by Ruskin, and the foundations of religious tradition and belief undermined by Darwin and Huxley. The Exhibition, indeed, although it seemed to those who visited it as the doorway to the future, was in reality the "Finis" to an age which was rapidly passing.

We may still linger a few moments over some of its aspects, which are amply portrayed in the novels of the time. As the Elizabethan period is that of the highest development of the drama, the mid-nineteenth century is that of the novel and no other period is so clearly mirrored in that form. In his *Vanity Fair* (1848) and other books Thackeray gives us unforgettable pictures of the London society of his time, as Trollope does of country life, and Dickens of the middle class and poor, mostly of the towns. If we add Mrs. Gaskell, whose classic *Cranford* appeared in 1853, we have an almost incomparable portrait of a society at a given time. We do not read about it; we live in it, as in no other period of English history. The world its authors created for us is three-dimensional, and their characters have a reality and vividness lacking in many of our living acquaintances. How much better we know Becky Sharp, Jos Sedley and Amelia, the Duke of Omnium, Mrs. Proudie, Doctor Thorne, David Copperfield, Dora, Peggotty, Sairie Gamp, Mr. Pecksniff, Mr. Micawber, and scores of others from the novelists of this period than we do our own neighbors!

IV. SOCIAL CONDITIONS

It was an age of strong individualism and "characters." Those of Dickens are not exaggerated, as neither were the conditions he described and strove to correct. It was still, in spite of the wonders in the Crystal Palace and of many reforms, almost incredibly crude and cruel. Every age is too complex to be described in a few paragraphs, and only hints can be given. To suggest something of the range to be described we may note that the ventilation of the Queen's apartments in Buckingham Palace still passed through the common sewer and as has been said "were less salubrious than King Alfred's primitive abode." The great houses in Belgrave and Eaton Squares, as well as in other fashionable neighborhoods, were built over "sewers abounding in the foulest deposits and emitting the most disgusting effluvium." Such physical conditions typify the social ones in which the highly educated and privileged upper society lived above the lowest strata in which conditions were still atrocious.

It was the heyday of the "great houses" with their retinues of servants, although the servant problem was beginning to be troublesome, and an estimate for 1850 suggests that on an income of £1000 only a cook, two housemaids and a manservant could be kept. A few years earlier on £5000 a year the possessor of that income could have maintained thirteen menservants, nine women, ten horses, and several carriages. We must recall that £12 a year was a good wage for an experienced maid and that the accommodations for these numerous servants were bad and crowded. In some great houses three and four footmen had to sleep together in a badly ventilated basement cubicle. One boon which the Exhibition year brought to servants and the poor was the abandonment of the iniquitous tax on windows, maintained long after by the French.

Ventilation brings us to one or two minor points in the development of the Englishman. For example, the English are supposed to be inordinately addicted to fresh air and the taking of baths, but as we have already noted not only in the homes of the very poor, where they might be crowded twenty to a cellar room, almost unventilated, but even in the great mansions, up to Buckingham Palace itself, the ventilation was often even noxious. The lack of water and bathing facilities was almost as bad. As early as 1812 the Lord Mayor's request for the installation of a shower bath in the Mansion House was refused on the old English argument that there never had been one and therefore there should not be one. By 1832 there were occasional fixed bathtubs to be found in such houses as that of Lord John Russell but they were not in general use even in the homes of the rich in the period of this chapter. Water closets which flushed came into common usage only after 1830, known with Victorian nicety as "necessaries." In the slums the poor often fought for pails of water from the general supply which was turned on for an hour or so only in the day, a Hogarthian precursor of the lines of guests who even yet wait for the few tubs available in many of the larger resort hotels and private country houses.

It was still a society in which each had his place and knew it in various hierarchies which not only extended from royalty and Dukes downward in fine gradations but had its counterpart in domestic staffs. My Lord and My Lady insisted no more on their precedence of rank than did the butler and housekeeper. If in great houses physicians and surgeons, except the most renowned, were expected to dine in the housekeeper's room and not with the family, on the other hand the etiquette demanded by the servants among themselves was quite as strict. In houses with large staffs the under servants even if they had their meals with the upper were not allowed to speak in their presence, and after the meat course the upper ones would adjourn to the housekeeper's room for their pudding and wine, leaving the first footman to preside for the remainder of the meal in place of the august butler.

The details might vary from house to house but the main point is that the gradations of precedence of the master class were not resented but copied and insisted upon among the working class themselves. It was all part of the close-knit texture of English social life to which we have already called attention, and if today Britain has in many respects outstripped the United States in political democracy it has in part done so by the tight fabric of its social life.

Individualistic and abounding in characters as it was, it was not the atomism of sheer individualism. The butler who indulged a love for the same niceties of precedence as did My Lord had no wish to see the lord lose his position and privileges lest in the process Jeems might lose his likewise. The farmer who might rise to the squirearchy and even the county gentry did not want those classes abolished, the workman who might become a manufacturer and the manufacturer a peer, all had no such detestation of the order of society and of social privilege as did those of similar standing on the Continent who found themselves barred from social aspirations by the closed phalanxes of caste.

On the other hand, there was no such dissolution of social bonds as took place on the frontiers of new countries where old ways, customs and relations rapidly disappeared. The frontier quickly brought, in its simple environment, political democracy, but it destroyed to a large extent social cohesion. In the old country, political democracy was slower in coming, but, because social cohesion remained, it was safer to encourage political democracy under complex social conditions than it was in the newer countries in which people had more largely lost their sense of social responsibility in an anarchy of individual opportunity and struggle.

V. LITERATURE AND THE ARTS

Meanwhile, in England, conditions in country life in especial were improving. Partly owing to the religious movements and partly to the example of the popular Court, the gentry and aristocracy were becoming more "genteel"; at least decent and less coarsely animal than in the Georgian days of John Bull. The clergy were also becoming more cultivated and more alive to their spiritual duties. Among the people generally reading as a habit was also rapidly expanding. If there was an enormous sale for religious and sentimental novels and tracts, such as the Reverend L. Richmond's *Dairyman's Daughter*, which sold 2,000,000 copies, the most widely read books among the people at large were still the Bible, *Robinson Crusoe*, and *The Pilgrim's Progress*, which are admittedly much better material for normal minds to feed upon than much of what is felling our forests for wood pulp today.

We have already spoken of the novelists, who formed the chief glory of the period from the point of view of art. Architecture was negligible and what monumental art could accomplish was unhappily to be displayed in the Albert Memorial, which when finally completed in 1866 had cost £110,000 and can best be described in the words of Professor Cockerell's young grandchild who, lapsing into the cockney of his nursemaid, said "Mamma, it's a hornament." In painting, Landseer was the most popular artist of a time which illuminates the history of art almost solely in the works of Turner, who in spite of Ruskin had long to await recognition.

In poetry the two outstanding figures are those already quoted, Tennyson and Browning. The first was essentially Victorian. If toward the end of the reign a middle-class woman, after a Shakespearean performance, could remark of *Antony and Cleopatra,* "How unlike the home life of our own dear Queen," Tennyson was much too like that home life. Highly skilled in the use of words and meters he was not profound in thought, but he most expressed the popular emotions of his day: "King Arthur," the British love of the mystical and the past; "religious faith," especially appealing in view of the religious revival; and "Liberal institutions," the ideal of the times. These three items taken from a memorandum of his may explain why he was the only English poet to be made a peer solely because of his poetical work. This may seem an inadequate appraisal, for he did write some of the most memorable and oft-quoted lines and stanzas in English verse, though his willingness to raise all the deeper problems of life only to leave question marks after them is indicative of the age of transition in which he lived. Deeply interested in the new science, he refused to face the answers or even to raise the problems too disconcertingly.

Tennyson was like a quiet afternoon in a country house, with lawns sweeping down to the tranquil meanderings of the Thames. In the gusto of Browning we find a wholly different note. Tennyson delayed his marriage for ten years to make sure he had enough money whereas Browning eloped with Elizabeth Barrett and carried her off to Italy on almost nothing a year. The work of perhaps no other English poet but Shakespeare is richer in characters than Browning's and his interest in human problems and personalities was infinite. In spite of a great lyric gift his poetry is often obscure and tortured, his dramas are for the study and not the stage, and one wonders why he did not try the leading literary form of the time, the novel. Among the lesser parts of the period we may mention Swinburne, with his intoxication of words and rhythms, Matthew Arnold, who turned from poetry to prose, and Edward Fitzgerald, whose free translation and rearrangement of the *Rubaiyat* of the Persian Omar Khayyam published in 1859 remains one of the most quoted poems in the language. It may be noted that Omar is considered by the Persians themselves a fifth-rate poet and that Rubaiyat is merely the Persian word for *quatrains,* but in his translation and arrangement Fitzgerald made a wholly new poem, which in its pessimism and agnosticism was to fit the mood of a later generation. In considering the mid-Victorian period the sensual paganism of Swinburne and the marvellously flowing verses of Fitzgerald cannot be ignored. They are as much part of the pattern of the time as Factory Acts, optimism, the atrocious household art, the whatnots in the corners of parlors, and the *Keepsakes* on the parlor table.

A reaction against the horrors of much of the household furnishing had set in under the lead of William Morris, also a poet who came near to high rank and was a precursor of the Pre-Raphelites in art. He was representative of the confusion of the day. Among other things a designer of wallpapers, a regenerator of the art of fine printing, poet, prose writer, Socialist, he expressed many of the artistic and social aspirations of his time, although in many ways ahead of it.

Another writer, of greater influence, who approached social questions through art and the artistic temperament was John Ruskin, whose rather too florid prose gained him a great following, notably among the young who were to be leaders in the next generation. His defense of art and of a communal life in which beauty, generosity, and a genuine community spirit should play their predominant parts as against the mere money-making motive which was causing modern industrialism to ruin much which was worthwhile in the life of the older England, had a profound and worthy influence, even though based on a naïve lack of sound economic understanding. Modern civilization could not retreat from the machine age to please Ruskin any more than Morris. Yet if in the welter of jigsaw Victorianism, of jerry-built towns and obscuration of the old, sweet countryside from the smoke of factory chimneys, their voices may have seemed those of prophets in the desert, they were to have effect at last, and the underlying thoughts of each are coming to be accepted in a new age filled with horrors of which they never dreamed.

The undermining of old accepted beliefs as to society and religion was beginning to be observable in such works as those of Herbert Spencer, the precursor of Darwin and Huxley, in his scientific views of the development of man; of Lyell in his *Principles of Geology* and *The Antiquity of Man;* and of Buckle in his *History of Civilization in England.* Lecky was soon to follow with his histories of Rationalism and of Morals in Europe. Compared with such books as these, which really changed the intellectual climate, Macaulay's *History of England,* in spite of its immense popularity and financial success, and his many essays were almost negligible in lasting, though not in contemporary, influence. Of limited vision he believed that all would be right with the world, not if "God's in His Heaven," but if the Whigs were in power, and he had none of the indignation with the evil aspects of the changing age which so stirred a Ruskin or a Carlyle.

The latter, always a hater of shams and injustice, came to adopt some himself, but at his best his pen was eager and potent to combat the easiest and worst assumptions of the Victorian Age as to the inevitable benefit of its economic system and to stress the value of the individual strong in his own personality. He stirred a whole age, as did J. S. Mill in his essay *On Liberty* (1859). To name and touch on briefly only a few leading writers is to run the risk of giving a false picture of a period, but possibly enough has been said to indicate the cross currents of the one we have been discussing. Tennyson, for example, as poet was as much intrigued by the problems raised by the new science as he was by the myths of King Arthur; Morris, rebelling against the crude household art, rebelled equally against the social system; Ruskin, championing Turner and art as a critic, was even more deeply stirred by the evils of the encroaching machine age of factories and railways. The list could be extended indefinitely. The breadth of interest points to one of the chief characteristics of the period. This was the belief in the "worthwhileness" of everything. People believed in the infinite possibilities of reform, political and social, in the new science, in peace from free trade. They felt themselves on the threshold of a new, freer, happier, and richer world, even those whose vision was limited to increased riches for themselves. This was the first half of the Victorian Age. Conditions in many ways might be bad but science and free government could set all right. The Public Health Act of 1848, a most important advance in the control of local government by the central one, was an example of how Parliament, like a *Deus ex machina,* could correct all evils, as Free Trade could bring peace to a warring world.

VI. FOREIGN RELATIONS

But the world was moving outside Britain also. On the Continent the second Napoleon had in turn become Emperor, and the uneasy balance of powers heaved like the sea in storm. In especial the Eastern Question loomed again, and the problem of Turkey, the "Sick Man of Europe," in the phrase coined by the Russian Czar.

There had been diplomatic movements on the part of both France and Russia for the possession of places dear to the Christian religion, especially the Holy Sepulchre, but neither nation was satisfied with what the Sultan proposed. There were indeed much larger issues involved in the web of international policies, and Russia proposed a division of the Turkish Empire, suggesting that Britain take Crete and Egypt as her part of the spoils, which Britain declined to do. The Turkish treatment of Christians and of subject races was unquestionably bad, but if the Turkish Empire disappeared there would be a vacuum in one of the most important sections of the world into which the wild winds of discord and world war might whirl. The eyes of Russia have ever been upon Constantinople as a warm seaport and a point of attack on some of the world's most important sea routes. On the other hand England has always dreaded the Russian menace to India, real or imaginary. Little by little the situation among the powers deteriorated, and after Turkey and Russia went to war Britain drifted into it, as an ally of France.

The war itself was inglorious, although it ended in the defeat of Russia. It was the graveyard of the reputations of diplomats, statesmen, and generals. The British Ambassador at Constantinople helped to bring on hostilities against the wishes of the Prime Minister, Aberdeen, who later resigned to give place to Palmerston, who was wholeheartedly in favor of war. The British commander in the field, Lord Raglan, was incompetent. The administration of the War Office broke down almost completely, and food and medical supplies for the mere 20,000 of the Expeditionary Force failed woefully. Only one person, an English woman, Florence Nightingale, made a reputation which will never die.

The effects of the war were out of all proportion to the operations, which need not be discussed, or to the formal terms of the treaty of peace. Louis Napoleon, with the ambitions but not the ability of the first Emperor, had played his hand shrewdly, and France came out of the conflict the leading power on the Continent. The consummate Italian statesman, Cavour, had also played his hand to the limit, and with Napoleon's aid had succeeded in making his complaints against the rule of Austria, which had chosen the Russian side, heard by all the world, and paved the way to the future independence and unification of Italy.

For England, the results were spiritual rather than material. Free Trade had proved not enough to keep world peace, and the smug complacency of the Crystal Palace was healthily shattered by the revelations of gross incompetency which the terrible "Crimean winter" of 1854–55 revealed. The conditions in the British force before Sebastopol, as given to the public by William Russell of *The Times*, first of modern war correspondents, were a dose of bitters after the soothing draught of the Great Exposition. Due to the ensuing anger of the British electorate Miss Nightingale, who had been sent out officially to help look after the sick, was given such power to organize her work as had never fallen to the lot of woman before. What she accomplished in the face of bewildered army officers is still almost incredible. At Scutari, where the British forces were melting away from sickness and wounds, she built the first modern base hospital, and the death rate fell from 42 to 22 in the thousand. How many countless millions she may have saved in the years since then it is impossible to calculate, for her work was not a mere incident of a minor war. She not only continued, after peace, the reorganization of the Army Medical Service but it was due to her influence that the international Red Cross developed from the Geneva Convention of 1864. Incidentally she so raised the status of women in the public mind that the woman's movement in all its many aspects felt the magic touch of her name throughout the world.

The names of the battles—Alma, Balaclava, and Inkerman, together with the siege and fall of Sebastopol—added to the roll of regimental honors, and helped to build the regimental spirit which has counted for so much in the history of the army. Even one of the worst mistakes in a long record of them crowded into the three years of the war was so magnificent in the heroism of the men sacrificed that it has been woven into the spiritual life of the nation as immortalized in Tennyson's *Charge of the Light Brigade*.

In the larger international field this centralized and comparatively unimportant war was to prove momentous. A unified Italy was eventually to develop from it. France had apparently become the leader on the Continent, with the imitation Napoleon at her head looking for glory, but had antagonized Austria and Britain. When a few years later the Germany rising under Bismarck should strike at her, Germany would be allowed to have her way and a broad highway opened for events to travel down to our own troubled times. The "Sick Man" was declared to be well again, and for the nonce there was no international vacuum on the shores of the Bosphorus. In connection with the Peace Conference the powers agreed to the Declaration of Paris, which abolished privateering, agreed that blockades must be effective to be recognized, and that a neutral flag should cover enemy goods if not contraband.

For the moment, and perhaps ominously for the future, the war appeared to have brought a Jingo spirit with it. When Palmerston with his usual high-handed way, especially with weaker nations, involved Britain in a second war with China and was defeated in Parliament on the issue, he was returned with a big majority by the electorate. Cobden and Bright, who had opposed the Crimean War also, went down to defeat in their home districts. France again joined in the fray, and the Chinese, no match for European forces with modern arms, were obliged to admit foreign representatives at Peking, open Tientsin and other ports to trade, agree to the regulation of the opium traffic which acquired official status, and as punishment for the killing of twenty foreigners suffer the burning of the beautiful Summer Palace of the Emperor.

It throws a somewhat unpleasant light on the character of the stormy Prime Minister that he took especial delight in this act of vandalism. Another interesting point, in view of the future, was that, although the French took part in the war, the feeling between them and the British had already become such that the question was raised in the British Cabinet as to whether the expedition should not be equipped with the old form of rifle, which would be good enough to shoot the Chinese, instead of with the new Armstrongs the secrets of which might thus be opened to the French. Meanwhile, momentous, and more gratifying, events had been happening within the British Empire itself. Before considering the most thrilling, that of the mutiny in India, we may turn to more humdrum but in the long run scarcely less important ones in Canada and Australia.

VII. Canada Comes of Age

In the former the year 1854 may be taken as an important dividing line in its history. It marked the departure of Lord Elgin, who had done much to lead Canadian politicians on their new path of responsible self-government, the last, as has been said, of the "proconsuls." After that date the center of politics shifts from the Governor to the Prime Minister. Canada had come of age and had learned how to handle herself as a nation and to use those political instruments of freedom which the mother country had willingly and peacefully bestowed upon her. Although the story was to be repeated in other far quarters of the world where Britain's sons had gone to build new Britains, there is something singularly inspiring in the story of Canada, for it had brought a wholly new idea and relationship into the long sad tale of empires.

It was natural that, in so far as economic interest was concerned, the small population of Canada, although occupying a territory larger though less productive and rich than that of the United States, would be drawn into the American business orbit as irresistibly as filings to a magnet. In the last years of Elgin's Governorship there was much talk of the benefits of annexation, and the adoption of a decimal system of coinage, like that of their great southern neighbor, in place of the immemorial pounds, shillings, and pence. These had been deemed ominous signs. They merely proved, however, that there could be diversity in unity. Elgin's long work for a reciprocity treaty with the United States bore fruit and he had the satisfaction of knowing that the matter was settled, though the papers were not signed, before he left for home. It solved at a critical time the pull of economic interests against political and sentimental interests.

As both nations, which between them divide the entire North American continent, except Mexico, have grown, the question of annexation has disappeared. Canada is rightfully proud of her position as a sister nation in the British Commonwealth, and Americans are proud of the undefended frontier of some five thousand miles and of her neighbor. Although from the nature of the case there can be no guarantee, I cannot imagine that the United States would fail to go to the assistance of Canada if attacked and on the other hand it is as impossible to think of the States as attacking Canada as of a man attacking his younger sister. If the relations now subsisting between the States and Canada form one of the few gleams of hope in a world torn by hatreds and fears of war, it is due in large measure to the wisdom of the British Government in the reign of Victoria and which had been so unhappily lacking in that of George III.

166

VIII. Changes in Australia

In Australia, as we have seen, the earlier colonies had all gained responsible government, and largely under the Wakefield system so much land had been brought into cultivation and the population had so increased, that any fears of foreign complications in the remote regions of the island continent had ceased. It was to be definitely all British and free. In the period of this chapter, 1850–60, the most important Australian event was the discovery of gold in quantity and the working of the mines. Scattered discoveries had been made from perhaps 1823, but it was only in this decade that gold changed the country. In the years 1851–61 inclusive approximately £124,000,000 of new wealth was dug from the ground. Naturally the results included all those associated with "gold rushes" anywhere in the world, and much experimenting with control of mines and miners, as well as the only rebellion (and that on a small scale) which the country has known.

But there were more fundamental effects. Wool had already become king, as cotton was in the American South, and Australian prosperity, with cries and setbacks, would have continued in any case. Railroads would have come, steamships would have carried freight in increasing amounts to the ports of the world and population would have increased had gold never been discovered. The point is that gold gave a tremendous acceleration to every movement. As has been said it "precipitated a colony into a nation." At the beginning of the period the population was only a little over 400,000. In ten years it rose to 1,168,000.

The change was not merely in numbers but in character. We have already noted the ideas stirring both in Britain and the Continent of Europe in the period immediately preceding this enormous influx which multiplied the Australian population nearly threefold. The liberal, democratic, and even revolutionary ideas of the Old World were thus transferred at a critical time to the new nation arising in the Antipodes. Combined with the attitude of the home government we find the results in a new sense of self-reliant nationhood in an Australia far advanced beyond the penal colony of a few decades earlier.

Between 1855 and 1859 the colonies of New South Wales, Victoria, Tasmania, South Australia, and Queensland were added to those possessing responsible government, and various Acts of the legislatures suggested a feeling of independence though no desire to withdraw from the Empire. Among such may be mentioned their insistence upon maintaining local control over the gold revenues; the stand by Victoria against the royal prerogative; the passage of the measures restricting Chinese immigration; and the beginnings of somewhat distinctive Australian labor legislation. Under the pioneering conditions of all new countries, as of the United States also in its earlier phases, there is little time, even if inclination, for the pioneers to interest themselves in the arts. In that sense therefore, it is at this period too early to consider any colonial culture, but by 1860 the various larger colonies, later to be Dominions, were already beginning to develop distinct characters. The British in Canada, Australia, New Zealand, and even South Africa, although still dominantly British were becoming under the changed conditions of each new land, something different in character and temperament from those who remained in the old settled and comfortable little island at home, just as the Americans, even of British descent, had become quite different in many ways.

IX. India and the Mutiny

India, with its vast native population and a British population which was scarcely more than a garrison, has always presented problems different from those of the Dominions and colonies. The terrible events of the year 1857 proved one of the major turning points in its history. It is well to remember that the great Mutiny was a military affair and not a rebellion of the civil population, although many things led up to it, some of which were of a civil nature. The period of the Governor-Generalship of Lord Dalhousie had seen many reforms as well as the completion of the general British framework of the country. The whole Indian Civil

Service, for example, was thrown open to competitive examination in Britain long before the Home Services reached the same point. But Dalhousie in many ways moved too rapidly for Indian opinion and prejudices.

Some of the Indian States were merely hereditary feudal powers in the hands of oppressive and degenerate rulers. There were also great landowners within the British frontiers who were not landlords in the English sense but wrung all possible wealth from the unfortunate tillers of the soil. To correct the first abuse, Dalhousie used his prerogative of not recognizing an adopted heir. By this method the native rulers, at great advantage to themselves, had been able to perpetuate their mismanagement even when they had no children of their own. Under prevailing conditions it was hoped that this policy of "lapse" would gradually bring about a more unified and simple government, the idea being that such a unitary government, with some nominally still independent native States, would be able to provide better conditions for a free peasantry, owning their own lands. To secure this end, a Commission was appointed to enquire into titles, which confiscated some 20,000 large estates in the Deccan. Naturally all these moves created a great body of discontent. The disregarding of adoption ran counter to old custom, and also landlords with however doubtful titles or however rapacious were infuriated at the loss of claimed property. Unquestionably there were also many cases of individual injustice in the proceedings.

Moreover, India felt it was being Westernized too fast and without regard to its own beliefs and customs. The new railways and especially the telegraph—which latter was to save India to the Empire in the Mutiny—were regarded as diabolical. Many new laws were considered by both Hindus and Muslims as tending to destroy caste and their religious and family lives, as were also many of the activities of the Christian missionaries. India, however, which has never been able to unite for centuries past, has always contained groups with grievances against one another as well as against the British. Had it not been for special grievances in the army it is likely that there would have been no uprising.

169

On the basis of the policy of "lapse" several native States had been annexed, as had the great province of Oudh, which had been taken over because of the gross mismanagement of its rulers. That province alone contributed about 40,000 troops to the Bengal army, and it was in that province and army that the disaffection was most pronounced. In any case the morale and loyalty of that army had been allowed seriously to decline, and when Lord Canning succeeded Dalhousie in 1856, and found it almost impossible to get troops to serve in Burma he changed the rules of service so that recruits had to agree to serve wherever ordered.

In such overseas service they saw the possibility of losing both their privileged position and possibly their caste. It must be recalled that caste did not depend alone on moral life or beliefs but on a vastly complicated assortment of purely physical acts, including contact with persons of another caste, the eating of forbidden foods, and others. The small British forces had been considerably depleted by the need for troops in the Crimean War and elsewhere. In the enormous area garrisoned by the so-called Bengal Army there was only about one British soldier to twenty-five sepoys, or native troops. The Indians had also absurd notions as to the real strength of Britain and it is said that many believed practically all the British were already in India. Although British officers still had almost complete confidence in their native regiments the Bengal Army was sullen and on the verge of mutiny when a stupid mistake in England supplied the spark.

We have already mentioned the incompetence of the army authorities in London in connection with the Crimean War, as well as the fear of loss of caste in India by the eating of certain forbidden foods. Be it recalled also that caste was not a social system but that loss of religious caste, even if innocently incurred, meant severest penalties, not merely in this life but in the lives to come. Just when the situation in the Bengal Army was at its worst, the new Enfield rifle was introduced which required for its use the biting off the end of a greased cartridge. It was said, and unhappily truly, that the grease used was obtained from the fat of cows and pigs, and that the British had done this purposely so as to break the caste of the Hindu soldiers and affront the Muslims, the cow being sacred to the former, and the pig taboo to the latter, so both were united in opposition. The British had had no such thought but the harm had been done.

When the 19th Infantry refused to use the cartridges and obey orders they were disbanded, as was also the 34th. But there was increasing insubordination, without anything being done to allay the feelings of the troops, and when eighty-five of the members of the 3rd Cavalry were sentenced to ten years' imprisonment, the storm broke. Delhi, where there was not a single British regiment, was captured by the mutineers, then Lucknow, except the Residency, then Cawnpore. Fortunately Dalhousie in 1855 with John Lawrence, one of three famous brothers to whom India owes so much, had made a treaty with old Dost Mohammed, and his capital of Herat had been defended for him against the Persians by Canning. In consequence Afghanistan and the Northwest Frontier were safe to the British, and also—something for those to consider who condemn all British rule in India—all of Sind, the Punjab, Assam, and Southern India, most of Bengal, all of Madras and Bombay, Mysore, Rajputana, Hyderabad, and the Maratha princes remained loyal.

Considering the insignificant resources of the British and the opportunity offered, then if ever would have been the time to throw off the British control if this was really desired. In point of fact it was not desired and the old factiousness of the Indian leaders prevented any general combination. No reinforcements came to India until the event was finally decided by the handful of British there and the natives who remained faithful. Against tremendous odds Delhi was recaptured in September, and a few days later Havelock and Neill, who had already restored Cawnpore to the British, reinforced the Residency at Lucknow, where until his death Sir Henry Lawrence had maintained a magnificent defense which is one of the proud tales that help to make up the British legend. Much remained to be done after the reinforcements arrived under the lead of Sir Colin Campbell but a mere handful of soldiers and civilians, with the aid of loyal Indians, had held the richest jewel in the Empire for Britain. They might well boast that "alone we did it."

Unfortunately the mutineers had set the example of murdering civilians, including women and children, and under the terrific strain of their seemingly impossible situation the British retaliated. Surrounded by overwhelming numbers and maddened by the brutalities of the mutineers, passion rose to a veritable blood lust, and neither side can look back with pride to the kind of war they waged. The massacre of the British women and children by the Indians at Cawnpore, and other diabolical outrages were to recoil upon the Indians, innocent or guilty, and for a time the forces of Hell seemed let loose.

Although the cleavage between the races after the Mutiny as contrasted with conditions existing before may be exaggerated, there is no doubt that it left an almost ineradicable scar on inter-racial relations. India had been always a vast sea on which the tossing waves of conquerors and dynasties rose and fell, but it now appeared that the rule of the alien British would be something different and something not to be thrown off. In the years later, as the Anglo-Indian colony increased and more British women came out, a new class system was formed in which the rulers were to be alien in religion, culture, and sympathies. Moreover, the English attitude changed. In 1858 the old East India Company was relegated to the lumber which had been useful in the past, and the British Crown assumed control, the Company's Governor-General becoming the Queen's Viceroy, and some years later (1876) the Queen herself assuming the title of Empress. The army also was at last completely reorganized. At the time of the Mutiny the natives had made up about 200,000 of all the troops. By 1863 they numbered 140,000 only to 65,000 British, and a large part of the natives were the Sikhs and Gurkhas, splendid fighting material and loyal in the war. The artillery was thereafter retained wholly in British hands.

There was also a change in policy as to native States. Since the Mutiny no more have been annexed, and there are still some six hundred separate ones, ranging in size from Hyderabad, which is larger than all Great Britain, to small States of actually only a few hundred acres each. It would probably have been better if the policy of the Dalhousie period could have been continued, and a more unified India resulted, but no one could then foresee that Britain would one day try to do for India what she had done for the growing Dominions of her own peoples. The welter of States, races, languages, and religions, frozen into the pre-Mutiny shape, enormously complicate the problem of an India with responsible self-government today.

CHAPTER IX

THE TURN OF THE CENTURY

I. The Turning Point

OUR STORY now reaches a marked turning point in 1867. That year was indeed one of the notable ones in Empire history. It witnessed the discovery of diamonds in South Africa with the great effects which were to flow from that event. It saw the establishment of confederation in Canada, and the beginning of a distinct change in imperial sentiment at home. It was the year, also, of the second great Reform Bill and was at the threshold of the long political duel between Disraeli and Gladstone which was to vivify politics and give them an interest they had not before possessed for nearly a generation. Between that year and the end of the previous chapter much was crowded in despite of peace abroad and lack of domestic issues to stir men's souls.

On the Continent modern Europe was fast taking form and in America the greatest civil war the world had yet known was taking place between the North and South in the United States, and Britain's stake was heavy in all these movements, in fact far heavier than she realized at the time.

II. Unification of Italy

There had already been several attempts made by the peoples of some of the numerous petty States which covered the Italian peninsula and adjacent islands to throw off the hated yoke of Austria but all had failed. Nothing could be done unless a first-class power could be induced to pit itself against the Austrians, and in 1859 Count Cavour, who had guided the movement with infinitely more statecraft than the more hot-headed revolutionists, induced Napoleon to play the required role with the King of Sardinia. Probably Napoleon's desire for military glory, and also the bait held out to him of French annexation of Savoy and Nice should Austria have to yield, had their influence with other motives.

The details of the long and sinuous story lie outside the main thread of ours. In brief, Cavour forced Austria to declare war on Sardinia, France came in, Napoleon won the victories of Magenta and Solferino, and then drew back. But the popular movement started throughout the peninsula had become irresistible. By 1861 Victor Emmanuel, King of Sardinia, was able to proclaim the Kingdom of Italy at Turin, ruling all of that country, including Sicily, with the exceptions of Venice and the Papal States, which were included in 1866 and 1870 respectively. Austria's power and prestige had greatly shrunk and a new great power had arisen. Few stories are more fascinating, in their personalities and the incredible drama of the whole, than the rise of united Italy again after centuries of division and oppression. With the altered balance of power in Europe, and the establishment of free parliamentary institutions in the new kingdom, it seemed as though the sun of liberalism was rising rapidly over the ebbing tide of reaction, it not then being foreseen that the Italians had created a form of government which they had not sufficient training or perhaps political aptitude to maintain. The way was unwittingly being paved which was to lead to a recrudescence of the old Roman imperialism and the dictatorship of Mussolini instead of the liberalism and freedom hoped for by the leaders of the *Risorgimento.*

Meanwhile, although Palmerston and the British watched the Italian rising with the greatest interest and enthusiasm, and while "Pam" had always been friendly with Napoleon, the annexation by France of Nice and Savoy aroused instant reaction against the nation. The ambitions of the earlier and greater Napoleon had cost Europe and Britain too much to be readily forgot. War with the new upstart seemed inevitable, and was only averted by Cobden, who with the backing of Gladstone, Chancellor of the Exchequer in Palmerston's Cabinet, went to Paris and proved Napoleon's real desire to avoid war with Britain by negotiating a commercial treaty which was a victory for free trade, and unpopular in France. Perhaps one of the best results of the effort to avoid war was the cementing of Gladstone's friendship with Cobden and the beginning of that with John Bright.

The struggle in Italy had been a wholly popular one with liberty and freedom as the goal, and in that respect it differed widely from the unification of another of the great powers of today. Germany, like Italy, had for long been a mere geographical expression and had consisted of a congeries of separate States of very varying size and power, with Prussia as the most aggressive. Although that country had nominally a parliamentary form of government, the King, fearing that his control over the army and taxation would be destroyed by the liberal elements, called Bismarck to his aid. It was then that the yet unended period and ideal of "blood and iron" began. Personal liberty, freedom of the press, parliamentary control of taxation were all thrown overboard, and the army under immediate royal control was wholly and efficiently reorganized. So far from being popular these movements were bitterly but unsuccessfully opposed. Bismarck was utterly ruthless, and "blood and iron" won. In less than ten years, in a series of unprovoked wars with little Denmark, then Austria, then, 1870, with France, he welded one of the most powerful of the new States of the time. His contribution to European civilization was to use brute force to suppress the liberalism and culture of the Germany of the 1840's and to build a power and to create a state of mind which seventy years later still spreads uncertainty and terror through the world. So, in the few years covered by this chapter the "shape of things to come" was emerging, though Britain, sympathetic to liberal movements and herself rapidly rising to perhaps her zenith of prosperity, did not realize it.

III. Britain and the American Civil War

Across the ocean in America another great new power was arising though threatened with extinction, and, again, British statesmen, including even the increasingly liberal Gladstone, did not realize what was at stake. Anglo-American relations in any case were bad, and to understand them we have to think ourselves back into the situation of 1860, largely different from that of 1940, though even now English lack of knowledge of American history, institutions, and culture is amazing. In the earlier period, however, the two peoples knew each other only by prejudice and rankling memories. There had been the bickerings leading up to the Revolution and independence, the years of quarrelling over the infringements of the Treaty of Peace, the War of 1812, the boundary disputes, the McLeod incident and others, and more threatened wars.

The United States, still young as a nation and to a large extent crude and raw though proud in the consciousness of its potential strength and unexploited resources, had the touchiness of youth and had deeply resented the unfair criticisms of such English travellers as Dickens and Mrs. Trollope. The days of trans-Atlantic tourism had not yet begun, or those of international marriages. Socially the first-hand knowledge which the two peoples had of one another was negligible. The English upper class, which has always tended to consider colonials as a breed inferior to themselves, looked upon the Americans as still lower, colonials who had broken away from the Empire and had also established a social democracy which was even more abhorrent to the English conservatives than the American political system.

Such was the position when after increasing tension for two decades the United States was at last rent by civil war. It was distinctly sectional, the free States lying, roughly, north of latitude 40° and the slave States south of that line, except Kansas which was free though south of the line. Maryland and Delaware, also south, were both slave but were saved to the Union in the struggle. In spite of more or less differences of individual opinion, which split families in the two sections, the Union and the Confederacy were practically units in their divergent views.

Each section had for a century and a half or so been developing an economic system and particular type of culture of its own. To this end soils, climate, education, and other factors had combined with slavery, which had proved economically profitable on the great plantations of the South but not in the small farm, industrial, and mercantile culture of the North. As part of the general reform and humanitarian movement of the mid-nineteenth century there had also been increasing feeling in the North against slavery as a system. The British Government and the Royal African Company in the earlier days had fastened the system on America, and Britain's contrasting of its own freeing of the slaves in the West Indies with the continued use of slaves in America was not justified. To free slaves in a single small section of empire and buy out a handful of owners for £20,000,000 was a very different problem from that which confronted America where 4,000,000 blacks, with a market value of about £300,000,000, formed the basis of the economic system and whole way of life of over 6,000,000 whites and to some extent that, through trade, of the entire nation. It must be recalled, also, that the freeing of the Jamaican slaves, noble as the act was, resulted not only in great economic difficulties but in the necessity of the whites yielding up their self-government and becoming a Crown Colony. Multiply the Jamaican situation by the American scale and it is easier to understand the American problem.

But there was also another issue at stake. Few Europeans grasp the fact that America has a dual form of government, and that it is at once a federal union of sovereign States and a nation which derives powers direct from the people as a whole and not as citizens of the separate States. The Southern States in claiming the right of secession stressed the federal nature of the Union, whereas the North stressed its popular basis. The question was whether the United States was a nation or merely a league of States which could be broken up at any time by the action of any one of them. In a country like the United States, with such a vast extent of territory and such diverse interests, the danger of sectionalism is always present, and if the right to secede were allowed, it would inevitably fall to pieces, and the experiment of self-government and democracy on the greatest scale the world has ever attempted would fail. That issue the British upper classes largely failed to recognize, and many who did recognize it would have welcomed the disintegration of the great democracy whose example they feared might have a dangerous effect on Old World institutions. They felt also that it would be impossible for the North to win or, if it did, to remake a free and united nation by force. This point, that of the saving of the great democratic experiment, although seen by some of the upper classes and statesmen, such as notably John Bright, was for the most part more clearly recognized by the laboring classes, even those who suffered most from the "cotton famine" incidental to the war, and America owes them and their leaders a great debt. For the most part, however, upper-class opinion, including such newspapers as *The Times*, turned against the North when Lincoln announced in his Inaugural Address that he had nothing to do with slavery but that his task was to preserve the Union.

It should be added that the issues of the war were confused even in the minds of many Americans themselves, and the evil effect, long to last, of what from across the ocean seemed the almost unanimous and hostile opinion of upper-class England, was due to its apparent unanimity and bitterness. The attitude of the government was for the most part, however, coldly correct. Russell promptly proclaimed British neutrality, which was maintained throughout the struggle.

In 1861 an incident occurred which nearly precipitated war. The Confederate States, wishing to enlist more active British sympathy, dispatched two agents, Mason and Slidell, to London. Having successfully reached Havana, they embarked on the *Trent*, a British vessel carrying mail, which was forced to stop by a United States warship, the captain of which, Wilkes, took off the two agents. His act was wholly unauthorized and of course illegal, but the North was jubilant. Although the two men were in fact never to accomplish anything of importance their capture was considered to be a blow to the enemy rendered all the more palatable by having involved a twist in the Lion's tail. The Lion, however, emitted a maddened and wholly justifiable roar. Approximately 15,000 troops were ordered to Canada and a sharp note dispatched to Washington, which was happily toned down somewhat by Prince Albert. Although a number of public officials, and even Congress itself, had acted hastily in praising the captain who had made the seizure, Lincoln had been dubious and had kept his head. The agents were turned over to a British vessel as requested, and the incident was happily closed though feeling on both sides had been made still worse. War had been narrowly averted, but Russell and Palmerston had stood out against enraged opinion in England, as Lincoln and Seward had in America, and in the absence of cable or radio the slowness of communication gave each side time to cool off.

Although from time to time the British Cabinet discussed the possibility of intervention as the struggle went on year after year, it never made any proposal, and Lincoln's proclamation freeing the slaves in the South as of January 1, 1863, had a favorable effect on a large section of British opinion. After the *Trent* affair the only time that the two nations came close to possible war again was in connection with vessels built at Liverpool, the most famous of which was the *Alabama*. Although it was illegal to equip any vessels of war in British ports for the use of belligerents in a war in which Britain was a neutral, two smaller ships had been built in spite of the protests of the American Minister and had been allowed to put to sea unarmed, taking on arms later and doing much damage to Northern shipping.

The more important *Alabama*, known in the building yards and records only as *No. 290*, was launched in May, 1862. While it was being completed, the American Minister, Charles Francis Adams, kept sending evidence regarding the mattter to the British Foreign Office, which was dilatory, and in some cases referred the documents to the port authorities at Liverpool, notoriously Southern in sympathy. Adams presented more evidence, which the distinguished solicitor Sir Robert Collier declared absolutely convincing and which Russell later admitted he should have accepted and stopped the ship, but the law officers of the Crown took a different view.

Finally a new case was presented which went to Sir John Harding, the Queen's Advocate, the law officer having particular cognizance of naval affairs. Unfortunately he had just gone insane, although no one knew except Lady Harding, who kept the fact, and unluckily the papers, secret for five days. As soon as they reached Russell he and other members of the Cabinet realized that the evidence was unquestionably conclusive and that the vessel must be seized immediately. Some one gave warning, however, and the *Alabama*, still unfinished, slipped out to sea, to inflict untold damage on the North, the direct damages being estimated, as we shall see later, at over £3,000,000. Adams later exonerated Russell and the government from any desire to let the vessel escape, but the affair, quite apart from Harding's insanity and Lady Harding's carelessness, was delayed and bungled throughout, and at the last moment, when haste and secrecy were essential, somebody must have let the secret out.

The very week that the *Alabama* sailed, the same builders, the Lairds, had begun work on two more vessels to be equipped with rams, and to be the most powerful vessels afloat. The danger was great, for Slidell had made it appear that the ships, which had been turned over to a French banking firm, were being built for the Pasha of Egypt. We cannot enter on all the complicated details of the transactions or of Adams' negotiations with Russell and the government. Finally a ram was launched and the other was nearing completion, when Adams tried one last desperate throw and sent a brief note to Russell, reiterating his demand that the rams be detained and adding that if allowed to go to sea "it would be superfluous in me to point out to your lordship that this is war."

The note was probably not the determining factor in the government's decision. Russell, having burned his fingers with the *Alabama*, was genuinely desirous of not getting caught again. He probably agreed with Adams that the evidence was conclusive to him but it was not capable of legal proof, and, if the vessels did not belong to the Confederacy, the government might lay itself open to heavy damage if it seized them. However, the North was at last beginning to win important victories, and a convenient rebellion started in Poland which might realign the relations of powers on the Continent. This time Russell decided to leave legal evidence alone, and the government bought the rams, paying £225,000 for them from the Lairds. Russell had in fact given orders to detain the rams four days before he got Adams' note but was waiting for the additional evidence which did not come. The most serious crisis in connection with the American war thus passed on the basis of expediency and not of law. Had Russell not taken the course he did there would almost unquestionably, in view of Adams' note, been a third Anglo-American war.

Instead, peace was maintained and the way opened for the North to win and for the Union to be preserved. Had it been split into two nations and the theory of peaceful secession become legalized by a decision of war, I think there is little question that the un-ravelling process might well have gone farther and the North American continent become split into a number of hostile nations. In any case there would not have been that vast free-trade area of 3,000,000 square miles and 130,000,000 people which more than almost any other factor has built up the power and wealth of the United States. One has only to consider the reservoir of wealth and resources which were utilized by the Allies both before and after the United States entered the World War, and the present relations between that country and Canada, to realize that the issue of the Civil War, and the reaffirmation of the Union instead of the Balkanizing of the continent meant much to the Empire as well as to the United States.

IV. RISE OF GERMANY

Incidentally the winning of the war by the North prevented the possible development of a French Empire again in the New World. Napoleon had been far more friendly to the Confederacy than had the English statesmen, but in 1861 Britain had joined France and Spain in an expedition to secure redress for foreign bondholders in Mexico. The immediate object secured, France alone remained, but Palmerston had no objections to Napoleon setting up an empire in Mexico under the unfortunate Austrian Archduke Maximilian as Emperor, believing that the American venture might divert his strength and attention from Europe. The United States, restored as a powerful nation, caused French withdrawal, and again Napoleon was left to spin his schemes in the new alignments of the old Continent.

Meanwhile the Prince Consort had died at the end of 1861, and Palmerston foresaw that the Queen would be more difficult to deal with than when Albert had been able to use his tact on occasion, as in the case of the *Trent* note to the United States. The position of a Royal Consort is always a most difficult one for a man and in Albert's case it was peculiarly so. The Queen had been utterly devoted to him and believed his opinions on every subject to be the only wise and correct ones, although she did not strain the constitution by opposing the Cabinet when it was united. The Prince was a serious-minded man who cared little for sport and society but much for the advancement of the scientific and commercial life of the country. Although essentially a liberal, Albert, who was German, had a better understanding of the difficulties in the way of German unity and of liberalism on the Continent than Palmerston, who, as Foreign Minister or as Prime Minister, had to fight for his own views against both the Queen and the Consort, who took a special interest in foreign affairs and insisted on seeing all the dispatches. Owing to her adoration of her dead husband it was clear that the Queen's views on such matters would become static at the point where they had been left by Albert.

Palmerston did not understand Bismarck and his policy, and because of that and the Queen's sympathy for everything German, England failed to intervene in the Danish war and the Schleswig-Holstein controversy with Austria. Britain had no allies, both Napoleon and Russia having been alienated by Palmerston and Russell, and she declined to enter on a contest with Prussia and

Austria, and left the field to Bismarck. It was the end of the Palmerstonian period of British interference, usually on the side of liberalism, on the Continent, and Palmerston himself died in 1865.

Meanwhile Gladstone as Chancellor of the Exchequer had performed the remarkable feat of lowering taxation for three years in succession and was becoming increasingly popular, though his impulsiveness was still mistrusted. Palmerston, facing death, is said to have remarked that "Gladstone will soon have it all his own way, and whenever he gets my place [Prime Minister] we shall have strange doings." It was indeed the end of an era but the strange doings were rather to be on the Continent, where Palmerston's policy as to Germany had unwittingly done much to help Bismarck create his empire of blood and iron and to overwhelm France in a few years and to create conditions which led to 1914.

V. Economics and Labor

At home the Empire was rapidly increasing in wealth in spite of the financial crises of 1857 and 1866 and the "cotton famine" due to the American war. Recovery from both the panics was rapid, but for a while the textile operatives in Lancashire suffered severely owing to the almost complete cessation of shipments of cotton from the Confederacy, which was the sole source of raw material for one of England's greatest industries. In the winter of 1861–62 it is said that 500,000 people were being supported by public and private charity, and by 1863 it was necessary to start public works, the government making a loan of £1,500,000 and private subscribers helping to the extent of about £2,000,000. As usually happens, however, scarcity and high prices developed new sources, and the situation began to improve when cotton came from Egypt and the East. That the suffering operatives during the two years of the crisis should have remained, on the whole, the staunchest English friends of the Union speaks much both for their ability to understand large issues and for their belief in democracy. We may well link their attitude with the passage of the new Reform Bill, which we shall discuss presently.

By 1860 Peel's work for free trade had been completed by Gladstone. All export duties had been abolished and practically all hindrances to imports. England had not only led in the Industrial Revolution and the Machine Age but she was the first to open the commerce of the rapidly expanding world markets to her traders. There were insistent demands for cotton goods in India, for iron and other manufactured goods in the rapidly growing United States, and in outer portions of the Empire whose development far outran their domestic capacity to meet their own manufacturing needs. British factories were roaring with activity and British shipping and commerce rose likewise until all reached their zenith, as compared with all other nations, in 1870, from which year the lead was to be lost.

An interesting point, unnoted by historians, was that two years earlier a discovery had been made which in time was to change the machine age into the chemical age of today with profound effects in all nations. In 1868 a new material, alizarin, a synthetic compound used in dyeing, was produced commercially. This proved to be one of the most significant events in world history, for it was the first substitution of a chemically produced article for a naturally grown one. Almost unnoticed by the public one new chemical substance after another was found until the process culminated in what some chemists consider the greatest discovery in the whole story of man, the fixation of atmospheric nitrogen by Haber and Bosch in Germany in 1913. This, by making Germany independent of Chilean saltpetre, helped to bring on the World War, and initiated a wholly new age. Though no one realized it at the time the world of old-fashioned politics, old-fashioned war, and opportunities for commercial success under machine-age conditions, was doomed by the discovery of 1868 and its successors.

Meanwhile the world went on unwittingly and prices were rising rapidly, owing to the discoveries of gold in California in 1849 and in Australia in 1851. The enormous addition to the world's supply had its usual inflationary effect, equalled only by the huge imports of South American gold by Spain after its conquests of Mexico and Peru in the sixteenth century. Almost more

185

important was the introduction in the 1850's of the use of checks, which had the same effect of adding to the currency.

In the same period came the invention of Bessemer's process for making steel, causing a complete transformation of the industry, with considerable changes in population. The 208 miles of railways in Britain in 1833 had risen to 14,000 by 1873, and steel as well as other products was being exported to all parts of the world. With the enormous exports of goods went an increasing investment in foreign countries, rising from approximately £300,-000,000 in 1850 to at least £1,200,000,000 by 1875. Britain had become not merely the work-shop but the banker of the world.

In spite of free trade, agriculture continued prosperous until after 1875, although the number of agricultural workers declined owing to improved methods of farming, and their wages did not advance as rapidly as those in other lines of work. The cities were growing fast as were the numbers engaged in manufacturing. One of the most notable features in changing incomes and position was the great increase in the middle and professional classes, and as an evidence of increasing wealth the number of domestic servants rose from 900,000 in 1851 to 1,500,000 in 1871, although as we have seen the cost of maintaining them had much increased.

In that period also the trades-union movement took on a wholly new aspect. The older men had been largely Chartists and Socialists but the young generation was much more conservative and, as the Amalgamated Society of Carpenters and Joiners announced, it was their object to become "respectful and respected." This was typical of the changed movement, in spite of some outrages which endangered it. It took on, indeed, the form it was to maintain for a half century or so, and the first Trades-Union Congress, which is officially recognized by labor as such, was held in 1868. From this period likewise date the great number of co-operative societies and shops which were specially favored by Parliament as contrasted with the unions. The work and propaganda of the Society for the Diffusion of Useful Knowledge, although it ended in 1847, had begun to tell heavily a decade later as a result of the millions of copies of its publications which had been read by the working classes. These had ceased to be militant, partly due perhaps to general prosperity and the rise in real wages, that is purchasing power, of nearly 33 per cent which occurred in this quarter of the century.

There was, however, comparatively little being done to improve the conditions of the working class either by laws regarding sanitation, working hours or other matters, except that the earlier Factory Acts were extended to cover more industries. Palmerston had had no interest in such matters and as long as he remained the dominant figure in public life little could be expected in the way of domesic reform. It was evident, however, that conditions in England were rapidly changing. By the Reform Bill of 1832 the middle class had become enfranchised to a considerable extent, but the working class had no representation at all. England had meanwhile become industrialized, and the working class had not only become enormously larger but better educated and more sober and conservative. This other of "the two Englands" of Disraeli could not be permanently left out of the account.

Parliament was hostile to the trades-unions, for which reason many of them called themselves Friendly Societies, but when the Court of Queen's Bench ruled that the Friendly Societies Act did not apply to them the workmen decided that for this and other reasons the only way to make trades-unionism effective and safe would be to secure a voice in making the laws. The question of a further extension of the franchise, which had slumbered as long as Palmerston lived, now became an active issue. Even before Palmerston's death, Gladstone had proclaimed that "every man who is not presumably incapacitated by some consideration of personal unfitness or political danger is morally entitled to come within the pale of the constitution." Because of this suggestion for a sweeping increase in the franchise he lost his seat for Oxford University.

VI. REFORM IN 1867

In spite of the earlier Reform Bill, the repeal of the Corn Laws, and all that had happened in the preceding quarter of a century and more, England was still governed chiefly by the landed interest. There were not only the magnates and county families of old days, but, as members of the middle class and mercantile or manufacturing new rich made money and acquired social and political ambitions, they bought estates and tried to assimilate themselves to the county society through which the way up in England has always lain and not through that of London. The anomaly of ruling a great industrial nation by the landowners alone was however becoming too great.

By 1865 Russell, now Earl Russell, had become Prime Minister with Gladstone as leader in the House of Commons, and despite the shock Gladstone had given the country by his 1864 speech he introduced a bill for lowering the franchise requirements in the boroughs and counties. The House was not interested, although the bill was so mild as to be entirely unsatisfactory to the reformers, and the Ministry resigned. During the debates, however, Robert Lowe, Conservative, had brought about a crisis by demanding the exclusion of all workingmen from the franchise on the ground that they were morally and intellectually unfit.

John Bright now led the working class in its infuriated opposition to the insult which they considered had been hurled at them. There was only one instance of violence, that of pulling down the railings of Hyde Park when the authorities would not allow a meeting to be held, but especially in the industrial north the size of the peaceable meetings and processions, numbering as high as 200,000 persons, which Bright addressed, made even the most reactionary among the rich pause as they had fortunately done in 1832. Again the English of all classes were to show their ability to prevent catastrophe by compromise and yielding.

The new Ministry was made up of Conservatives, but they did not dare to appeal to the country in a general election although they had only a minority in the House. Something had to be done first to allay the storm which Lowe had raised for them, though they would have to reverse themselves in the process. They had come into power because they had opposed a mild reform bill and now they would have to enact a much more drastic one.

In view of the state of the nation Disraeli, who was the moving mind of the Cabinet, although Lord Derby was Prime Minister, did not hesitate long. The bill which he introduced and which was much altered in the House and finally passed by the Lords marked by far the longest step England had yet taken toward democracy. In the towns household suffrage was practically established and even lodgers were allowed to vote if they paid £10 rent a year and had spent that length of time in one place. In the boroughs all men who paid any rates secured the franchise, which was also much enlarged in the counties. Unfortunately the agricultural laborer was still excluded, but the workingman had at last secured direct representation, and this was extended to Ireland and Scotland the next year, 1868.

VII. Attitude Toward the Empire

Meanwhile important events had been happening in the Empire overseas, though the British people were taking little or no interest in them, save as they affected trade. The decade of the 60's indeed marked perhaps the very nadir of British interest in colonial possessions and in colonization and imperialism. Practically every one, including such statesmen of varied parties and outlooks as Disraeli, Gladstone, Cobden, the jingo Palmerston, and Lord Blachford, permanent Under Secretary of the Colonial Office, all believed that it was a mere question of time when the colonies would become independent as the original thirteen American ones had. It was one of those things that was taken for granted and accepted generally without argument.

Meanwhile, as long as the connection should be maintained they were to be honestly administered with as much profit and benefit for both parties as possible, and allowed to go much their own way. Feeling was to change very rapidly in the next few years, but nothing could be farther from the truth than to think of the British Government or people as having pursued through the centuries a consistent and steady policy of trying to grab any outlying land they could lay their hands on. In this decade they were quite willing to let most parts of the Empire secede peacefully whenever they wished, and in 1863 Britain presented Greece with the Ionian Islands because the Greek inhabitants desired it. There was no pressure of any sort, and the act, on the advice of Gladstone, was consummated by Palmerston, of all men the most tenacious of British rights abroad. On the abdication of the Greek King in 1862 the Greeks had asked Prince Alfred of England to take the throne, which he declined. It was accepted by the Danish brother-in-law of the Prince of Wales, but there is nothing to indicate that the gift of the seven and more islands was part of a political bargain. The cession indicates rather the almost numb indifference at this time regarding overseas possessions.

VIII. Federation of Canada

In Canada development had been rapid since self-government had been inaugurated but the situation was difficult. The huge central plain portion was owned by the Hudson's Bay Company and was almost uninhabited save by scattered Indians, half-breeds, and whites engaged in trapping. East of this were the old provinces already mentioned, and on the Pacific coast was the fast-growing colony of British Columbia. We can thus picture the map of the present Dominion as showing a group of separate colonies in the east, then a vast empty space, and the new colony on the west coast. There were no lines of communication across the Hudson Bay territory, and each section of Canada, divided by wilderness from the other, was tending more and more, especially since the reciprocity agreement of 1854, to be drawn into the economic, and possibly the political, orbit of the enormously richer and more populous United States, then rent by Civil War.

That war, although it ruined the Confederate States, was making industry hum in the Union, which adjoined the Canadian line, and there were some in the United States who desired the absorption of Canada although the American Government had no such designs. We have already spoken, however, of the bad feeling between America and England, and the troops which had had to be sent to Canada at the time of the *Trent* affair. Although most Americans did not dream of forcibly annexing their small neigh-

bors to the north, and the vast majority of Canadians much preferred remaining in the Empire, there were threatened dangers,
and the war undoubtedly greatly accelerated the movement toward
Canadian federation which had been recommended by Durham
but had long been left in abeyance.

There were also other considerations. The union of Quebec and
Ontario was now raising new questions, owing to the great increase
of English immigration into the latter, which tended to make the
racial problem again acute and the working of party government
almost impossible. It became increasingly clear to the wiser Canadian statesmen that some sort of union, preferably a federation,
was essential from every standpoint—economic, political, and even
military. It was considered that two things would be necessary:
first, the acquisition of the Hudson Bay territory and especially
the building of a transcontinental railway which would bind all
the colonies together, though, as it turned out, both these projects
followed instead of preceding political union.

As in the case of the formation of the United States, localism
threatened to ruin the plan, and in fact Newfoundland never
joined the federation and Nova Scotia only with the greatest
reluctance. In 1864 however the plan was drawn up at a conference
of all the eastern colonies and finally accepted by their legislatures,
except Newfoundland. Three years later it was accepted by the
British Parliament, which passed the British North America Act, a
landmark in imperial history. The way was now clear, and the
Dominion of Canada established, though the newly organized
province of Manitoba did not join until 1870, British Columbia
in 1871 and Prince Edward Island in 1873. Meanwhile, in 1869,
the Hudson's Bay Company had been induced to sell its lands,
though retaining its trading rights, and the Dominion had taken
its general final territorial shape.

If the impact of the American Civil War had been an important
factor in speeding up federation, it had perhaps an even more important repercussion on the development of the British Commonwealth. The federal form of government adopted in Canada was
that later to be followed in Australia and South Africa, though

with the variations which will duly be noted, and is therefore of special significance, and that form was to some extent determined by the great crisis which the United States was passing through at the time the Canadian form of government was being drafted. The Union had been threatened and almost disrupted by the excessive stress laid upon the sovereignty of the component States. We have already spoken of the type of federation devised for the American system and need only add that according to it the Federal Government was one of limited powers only, all powers not expressly delegated to it being reserved to the several States or to the people themselves. Realizing that the constitutional questions which had in large part led to the Civil War arose from this scheme of the location of powers, the Canadian plan reversed it, giving the "Provinces," as members of the federation, only limited powers and reserving all others to the Dominion government. There could be no question of the secession of a province in Canada or of its powers being paramount or even coequal as regards those of the central government.

Moreover, as Canada had not had the experiences which the revolted American colonies had had and which had led them to fear the power of the executive, the Canadians followed English tradition and not the American innovation of divorcing the executive from the legislative branch of government. In other words they adopted the Parliamentary instead of Congressional form and made the executive dependent on and immediately responsible to the legislature. In many ways this form has advantages over the American one, though in a single country there are points to be made in favor of each.

The evolving British Commonwealth, however, is not a single country, and the system adopted locally by the Dominions has had the great advantage of allowing them to be represented at Imperial Conferences in London by Prime Ministers who can speak with the authority of the majorities in their several legislatures behind them. Under the American system a chief executive, often in opposition to the legislative majority, could not possibly do this. This is not the place to discuss the advantages or disadvantages of the American form of government with regard to peculiar American conditions, such as the vast size of the country, its furiously rapid rate of change, and its enormous and heterogeneous population, but there is no question that the adoption of the British system in the Dominions has been of great import for the free working of the Commonwealth system and mutual understanding among its component parts.

On the other hand the British system afforded no lessons in federalism, whereas the United States did, and on one of the most difficult points, that of representation, Canada followed in part the famous "great compromise" of the American Constitution. In the United States the lower House consists of members elected according to population, whereas the upper, or Senate, has two members from each State regardless of population. In Canada the lower House is like that of the House of Representatives in the American Congress, and the upper consists of members appointed by the federal government. In both cases the idea had been to make the upper House a more conservative body and non-elective, the original American system calling for election of Senators not by the people but by the State legislatures. This has been changed by amendment so that Senators are now also popularly elected, although for longer terms than the members of the lower House, but to a considerable extent the evils which the Canadians feared in their own case have come to pass in the United States. The character of the Senate there has greatly changed, because a Senator, like a Representative, has now to go through the rough and tumble of a popular election campaign.

The system, however, appears to have worked well in Canada, and after its installation the progress of the Dominion was rapid. In 1870, in the newly acquired territory of the Hudson's Bay Company, there was a rebellion under the lead of a French half-breed, Louis Riel, which required troops to be sent from England before it could be suppressed. It finally collapsed, and with the aid of the famous Northwest Mounted Police, one of the finest forces of men in the world, law and order were maintained in the great empty stretches acquired from the Hudson's Bay Company with resultant growing up of settlements to connect East and West Canada, although the transcontinental railway did not materialize until the 1880's.

In spite of the abrogation of the Reciprocity Treaty by the United States in 1866 that country still remained Canada's largest customer, with the United Kingdom next, the two together accounting for approximately 90 per cent of Canadian foreign trade. Canada, which had entered on the road of protection of home industry as contrasted with the free-trade policy of England, had hoped that the fisheries dispute might be used as an inducement to the United States to renew the reciprocity agreement, but this was settled directly between the British and American governments to a way which the Canadians thought was to their own distinct disadvantage. There have naturally been many matters in dispute between the neighbors in North America during their histories, and the fact that in most cases each has thought that the other got the best of the bargain is perhaps the best evidence that the settlements have been reasonably fair to both.

In this case, however, Canada was extremely angry, and it was evident that as the future Dominions should become stronger and more independent they would demand from Britain such a share in the management of their international affairs as would eventually bring about creation of their own diplomatic services and the acknowledgment of their right to make treaties and settle disputes for themselves. One great difficulty for the British Empire has always been that of balancing the interests of one portion against those of another, or of the Empire as a whole. In the last analysis the immunity of every portion of the Empire from being the victim of foreign aggression has been due to the military and particularly the naval power of Britain. The center of empire must be rich and strong or there is no safety for the outlying sections. Naturally, also, people like to feel themselves rich and strong, but aside from natural selfishness and of legislation by Parliament in the early days in favor of England as against the local interests of colonies, the problem has always been a real one.

Not only must the trade interests of colonies conflict at times with those of the mother country but also those of one colony with those of another, as in 1730, when those of New England were in direct opposition to those of the West Indian sugar islands, with legislative results that were among the contributing causes of the Revolution. Problems of trade and of mutual defense are among the thorniest in such an empire as the British, which is unique in world history. By the period we have now reached in our story, the trade problem had been to a considerable extent quieted by allowing the larger colonies a free hand in settling their own trade terms. Canada and Australia both had protective tariffs, which were directed against British as well as foreign imports. The military measures, however, which Canada refused to take during the American Civil War left a bad impression, and the problem of joint imperial defense yet remains a vexed one.

IX. Significant Development in New Zealand

We have already spoken of developments in Australia during this period. Those in New Zealand were particularly significant and illustrate some of the best traits of the British in their empire building. As we noted earlier, the land question had been a difficult one and its unwise temporary settlement had left the seeds of future trouble. The native Maoris lived mostly in North Island, which was the first settled by the whites, and for a while that to which most settlers emigrated. Increasing population and the pushing of new settlers onto Maori lands precipitated a clash between the two races, just as the constant advance of settlement in the United States raised incessantly the land question between the frontiersmen and the Indians.

The Maoris had far more land than they could use, and the different concepts of landownership of barbarians and civilized agricultural and industrial peoples always create difficulties and a problem as much ethical as legal. It is easy for moralists to say that a wild tribe in possession of land "own" it and that it is immoral to despoil them of any of it. On the other hand, is it better or worse for example for the world that the territory of the present United

States should have been left to the 500,000 or so savages who roamed it mostly in the hunting stage in 1600 or that it should have become the home of the 130,000,000 who are using it today and contributing in many ways to the civilization and happiness of the world?

In North Island the problem was settled by the dreary decade of wars with the Maoris from 1860 to 1871. The Maoris are, as we have said, a magnificent race, probably the finest in the savage state in the world. Stung by pride and many cases of undoubted individual injustice in relation to the land treaty which had been made with them, they formed an alliance among themselves and fought the British with splendid gallantry. The conduct of the combatants in the struggle reflected equal credit on both races, as did the final settlement, although, owing to the ill-advised action of the legislature in confiscating 2,800,000 acres as punishment in 1865, the war was prolonged and left a legacy of resentment. The fighters on both sides, however, were chivalrous and natives on occasion even risked their lives to get water for their prisoners. Although the main cost of the war was borne by England, the addition to the local debt was well on to £4,000,000, and the wise opposition of England to the confiscation policy created so much feeling in the colony that there was even talk of secession from the Empire and applying to the United States for protection.

Looking at the period in the large, however, we get a different picture. New Zealand has not only become one of the most loyal of the Dominions today but it is the only one in which intermarriage, among all classes, with the aboriginal inhabitants is common and not frowned upon. In war the latter had so fought and conducted themselves as to win the admiration of their conquerors, and at the end not only was a wise land policy finally adopted but it was agreed that four Maori representatives should sit in the colonial legislature. Some of the tribes and chiefs had remained loyal throughout and rendered notable service, especially such men as the magnificent-looking chief known as Major Kemp. The fact that intermarriage takes place between the British, most race-conscious of peoples, and the Maoris is the best proof of the esteem in which the latter are properly held, and I know of no other case in which a conquered native and alien race was at once offered seats in the legislature ruling both peoples. The magnanimous settlement with the Boers after the South African War at the end of the century was to be one of the wisest and most notable events in the history of empire, but a precedent on a small scale may be found in New Zealand at the end of the long native wars.

Meanwhile, constitutional government had proceeded rapidly and in British fashion. Responsible self-government had been granted in 1856 to each of the far-scattered six provinces of the federal union. Owing to distance and lack of communication the provinces were far more important and the central government less so than in Canada, but by 1876 population and communication by rail had so increased that the local provincial governments were abandoned entirely and instead of a federal state New Zealand became a single unitary one. The islands are so much smaller in extent than either Canada or Australia that as settlements became connected with one another this was a natural development and is an example of how, in the vast variety of the Empire, institutions can be made to fit local conditions. If the first Empire was lost by attempted administrative rigidity, the second has been saved and developed by flexibility.

Each race has its individual characteristics. Perhaps no other has so strong an instinct for the art of governing as the British, but also no other has ever been called upon to administer so enormous and varied an empire. Just as in America the forty-eight individual States of the Union act as laboratories for political experiment, so the unexampled number of British possessions—forts, ports, islands, great continental tracts, and even a continent itself—with all conditions of climate, race, religion, and economics, have given the British a world laboratory in which to experiment and train themselves. They have been in the happy position of a man who has certain innate abilities and has found himself from circumstances through a long and rich life experience in one situation after another in which he has had to adapt his capacities to constantly changing conditions. It is this, and not mere romance or

197

historical detail, which renders the story of the Empire of interest to all the world and not only to the British themselves.

X. Difficulties in South Africa

In South Africa we find in this period the same forces at work as elsewhere. There was the same lack of interest in extending the Empire or desire to assume further responsibilities. The government, in addition, was tired of the difficulties between English and Dutch and between the blacks and both. However, the form of government developed as usual, and Cape Colony was granted first representative government and then full responsible government by 1872. Not only the two white races but also the natives were given the franchise with a small property qualification. In Natal, the second of the four European South African states, the situation was wholly different. The white population was very small as compared with the natives within its borders, and just across these was the land of the powerful and warlike Zulus, who were rising to power again under the new chief Cetywayo. It was uncertain whether, when he might get ready, he would attack the British or the Boers in the Transvaal but in any case the native problem was an imminent danger of the first magnitude. Even in Natal the blacks outnumbered the whites over twenty to one and should the vast hordes of Africa be put in motion the result might be massacre on a colossal scale.

For this reason Natal remained a Crown Colony and did not join Canada, Australia, New Zealand, and Cape Colony on the road to self-government until 1893. The two Boer republics, and the two British colonies, with the mixture of Dutch and English, and the native question seemed to make an almost insoluble problem. Yet it would not have been had England not been opposed to imperialism. There was a moment when the whole question could have been settled and the later tragic and unhappy story of the Boer War been avoided.

Just as in colonial America the selfishness and jealousies of the colonies prevented any common policy being adopted toward the Indian menace, so in South Africa the four colonies or states could not agree, though what each did might menace the very life of the others. In 1858 Sir George Grey, who had vision and had done excellent work in Australia and New Zealand, advised that the four states should join in a federal union. Although, as we have seen, federalism was the order of the day, the experiment was a bold one to put forward for South Africa, where the Boer republics would have to federate with the British colonies. The moment, however, was propitious. Natal would willingly have joined with the Cape, while the Orange Free State, which had never craved independence on account of the menace of the wild Basuto tribes between her and Natal, would have come in. At that moment, in spite of the strong anti-British feeling in the Transvaal, that state would also probably have agreed.

Unfortunately the British Government saw no use in colonies; it wanted to reduce expenses; it did not want the added responsibilities which incorporation of the Boer republics might entail; and the moment for the happy solution of all the problems passed. Such moments rarely recur to give humanity a second chance, and did not in this case. The failure to assume responsibility in 1858 eventually entailed far more in the future and one of the most unfortunate wars Britain has ever been called upon to fight.

Within a few years the farming republic of the Free State had its fourth struggle with the Basutos, who appealed to the Governor of Cape Colony. Basutoland had once been a British protectorate and in spite of the resentment of the Boers a treaty was made by which, reduced in size, it again passed to Britain, and the natives were taken under British protection. The arrangement proved greatly for their good but alienated the Dutch.

Next, in 1867, came one of the fatal accidents of history which no one could foresee and the effects of which proved illimitable. Diamonds in quantity were found in the valley of the lower Vaal near the modern Kimberley on the edge of the uncertainly defined borders of the Free State. There immediately ensued a rush of characters of all sorts and in great numbers to the new source of wealth. Although there was a question as to whether the Free State or the native tribe of Griquas owned the territory, the Free State claimed it and tried to maintain a semblance of order but failed. The Boer government, adequate for the ordinary farming population, was not so for the new conditions. Confusion ensued. The chief of the Griquas, in the hope of peace, offered their lands to Queen Victoria, and Britain accepted both the diamond field and the responsibility of maintaining order in it. In 1871 Griqualand West was annexed to the Crown on the theory that the Griquas and not the Boers had valid title to it. It would be difficult if not impossible to decide which did, and the payment by Great Britain five years later of £90,000 to the Free State indicates that the question was at least debatable.

There are, however, two points to consider and one is reminded of the story of India. England had shown within the few previous years that she did not want more territory or responsibility in Africa. It had, indeed, even been suggested by Lord Grey that she retire entirely and merely maintain a naval station at the Cape. Nevertheless she did have responsibilities whether she wanted them or not. There were already some 200,000 British and Dutch living harmoniously in Cape Colony and perhaps another 10,000 in Natal under the British flag. There was also the native question and the new one of Europeans of all nationalities who were rushing to the diamond fields. Whether the Free State held a valid title or not it could not maintain order. The few hundreds of thousands of white men, British, Dutch, and other, living in South Africa were nothing compared with the countless blacks who could roll southward from the vast interior of Africa like the endless waves of the sea. As in India the British started with no wish to become the "paramount power" but they were the only power which could maintain order.

This was shown even more clearly in the case of the Transvaal. We speak of it as a unit, but, although the men who had trekked into it, and who were the most stubborn and recalcitrant of the Boers, numbered perhaps not more than 10,000, there were practically four governments in the so-called republic, and civil war between the parties for some years. Martin Pretorius tried to effect unity as President with Paul Kruger, "Oom Paul," as head of the military forces, but the state, if it may be so called, remained in a condition of more or less anarchy, bankrupt, unable to collect taxes or to enforce law. To their own misfortune and to the great danger of all the other states, the Boers were constantly starting wars with one native tribe and another, in which they were unsuccessful. There was only one power to which the natives looked with trust, and that was the British.

As the difficulties increased and the Transvaal Boers resorted to atrocious cruelties in their raids on the natives, chiefs of many tribes petitioned the British Government for protection. When finally the Boers attempted to seize territory claimed by the Zulus it was clear that something had to be done, for, if the powerful Zulus were forced to fight the whites, the ear of imagination and statesmanship could catch the rumbling of the war drums from far up into central Africa and the mass of black humanity might roll over the states of all South Africa like an engulfing tidal wave.

To complete the story of the British in Africa in this period we must trespass a few years into the next. In 1874 the then ministry of Disraeli sought to solve the problem by the plan of federation which England had turned down nearly twenty years before, but it was too late, and so able a negotiator and administrator as Sir Bartle Frere could not recapture the lost opportunity. Meanwhile, however, many even of the Transvaal Boers themselves were alarmed over their situation and in their fear of the Zulus had asked to be taken under British protection, as many of the native chiefs had. Others were still opposed, but in 1877 the Transvaal was declared annexed to the Crown as a step toward possible federation and as a gesture toward the natives. Unfortunately the belated move of the government solved neither the Boer nor the Zulu problems, and with the end of this chapter we enter upon a wholly new period in world politics.

The high hopes of the early fifties and of the Great Exhibition were turning into ashes. The period had seen the union of a free Italy, the unification of Germany, and the solidifying of the Union in America, with the slaves freed, as well as long steps taken toward the unification and freedom of important parts of the Empire. The stage of idealism, however, had passed, to be replaced by high finance instead of business, by restrictive tariffs instead of increasing free trade, by power politics instead of intellectual liberalism in international affairs, and of a new and sordid imperialism instead of the former indifference.

Owing to her long seclusion after her husband's death, the Queen had lost her popularity, and the trend toward a republican form of government, under the leadership of such men as Joseph Chamberlain, Charles Dilke, Charles Bradlaugh, and others was stronger than ever before or since, if we except the Cromwellian period. This was to pass, but although the period was to be one of great prosperity, activity, and false advance during the whole of it, from 1871 to the World War in 1914, none of the nations solved satisfactorily a single problem of the first order. A mechanistic philosophy of the universe, an undermining of old religious beliefs and of morality, policies based on power, prestige and race, and a wholly materialistic view of progress, all worked together to bring on the great catastrophe which was to change the world and endanger the foundations of civilization itself.

CHAPTER X

NEW POWERS AND NEW FORCES

I. THE THRESHOLD OF OUR OWN DAY

WE HAVE now in our story definitely reached the threshold of our own day and its problems. As we have often said, history is a continuous stream. It is not cut into definite periods, such as ancient, medieval, and modern, or short ones such as reigns of monarchs. But just as rivers may at certain points definitely change their direction and even character so may the stream of history be deflected and alter though the fact may not be recognized at the time. We have already mentioned some of the determining factors which came to the front in the overlapping decade discussed in the previous chapter and in this.

One of the most powerful and ominous was the Franco-Prussian War of 1870 with its immense effects. Among these was the passing of the concert of Europe organized in Vienna after the defeat of the first Napoleon. Although the Danish question had apparently been settled by agreement among the Great Powers in 1852, no power intervened when Prussia and Austria broke the agreement by sheer brute force. Prussia had learned the lesson that if she struck powerfully, swiftly, and ruthlessly enough the world would stand aside. When four years later she struck at France, again she had her way. France had created bitter feeling in England by earlier suggesting to Bismarck that she be allowed to annex Belgium. Therefore, Britain, so far from supporting her when the swift Prussian attack was made upon her, merely intervened to an extent sufficient to secure from both the combatants a new guarantee of Belgian neutrality.

In fact Britain was afraid of France and of the rising Germany. Louis Napoleon had failed in his policies both at home and abroad and had abandoned his liberal tendencies. The English saw this, but with rare exceptions failed to see the growing German menace for the future. Bismarck had developed a new form of tyranny unlike that of the old absolutist monarchs or of statesmen like Metternich. Although ruling with a rod of iron and suppressing freedom and all liberal movements, he at the same time built up an overwhelming following by appealing to the desire on the part of a large part of the people for national power and prestige. It was a sinister warning of the dictators and their methods in our own post-war world.

The overthrow of Napoleon and the crushing of the new French Republic had solidly united modern Germany, which now took the place occupied for two centuries by France as the most powerful nation on the Continent. A nation essentially liberal and civilized was replaced by one that was to pursue the policy of "blood and iron." The speed and completeness of the victory, and its spoils of Alsace-Lorraine and an indemnity which paid all costs, also showed the possibilities of modern warfare as an instrument of policy. Further it indicated the superiority for quick success of large bodies of conscript reservists over the small professional armies which had hitherto been the standing military forces of Europe, and marked the beginning of conscription among most of the large Continental nations, and of the modern arms race. German teachers, historians, and even philosophers set themselves to inoculating the German people with the Bismarckian *Realpolitik*. This rise of a new Germany with such ideals to the position of the leading power in Europe, combined with the new imperialism which we shall discuss later, led straight from 1870 to 1914 and on to the Hitlerian savagery of today.

On the other side of the world there was also a great new power emerging. Japan had been forced out of her isolation to learn something of Western civilization by an American fleet in 1853. Others followed and taught her more by bombarding her ports. By 1868 the decision, so fateful for all the world, had been made. Japan determined to change a culture which had endured for two thousand years and to remodel herself completely. Specialists from many countries, the United States, Britain, France, Germany, and others, were brought in to help with the unique transformation. In the next quarter of a century it had been accomplished, but so rapidly that the Western world did not yet realize its reality or significance.

II. THE PARTITION OF AFRICA AND THE NEW IMPERIALISM

Nevertheless everywhere a new alignment of forces was taking place. Even geography was being altered. The opening of the Suez Canal in December, 1869, changed the trade routes of the earth, and the significance of the Mediterranean, through which now lay the way to India, instead of around Africa. However, that continent was about to assume a new importance. Although ships had been cruising along its coasts for centuries little was known of its vast interior, but by one of those curious coincidences by which one phase of history grows from another, for about twenty-five years after 1850, a succession of great discoverers, the most notable of whom were British, opened the secrets of the dark and unknown continent. Among the leaders of the British were Livingstone, Stanley (first sent out by an American newspaper), Speke, Cameron, Baker, and Grant, who with others were exploring and mapping the whole central region, crossing the Sahara, charting such great rivers as the Niger, the Zambesi, and the Congo, discovering the vast lakes such as Nyasa, Victoria, and Tanganyika, all in what had hitherto been only an empty white space on the maps.

Although the work more or less coincided with the exploration of the interior of Australia, which makes this one of the great exploring periods in all history, Australia had already become definitely British. The populous and vastly rich interior of Africa, however, was still a no man's land and unclaimed by any nation save in so far as such shadowy demands as that of Portugal might afford basis for the ownership of what was now being brought to light by other peoples.

The discovery of the non-European-owned resources of the territory now opened to the world came at a critical moment. We shall note presently how other nations were increasing their relative industrial and trading positions at the expense of Britain. Other "workshops of the world" were rising with a resultant scramble for both raw materials and markets. An imperialism of a wholly new type was in the making. In earlier centuries Spain had been a great imperial power, as had also France, but Spain had decayed, France had lost India and North America to the British, and the British themselves, in spite of their wide-flung empire, had, as we have seen, come to consider most of it as of negligible value.

However, the new type of industrial competition between nations developed a new attitude in all toward the ownership of the remaining empty spaces, speaking in terms of spaces not definitely controlled by some of the European powers. Even in 1866 there had appeared the *Greater Britain*, by Sir Charles Dilke, which advocated the value of imperial possessions, and only a few years later W. E. Forster was advocating the impossible but for a time popular idea of imperial federation as the future Dominions were rising in importance. Even Disraeli, who had sneered at the Empire but was now entering on the great period of his career, made a complete *volte-face* and became rampantly imperialistic.

What was happening in Britain was happening in other countries, partly due to their becoming industrial states and partly to the fact that in the rush to seize valuable portions of the non-civilized world, prestige was now involved. To be reckoned as a "great Power" meant no longer a great Power in Europe but a great imperial Power on the globe at large. The race was so swift that in the next quarter of a century, practically all the inhabitable world, unoccupied or occupied by races with a low grade of culture, became portions of one of a half-dozen great empires dependent on one or another of the European Powers.

The newly explored and enormously rich continent of Africa was the first to feel the impact of the new forces and ideals motivating the imperialist nations. The Egyptian question we shall consider later, as the British occupation was not intended to be permanent, and in fact has not been, and it falls in a different category from the partition of the rest of the continent. Moreover, the north coast of Africa from the earliest days, including the history of the Roman Empire, has been within the normal sphere of European relations and policy though a cause of strife between nations. Southward from this Mediterranean coastal region lies the great barrier of the Sahara desert, but between that and the settlements of British and Boers at the extreme southern tip of the continent was the huge interior unclaimed in the early 1870's save by its savage occupants. There were, indeed, some ports claimed by various countries, and the vague and unsubstantial claim of Portugal to much of the whole continent when the scramble began.

Twice there was a chance of orderly settlement of the problem, which, like the opening of Pandora's box, had let loose all sorts of ills, even though the legend tells that the lid was covered in time not to let Hope escape. In 1876 the Belgian King, Leopold, called a conference to discuss the partition of Africa, but the ambitions of the various nations involved prevented any equitable settlement by international co-operation. France, Italy and Germany were all active in making "treaties" with native chiefs and staking out their claims to vast territories. Belgium itself had founded the Congo Free State, so called; Italy had placed a small colony on what became Eritrea on the coast of the Red Sea; France was trying to establish her claim to a possible empire extending across the entire continent; Germany was claiming a protectorate over lands close to the Cape Colony on the southwest coast, and to save British trade Great Britain proclaimed a protectorate over Nigeria in 1886.

A general European war seemed possible over a non-European question. In 1884, for the second time, a conference was called, this time at Berlin and participated in by fourteen nations. It did succeed in avoiding war at the time but otherwise did little except lay down the rules for the game of grab. By decreeing that occupation of a "protectorate" to be valid must be effective, it not only voided the vague Portuguese claims but, what was more important, started a period of anxious haste in staking out claims by effectively occupying the territories chosen.

The continent was on a great scale and the portion now open to the greatest international land rush the world has known contained enormous riches for trade and also teeming millions of blacks with all the horrors of local slave trade, constant wars, human sacrifice and cannibalism. The Berlin Conference had ignored the native question. In spite of the changed attitude toward imperialism in Britain, the British had always preferred settlement in a "white man's country" to assuming tropical possessions and the responsibility of governing alien and lower races. Even after the scramble for territory was obviously begun, Britain showed little haste at first.

As we have pointed out her people and statesmen did not grasp the meaning of the new Bismarckian Germany, and Britain was perhaps more friendly to that nation and trustful of her than of any other. Britain allowed her to seize all of what became German Southwest Africa, although she might easily have taken it in advance herself. She also allowed the Germans to establish a protectorate over the whole of the lands of the Sultan of Zanzibar in spite of the facts that the entire trade of the area had been in the hands of British merchants and that the Sultan had asked to be taken under British protection as he strongly objected to the Germans. When Germany enforced her claims by sending a fleet to the coast Britain not only made no objection but commended the action.

British merchants, however, became restive, and fearing that they might be shut off from the trade they had established began making treaties with the chiefs farther north in Kenya. Even then the government refused to lend its backing to them until Germany agreed to what had been done. At this stage it certainly cannot be said that Germany was not allowed a completely free hand in securing her "place in the sun," for by the agreement of 1886

Britain fully consented that Germany should have the four great districts of East Africa, the Cameroons, Southwest Africa and Togoland, though British trade had first opened them up and was dominant in all of them. The later and more aggressive stage of British activity, after the advent of the Salisbury ministry, belongs to the next chapter.

Looking ahead for a moment, we may note that in the twenty-five years between 1875 and 1900 Germany was to confine herself for the most part to acquiring colonies in Africa only, where she brought under her sway approximately 1,000,000 square miles and 17,000,000 subjects. The enormous expansion of imperial possessions, however, was to be felt in all quarters of the world, with Britain leading by adding to her territory and population nearly 5,000,000 square miles and 90,000,000 people. How vast the changes were to be in this period is indicated also by what other nations were doing. France grabbed about 3,500,000 square miles with 40,000,000 inhabitants without counting the huge Sahara; Belgium 1,000,000 square miles and 30,000,000 inhabitants; Portugal 800,000 square miles and 9,000,000 new subjects; while Russia opened up the enormous resources of Siberia and conquered various minor Asiatic states.

Just as the energies let loose by the Renaissance and Reformation in earlier centuries had resulted in the outburst of exploration and the subjugation of the American continents, so the extraordinary increase in population and the industrial revolution of the nineteenth century had resulted in a second sudden manifestation of forces which called for expansion or explosion. On both earlier occasions empty spaces or those occupied by natives who were no match for Europeans with their superior weapons offered the safety valve demanded. Today, with the whole world claimed and occupied, there is no safety valve save possibly in man's intelligence alone. Pandora's box may or may not still contain Hope. As we watch, however, the complete division of the non-European and American worlds, the closing of opportunity for expansion, the increasing of population, the innumerable new points and occasions for friction, and the temporary overwhelming of the rest of the world by Europe, although the United States also took a hand, we can trace, as in a Greek drama, the weaving of the threads of Fate.

III. Britain Falls Behind

Meanwhile we may turn to what in our period was happening in Britain. The year 1870 marked, as we have said, the approximate zenith of British supremacy in trade, and the period since the end of the Napoleonic wars had also shown striking changes in population. The comparative trade figures, in pound sterling millions, for the two decades from 1870 are:

	1870	*1880*	*1889*
United Kingdom	547	698	740
France	227	339	311
Germany	212	294	367
United States	165	308	320
Belgium and Holland	136	237	310
British Colonies	128	203	298
Italy	68	91	94*

That the United Kingdom was losing rapidly, especially in relation to Germany, Belgium, Holland and the United States is now clear. This was not appreciated in England at the time. Various factors combined to obscure the truth. The period up to 1870 had been enormously profitable and the trade of Britain was still far ahead of any competitor even though falling behind comparatively. In addition she had invested huge sums abroad, estimated in 1885 at about $6,500,000,000. In spite of misjudgments and losses the income which rolled into her coffers from all over the world was immense and gave a sense of tremendous wealth. Thus, what is obvious to us did not disturb the Britisher of the period, who thought Britain would continue to forge ahead as in the past.

The changes in population figures are also important as showing the changes in one aspect of power alignment. They are given in round figures, less than a half million not being entered and more than a half being counted as one.

*The tables are Mulhall's, taken from R. C. K. Ensor, *England 1870-1914*, Oxford Press, 1936.

TABLE I

France (1821) .... 30 millions
Germany (lands of later Reich,
      1815) .... 21 millions
United Kingdom (1821) .... 21 millions
United States (1820) .... 10 millions

TABLE II

Germany (1871) .... 41 millions
United States (1870) .... 38 millions
France (1872) .... 36 millions
United Kingdom (1871) .... 32 millions

TABLE III

United States (1880) .... 50 millions
Germany (1880) .... 45 millions
France (1881) .... 38 millions
United Kingdom (1881) .... 35 millions
Italy (1881) .... 28 millions†

The United Kingdom, of course, included Ireland, whose disaffected population had fallen to scarcely over 5,000,000 at the time of the last table, and the population of Great Britain alone was only 1,500,000 more than that of Italy. Moreover, perhaps owing to the birth-control movement started in 1877 by Bradlaugh and Mrs. Besant, the English birth rate began to decline as the French had been doing for a long time in relation to the German. This was obscured for a while by the lower British death rate but was to have its effect.

Although by the various education Acts the people in general had far better educational facilities than in the preceding generation, higher education was lagging behind that in other countries, particularly Germany, and notably in the field of science. Both Germany and the United States were running ahead of Britain in all that pertained to success in the new electric-chemical age on which the world was entering. In the early part of the century England had been the market for new ideas but this was no longer

†*Vide*, R. C. K. Ensor, *England 1870–1914*, Oxford Press, 1936, pp. 102 f.

true. Inventors and scientists went elsewhere. England had lost her lead.

This by no means signifies that the Empire was doomed, either then or now. Personally I most emphatically believe the contrary, but the period of ease and optimism was soon to be over. In the years covered by this chapter, 1870–1886, there were two severe financial crises and industrial depressions. This was not unparalleled in the past but conditions had altered. We have already noted the new relation between employer and employed which the rapid rise of the factory system had brought about, but after the first severe dislocation had occurred and the greater firms passed down through another generation or two in the same family, to some extent the patriarchal relation of the age when agriculture was the main source of wealth was restored. Management and ownership being united in the same person or family bred a sense in many cases of personal responsibility and personal interest with regard to the workers.

In the latter part of the century, however, the rapid spread of the limited liability stock company, with nominal ownership distributed among thousands of stockholders who never saw the plant or knew the workers personally yet demanded returns on their money, brought about a new and worse relation between capital and labor, varying in different localities and industries. The word "unemployed," first used as a noun in 1882, took on a more sinister meaning. Company development also brought into being a quite new class of small *rentiers*, who did not earn their income by labor nor had the responsibilities of landowners or of businessmen but had nothing to do but to live agreeably, largely in suburban villas or in new towns built for them, such as Bournemouth or Eastbourne, both dating from about 1870.

To a considerable extent, members of this fairly large social group were without ambition other than to conserve their position of smug Victorian respectability. They added little to either cultural or economic advance and served rather as a drag than a spur to England's progress. We may note also that the movement toward merging private banking houses into large limited-liability incorporated institutions, while useful in some ways, also militated against the old personal relationship between the banker and his client which had been based on character rather than on collateral. This made it more difficult for the sound ambitious man of small resources to get a start, much as in the United States today.

While these retarding tendencies, with others, were notable in industry, agriculture was on the road to ruin, almost completely altering the position of Britain in times of both peace and war. In the earlier centuries she had been practically self-sufficing in the matter of food. The great increase in British manufacturing and trade in the nineteenth century had been partially due to improvement in transportation and lowering of freight costs, but this same factor was to militate against the farmer, who in the 1870's was buried under a flood of cheap American wheat. In the West of the United States vast quantities of land were opened to settlement and there was a rush of population to take it up after the disbanding of the armies of the Civil War and during the deep depression after 1873. Moreover, there had been a great development of agricultural machinery which cheapened production, of railway mileage which brought the new supply to market, and a lowering of ocean rates due to improvement in steam vessels. The results were an enormous and sudden increase in the world wheat supply, which would have lowered prices in any case, and an unexpected and disastrous differential in favor of the American producer in the decline in the freight rate from Chicago to Liverpool from £3 7s. per ton in 1873 to £1 4s. in 1884.

In a decade the number of farm laborers in England and Wales decreased by more than 92,000, and a million acres less were under cultivation for wheat. In 1830–40 Britain had imported only 2 per cent of all its cereals for food; by the decade of the 80's it was forced to import 45 per cent, and had become dependent on foreign sources for 65 per cent of its wheat. Naturally with the decline in farming generally went a decline in the home supply of meat.

The effects were far-reaching in many directions. Obviously a nation dependent for a large part of its necessary food supply on imports over thousands of miles of sea routes from America, the Argentine, New Zealand, Australia, and elsewhere, would be in a far more vulnerable position in case of war than when the island had been practically self-sustaining. Moreover, the shift in employment and population, with the drift from country to city, completed the urbanization of England, although the Englishman remains still essentially a lover of the country and of nature. In spite of the industrial revolution agriculture had remained until this fatal period the leading industry in the island and its fall entailed a genuine revolution in English life.

Land had not only been the main source of national income but its possession had spelled political power and social prestige. As wages and employment fell and the more energetic and ambitious young people drifted to the cities, rents and profits fell likewise. For the rich, land remained a costly and ostentatious luxury, a badge of social position, but the blood had been drained from the life of the old England which had persisted for centuries. A great country estate became something like a title, kept as a mark of distinction but reality had gone out of it and had left only the shadow. The day of the great landed magnates, such as Trollope's Duke of Omnium, had gone, and a collapse of their economic power was bound in time to be followed by that of their political control. The day of the financiers and great business magnates lay not long ahead.

IV. DISRAELI AND THE CHANGING ORDER

The old order found its defender in Benjamin Disraeli, for a generation or more leader of the Conservative Party, though he had begun as a radical, and as we saw in the previous chapter had aided in the passage of the Reform Bill of 1867. Descended from a family of Spanish Jews who had fled from Spain to Venice and in 1748 moved to England, he seemed a most unlikely person to head the party of the landed aristocrats. It is difficult to conceive of a more un-English figure than this Hebrew, scarcely rooted in

British soil as the British count descent, with his exotic appearance, his clothes, his ringlets of hair, his romantic imagination and Oriental cast of mind.

Heading the Conservatives and in opposition to the Liberals (the term was first used in its modern meaning in 1868), he had perforce to take a negative position on reform, and he made his cause the enhancement of the monarchy and the Empire. Both appealed to his Orientalism. The real power of the Crown, however, was steadily to decline after 1870, while its symbolic value increased. One of the strongest traits in Disraeli's mind was irony and it was one of the ironies of his life that by helping to pass the Reform Bill he had made the Crown politically less influential. Nevertheless it was largely due to his imagination and acts that by the end of the century Victoria was almost deified and imperialism had become rampant.

In 1868 the lists were opened for the long duel between Disraeli and the Liberal leader Gladstone. Lord Derby had resigned as Prime Minister and was succeeded by Disraeli, while at the same time Lord Russell also retired and left the Liberal leadership to Gladstone. No contrast could be more striking than that between the two men who were long to dominate the political scene. Both had enormous courage and could make the most daring of political moves, but, whereas Disraeli was a most subtle calculator, Gladstone, once he had made up his mind as to the end, could rush toward it as madly as a bull. The difference may be noted in the massive square-jawed head of Gladstone and the long, lean, aquiline-nosed face of his opponent. Disraeli accomplished many brilliant things for the Empire, but one senses in him a strong strain of the adventurer. Practically all political leaders are personally ambitious, and properly so, but in the case of Gladstone, in spite of his many inconsistencies, we sense a unity of unusual political character. John Morley wrote of him that he was "not only a political force but a moral force." Throughout his life he saw things from the moral and religious standpoint rather than through political glasses. That such a man, even with his consummate abilities in the fields of finance and oratory, held the office of Prime Minister for a longer aggregate period than any other in the long Victorian reign illuminates the time.

When Disraeli assumed the office in February, 1868, it had become evident to the Liberals that something genuine would have to be done to allay the unrest in Ireland. The eternal Irish question had never been settled, and had been brought again to the center of the stage by a series of outrages. A secret society had been formed whose members were known as Fenians, and had been largly recruited by Irish immigrants to America who had been serving in the army during the Civil War and on the disbanding of the forces had drifted back to Ireland to use their military experience in making trouble for the British authorities.

V. GLADSTONE AND IRELAND

Among many other grievances was the fact that the Irish had to pay tithes to the English Church, and during Disraeli's brief Ministry Gladstone introduced a bill for disestablishment in Ireland, though there was no more devoted member of the Church. However, he felt that what was just and right in England was unjust in overwhelmingly Catholic Ireland. Disraeli dissolved Parliament, as he would have had to do in any case according to the terms of the recent Reform Bill, and in the general election there proved to be a large Liberal majority, and Gladstone, as Prime Minister, who had formed his Cabinet in December, 1868, succeeded in the session of 1869 in wholly disestablishing and more than half disendowing the Church of England in Ireland. In doing so he met with little opposition even in the Lords where sat the Bishops. The nation, including the new electorate of the 1867 Reform Bill, had voted on the question, which was a leading issue in the election, and the first action of the broadened democracy had been an act of justice. A generation earlier such a measure would have been doomed to certain rejection. Gladstone, now almost sixty, was at the height of his ability though in his amazing career he was again to become Prime Minister at eighty-four.

If in general the people of England and the vested interests of the Church supported Gladstone in removing the religious grievance in Ireland, the landed interests in both islands were too strong to permit him to do much for the agrarian problem. The Irish landlords naturally did not wish to be disturbed and the English did not understand how different the landlord-tenant relations were across the sea and feared lest they themselves might lose some of their rights and privileges if the government removed the just grievances of the Irish peasants. Gladstone was able to ameliorate slightly certain conditions by legislation, but the fundamental injustices remained for another generation. The Land Act of 1870 required landlords to pay the tenant some compensation for improvements he had made at his own expense, and also for eviction for reasons other than non-payment of rent. Owing, however, to the influence which could be exerted by the landowners even this slight step forward had less practical effect than had been hoped.

VI. Educational and Other Reforms

Besides the disestablishment of the Church in Ireland, the first Gladstone Ministry had other notable reforms to its credit. The first was the great Education Act, introduced by W. E. Forster. In England the Church had always clung tenaciously to its control over education, but the entire system, partly of Church and partly of State, was haphazard and only about half the children in the nation received any education, however inadequate. The wide extension of the franchise among the working and lower classes by the Reform Bill of 1867 had raised new problems, and it began to seem an anomaly that a man should be denied the opportunity to learn to read and write and yet be given the power to choose the rulers of the Empire. Moreover, a large part of the support of the new Liberal Party came from these same classes and from the Non-Conformist elements which had always been opposed to the stranglehold which the Church had on both schools and universities. The problem was not merely one of taxation and educational theory but was tinged with all the bitterness of age-old vested interests and of religious strife.

The Forster Bill, passed in 1870, was aimed to please both sides and like most straddles pleased neither, although it was a great advance and a landmark in the history of English education. The grants to the Church were doubled, so that it became apparently ensured of remaining a permanent part of the national educational system, but at the same time the empty spaces in that system, geographical and other, were filled by a system of non-sectarian schools paid for by local taxes and managed by popularly elected local boards. Education for every English child was not made compulsory until 1880 and was not wholly free until a decade later, but the disgraceful conditions of the earlier part of the century were being bettered at least, and between 1870 and 1890 primary-school attendance was more than tripled.

Although England was to lag far behind Germany and the United States in scientific education, nevertheless, between 1850 and 1882 the universities of Oxford and Cambridge were stirred to some extent out of their eighteenth-century indifference. By the new Tests Act of Gladstone's Ministry in 1871, academic positions were opened to scholars regardless of their particular religious belief. In another dozen years, under the guidance of Parliament and not the Church, the universities had taken their modern form, but England had paid, and was to pay dearly, for her slowness in meeting the educational needs of a rapidly changing era.

Higher education, including that for women and the university extension movement for the provinces, in addition to the new provincial universities without Church connection, all had a profound influence on many departments of English life. We have already noted the improvements in the Indian Civil Service, but the home service remained, as that in the United States has too largely to the present day, a preserve for family and political favoritism. In 1870, however, Gladstone, whose hobby was chopping down trees, chopped down this vast upas tree of patronage, and practically all public offices were made to depend on competition in examinations. It is said that now with a change of government in Britain scarcely a hundred officials lose office. Any practical politician will realize the difference between this situation and that of the United States, where hundreds of thousands of officeholders of all sorts and ranks depend on the party in power for their jobs and will certainly be ousted with a change of party in an election. Perhaps an American can understand better than an Englishman, accustomed after two generations to his own system, the prodigious effect of this measure on public life. Not only was the quality of the public service greatly improved but one of the most debasing factors in political life was removed.

Another reform, in line with the others mentioned, was the abolition in 1871 of the purchase of commissions in the army. A commission of any grade was a property and no officer could be commissioned or advanced in rank unless he could pay the price asked by the previous holder of the commission, although prices were standardized. The ramifications of the effects of this system were obvious but not only did the officers, as was natural, object to any change which would deprive them of their property, but even the Queen and her cousin the Duke of Cambridge, who was Commander in Chief, objected likewise.

In this system, which was typical of the eighteenth-century attitude toward public service, there was a strange and dangerous exception. Only a living officer could sell his commission. If he died or were killed in action his "investment" became worthless and his family got nothing. No worse system, either for the efficiency of the army in selection and promotion of officers or for conduct in war, could possibly have been devised. The fact that when it was abolished it could be so only by allowing the incompetent Duke to remain until 1895 as Commander in Chief shows how much of the eighteenth century survived into the late nineteenth.

Gladstone had lost the sympathy of many of his supporters by the disestablishment of the Irish Church, his Land Bill, the Education Act and the Army Reform, but most members of the Liberal Party supported him in another reform. The extension of the franchise to the working class had raised the problem of free voting. Members of that class were largely dependent on their employers, and so long as the employer knew how a man voted the vote could not be free. In 1872 the Gladstone government passed the Ballot Act which established secret voting and marked another great step forward in the independence of the electorate.

Another act to the credit of the government, of great significance for Anglo-American relations and in world history, was the decision to agree to arbitration of the claims made by the United States for the damages inflicted by the vessels built in England during the Civil War, chiefly by the *Alabama*. The sums claimed by some of the American statesmen and officials were obviously absurd, but Russell's admissions had made it clear that there was some claim for a reasonable amount. That the two English-speaking nations, who had long been on bad terms with each other, should agree to abide by the decision of a board of arbitrators, marked a new and happier stage in their mutual relations. The arbitrators, sitting at Geneva, awarded approximately $15,000,000 to the United States, and the award, with some grumbling as to unfairness, was peacefully accepted and paid by England.

As often happens, a rapid forward movement of reform brought about a reaction, and the various matters noted above had reduced the popularity of both Gladstone and Liberalism. In the general election of January, 1874, there was a turnover and a large Conservative majority was elected, with the result that Disraeli replaced Gladstone as Prime Minister.

VII. Disraeli—Reform and Empire

Disraeli's term of office, 1874–80, largely coincided with the world depression of the 70's, but much was accomplished both at home and abroad, several of the most striking and far-reaching events being the result of the peculiar qualities of Disraeli alone. In domestic affairs, while in opposition, he had taunted the Liberals with not carrying out the promised reforms, and now in office, and with growing depression and unrest in the country, the Conservatives under his leadership were forced particularly in the session of 1875 to a series of measures which would have done credit to their opponents.

A Trades Union Act materially improved the legal position of the unions and of labor; the Artisans' Dwelling Act was an important milestone in the history of housing legislation; the Food and Drugs Act was not only the first comprehensive piece of legislation on the subject, but remained the principal one until 1928. Even more important was the Public Health Act, which is the real basis of English sanitary law to the present day. When we add to these the establishment of the Sinking Fund for the public debt the year stands out as one of the most remarkable in the long annals of Parliament. *Laissez faire*, which had ruled since the later eighteenth century, was dead. The daily life of the common man was again becoming a matter of concern to the lawmakers.

There had also been a significant change, not fully recognized, as such changes rarely are, in the membership of Parliament. In spite of the broadening of the franchise by the Act of 1867, there had been no immediate attempt to return what we would now call Labor members, but in 1874 two miners were elected, portent of the future Labor Party. To the same Parliament came also fifty-eight Irish members who refused to be called either Conservatives or Liberals, their sole objective being to secure Home Rule for Ireland by obstructing the working of the party system.

In spite of what was accomplished in the way of social reform instead of political reconstruction in the earlier years of Disraeli's Ministry, his genius lay rather in the more grandiose conception of empire, and the Palmerstonian belief in Britain as the deciding voice in international affairs. He had for some years been the prophet of the new imperialism and had even spoken of Great Britain as being more of an Asiatic than a European power. The cast of his mind, as we have said, was in many respects Oriental rather than English, and the Empire he envisaged was not the Commonwealth of free nations which it has become but a closely consolidated empire with a universal imperial tariff, a military code, and centralized in London through some sort of representative council—a theory which was to be much in vogue in the latter part of the century.

Overseas, Disraeli had inherited from Gladstone the war with the Ashantis, a warlike, human-sacrificing and cruel Negro tribe living in the fever-haunted jungle back of the Gold Coast. In 1871 the Dutch, in exchange for all British claims in Sumatra, had transferred their Gold Coast forts to Britain, thus consolidating

British control over the territory and allowing England to put an end to the slave trade from the interior. One of Britain's innumerable "little wars," this was of peculiar interest on account of the unusually low and cruel qualities of the natives, the atrocious physical conditions under which the expeditions had to be carried out, the character of the group of men involved, and the improvement which resulted. A war in which only about 2400 white troops were involved but which included such officers as Sir Garnet Wolseley, Field-Marshal Sir Evelyn Wood, Field-Marshal Lord Methuen, General Sir Redvers Buller, and General Sir J. Frederick Maurice, with such correspondents reporting it as Winwood Reade, author of the *Martydom of Man*, and Henry M. Stanley, would be notable simply from personnel, but its success also saved the unpopular Gold Coast to the Empire, with slavery abolished. On the other side of the globe the unowned group of the Fijian Islands was annexed for the preservation of order among the natives and as a stepping stone to Australia and New Zealand.

Perhaps the most famous and dramatic act of Disraeli in these years was the purchase of the shares of the Suez Canal owned by the Khedive of Egypt, who was in serious financial straits. There had been opportunities to do so before, but Gladstone and other statesmen were opposed to it. The courage, daring, and success belong to Disraeli alone. In the following half century not only was the cost repaid by income nearly eight times over but, although the interest acquired was not controlling, it gave Britain a new position with regard to Egypt and eventually led to her assuming responsibility for that country, much to its benefit. The canal was also the route to India, and it was that part of the Empire which appealed most to Disraeli's imagination.

In the winter of the year 1875, in which he later electrified Europe by buying out the Khedive, he had planned the visit, which proved highly successful, of the Prince of Wales to India in order that the princes and other rulers should come into personal contact with their future suzerain. The splendor and glamor of the tour proved the Minister's understanding of the Oriental mind, as did his next move which was to force through a somewhat unwilling Parliament the addition of "Empress of India" to the Queen's other titles (1876). Most Englishmen, though they spoke of "the Empire," did not like the imperial title. It had for them bad connotations—the Emperor of the French, and the unfortunate Emperor Maximilian of Mexico—and was considered un-English, showy and tawdry. But Disraeli, himself so un-English, knew the Oriental mind better and realized that the Indian rulers would have a different and more loyal feeling for an Empress of India than for a Queen of Great Britain.

Psychologically the step had two effects. In India it helped to develop loyalty and nationality; and in England the opposition to her assumption of the title so irritated Queen Victoria that it contributed to the anti-Liberalism of her later life. The Crown, however, was again becoming more popular, partly due to the success of the Prince's tour of India and partly to a serious illness which threatened his life. Relief at his recovery, and growing realization of the value of the Crown as symbol rather than power in the evolving Empire were among the factors making rapidly for its modern position.

Meanwhile, Disraeli (in 1876 to become Earl of Beaconsfield) pleased the Queen with an obsequious flattery which no other Englishman of the day would have used, and which was more suited to *Gloriana*, Queen Elizabeth, than to a constitutional sovereign in the nineteenth century. Gladstone was as heartily disliked as Disraeli was relished by the aging woman and might never have come to office again had the Crown possessed the power of a few generations earlier. The Queen objected to be talked to by the respectful but absorbed and blunt Gladstone "as though she were a public meeting."

VIII. The Eastern Question

The last few years of Disraeli's tenure of office saw the reopening of "the Eastern Question." Like Palmerston, whose attitude and policy were in many points akin to his own, Beaconsfield, as we may now call him, was fearful of any increase of Russian power and influence. The Turkish Government had long been notorious for its ill treatment of the Christian minorities under its rule, but in the Russo-Turkish War, which ended with the collapse of Turkey in 1878 and the Treaty of San Stefano, Beaconsfield's sympathies had been wholly against Russia, if not with the Turks, and he demanded a general European Congress to settle the questions at issue.

The treaty had reduced the size and power of Turkey in Europe to much as it is today. It undoubtedly included some injustices but not those which Beaconsfield believed it did. Opinions may differ on so complex a problem and conditions shift in a manner often unpredictable by the most astute statesmen, but it would seem in the light of after events that Disraeli was wrong in the revision of the treaty which he secured at the conference. The whole Balkan question was and has remained not only a puzzle but a constant threat to the peace of Europe, and the Beaconsfield solution planted many of the seeds of future trouble. In continuing the policy of misplaced trust in Turkey and perhaps of equally mistaken fear of the old Russia, he restored the Turkish power by the return of some 4000 square miles of territory, with their inhabitants. Macedonia was returned to her although Bulgaria was liberated, and Bosnia and Herzegovina transferred from her to the rule of Austria-Hungary, presaging the eventual clash between that empire and Serbia as defender of the Jugo-Slavs. The complete and high-handed annexation of these provinces by the dual monarchy in 1908 was one of the events which led directly to the World War, and the whole Austro-Hungarian and German *Drang nach Osten* had been given a great impetus by the Beaconsfield policy of 1878. Even Lord Salisbury, who was with the Prime Minister at Berlin, admitted later that they had "backed the wrong horse." Incidentally, as a side result of negotiations, Britain received the island of Cyprus.

Beaconsfield returned claiming that he brought with him peace with honor, and the people heaved a sigh of relief at having avoided being drawn into a general European war, although in 1878 it would have been far less disastrous than in 1914.

Meanwhile, however, there had been a violent public debate

and conflict of opinion as to the fundamental issues. Beaconsfield cared nothing about the atrocities and stupefying effects of Turkish misrule. For him, "peace with honor" meant Britain dictating terms and increasing her strength internationally by what he believed was the right Russo-Turkish policy for her to pursue. On the other hand Gladstone, filled with rage and righteous indignation at what he considered the betrayal of the subject Christian peoples of the Porte, had come out from his proclaimed retirement. He took his stand on moral and not political ground and denied that any one nation should demand for itself a dominant position in the general councils of Europe and that the weight of Britain should have been thrown on the side of the weak and oppressed, and not used to force liberated peoples who had won freedom to place their necks again under the yoke of tyranny.

For the moment, peace, any peace, turned the scales in favor of the Government, but the Ministry was fast losing popularity. Gladstone's cyclonic moral force probably had deeper effects than appeared on the surface at the time, and the anti-Russian foreign policy of Beaconsfield, which involved England in another Afghan war, which will be noticed later, was becoming unpopular. A war with the Zulus and the deepening agricultural depression were also contributing factors in lowering his prestige, and times were changing in a way he did not realize.

IX. THE NEW RADICALISM

Joseph Chamberlain in Birmingham had organized the National Liberal Federation, made up of small local organizations in which the newer working-class members of the party who had been given potential power in 1867 were now given the opportunity of making their voices and desires heard in the party councils to an extent which would have been believed impossible and revolutionary in the earlier days of aristocratic control. Gladstone understood the change in the political air and in his whirlwind speaking tour known as the Midlothian campaign in 1879 he was acclaimed by such multitudes as had never cheered any other statesman. They not only cheered but voted, and the new Parliament of 1880 had a handsome Liberal majority. The political duel with Disraeli, who died the following year, was over and Gladstone again headed the government. The campaign in which the new democratic forces had been marshalled and democratic machinery used in a modern way had scandalized the Queen and even many of the older line statesmen.

Indeed, by the 1880's we find much that was beginning to scandalize conservative people outside the realm of politics and politicians. If the Queen did not like the goings on of Mr. Gladstone, who actually so far disturbed her as to address a great audience from the unseemly forum of an open window in a railway carriage, neither did she like those of her own son, the Prince of Wales. Excluded by her from any real share in affairs of state, and being a man who with all his ability did not much enjoy intellectual or æsthetic pleasure, he perforce had to content himself with those of another sort, and became the leader of the gayer part of London society. In spite of early unpopularity, and widely whispered sex and gambling scandals, he became popular with people of all classes, perhaps as part of a general reaction against the excessive strictness of mid-Victorian family life. The first breach in social observance of the English Sunday was made by the Prince's innovation of giving Sunday-night dinner parties at Marlborough House, followed a little later in the 80's by the week-end parties in country houses. The "week-end" has been considered so distinctively English that it will surprise many to learn how recent it is, but obviously the week-end and the old-fashioned Sabbatarianism could not go together.

The year 1880 also saw another portent. The press was still mostly made up of dignified daily newspapers, of a few serious weeklies and of the formidable and very able quarterlies. But in 1880 George Newnes started a small weekly journal, *Tit-Bits*, in which gossip news of all sorts was served to those who were literate but who did not want to disturb their minds by concentration. It was the harbinger of a new era of mass thought.

There were other disturbing factors. The Radicals were now recognized as a wing of the Liberal Party, and Joseph Chamberlain, Dilke and others were making alarming suggestions. Indeed, Chamberlain was soon to be saying that private property, because it had replaced communal ownership and management, should be subject to a "ransom" in the form of taxation for the good of all the people. Those who recall the excitement caused by the earlier speeches of Mr. Lloyd George in our century can readily understand the shivers created by Mr. Chamberlain in the newly invented week-end parties.

Everything seemed to be shifting, even the architectural style of houses, or at least the smaller country ones. England is a small country, "half an island," as it was called in the Elizabethan period, but the happy visitor from abroad is always amazed by the extraordinary variety, not only of scenery but of its older village architecture. The variety of brick, many kinds of local stone, wattle-and-daub, and what-not, was due in earlier days to what always governs the building of the houses of the less well-to-do, namely convenience and cost. When transportation of building materials was expensive, even when possible at all, builders turned to the materials at hand in each locality. With the era of surfaced roads, canals and railways, many standardized materials, even with transportation added, became cheaper than the local ones, and the enormous change for the worse in village building may have been due rather to economic causes than any original sin in the Victorian soul, much as in the case of the epidemic of corrugated iron after the World War in our own day.

What happened in architecture also happened with furniture turned out by machinery instead of craftsmen, and the cheap colored prints manufactured in quantity. The machine served economy but had not yet been controlled to serve beauty, and if the effect on taste was utterly deplorable it is understandable. There had also been a great shift in wealth, and just as a new class had learned to read without being able to concentrate, so new classes had come into being who could buy comforts and knick-knacks without any training in what to buy.

On the other hand, a reaction was already in progress in these years under the leadership of such artists as William Morris,

Rossetti, Burne-Jones, and Watts, and the struggle against the damage done to pictorial art by the earlier photography was led by the American, Whistler, already domiciled in London. Literature, which had practically collapsed, in 1870 was beginning a new start, though poetry was notably lacking, and for the most part the rising novelists of the new day, such as the American Henry James, George Meredith, and Thomas Hardy, had very limited audiences—although Stevenson had published *Treasure Island* and *Kidnapped* by 1886. All the early Victorian novelists—Dickens, Thackeray, George Eliot, and others had been best sellers, but that rank was now held only by now forgotten mediocre writers or worse. The Queen read Marie Corelli. The heir to the throne read nothing.

CHAPTER XI

THE EIGHTEEN-EIGHTIES

I. Difficulties of the Gladstone Ministry

IN THE period of vast change and incubation of new forces from 1880 to 1902 (except for the short interlude of Rosebery, March, 1894 to June, 1895), there were but two Prime Ministers, Gladstone and Lord Salisbury, who alternated in office much as the two figures in a certain type of barometer used to come in and out of their boxes. In this and the next chapter we shall consider the period down only to 1892, and in the present one chiefly home affairs together with those of Egypt, never considered a permanent part of empire, and of Ireland.

During Beaconsfield's Premiership Lord Granville had been the leader of the Liberals in the Upper House and Lord Hartington in the Commons. After the party had been swept into power in the campaign of 1879 the Queen, who intensely disliked Gladstone, asked each of them to form a government but both declined. Gladstone refused to join any Ministry of which he was not the head and obviously none could be formed in which he might be left out. The Queen therefore had to conquer her personal feelings and send for him.

For the first time, in the portentous Midlothian campaign, already noted, the new electorate was largely radical. Parliament had become split into three instead of two parties, the Conservatives, Liberals and Irish Home Rulers, but in fact the Liberals were also becoming divided into those of Whig and Radical types.

Gladstone himself, now past seventy and beginning to display some of his less able qualities, belonged rather to the former group, and in forming his new Cabinet selected eight Whigs to three Radicals, though it had been the latter wing of the party which had largely contributed to its success at the polls. This split, which was to widen, was to hamper the success of the Liberals when in power and eventually to drive them into the wilderness for nearly two decades.

The new government made at once a bad start. The atheist, Charles Bradlaugh, had been elected member of Parliament for Northampton but was not allowed to take his seat after a mere affirmation of allegiance, as he requested, or the ordinary Parliamentary oath which he agreed to. The case was stupidly handled and although he was re-elected by his constituency three times it was not until 1886 that he was permitted to sit. Meanwhile, religious feelings were aroused, politicians made use of the situation, and the trouble in which the government had involved itself was a continued weakness to it. The undignified proceedings as well as the frequent disorders in the House began the process of lowering respect for Parliament.

Although most of the imperial history of the period will be considered later we may here mention two brief incidents which helped to make the government unpopular. Gladstone had inherited from his predecessor the problem of the Transvaal. When out of office and also in his campaign speeches the now Premier had been in favor of restoring independence to the Transvaal Boers, a policy favored by most of the Boers in all South Africa. A plan for federation had been rejected by representatives from the Transvaal, Kruger and Joubert. The latter was a good soldier and the Transvaal Boers had become far better troops than the British commander in Natal, Sir George Colley, realized. Finally the Boers broke into armed revolt and besieged the four small British garrisons in the Transvaal. General Colley marched to their relief with 1500 men, only to receive a severe check at Laing's Nek and to be decisively defeated, at Majuba Hill in February, 1881, where he was himself killed.

Gladstone had the choice of engaging in larger operations and perhaps bringing on a general revolt of the Cape Boers for the sake of forcing a continuation of the annexation policy which he had publicly opposed or of conceding defeat with loss of British prestige and allowing independence to the Transvaal, whose inhabitants would feel themselves superior and at the same time retain a sense of injury. He chose the second course, and the independence of the Transvaal (to become the South African Republic) was recognized in the Pretoria Convention, 1881, Britain retaining control of its foreign relations and maintaining "suzerainty," a word left out of the London Convention three years later.

Kruger, stubborn and now an inveterate foe of the British, became President of the new state, and was to remain so as long as his country retained its independence. The choice for Gladstone may have been difficult but the matter had been fumbled and as a result of delay Britain had yielded to force what it might have granted willingly. The seeds of much future trouble had been sown and the reputation of the new government tarnished again at the start.

Afghanistan was another problem which Gladstone inherited from the Disraeli Ministry. The new Viceroy of India, the Marquis of Ripon, was promptly instructed to arrange for British withdrawal from that country. An Afghan claimant, Abdurrahman, was recognized as Amir and at once installed at Kabul, but another claimant arose and started to attack the British forces still at Kandahar. The commander there, General Burrows, marched out with 2500 troops, to stop him, but was defeated heavily at Maiwand, and had to retreat to Kandahar, where he was besieged by the Afghans. He was happily relieved by General Roberts, who with 10,000 troops and 8000 camp followers made an extraordinary march of over 300 miles in twenty-three days. The victory was complete and the British eventually withdrew as planned, though Abdurrahman, who finally unified his control over the country, agreed to be controlled in foreign relations by Britain in return for a subsidy and a guarantee against aggression from other powers.

These two withdrawals, from the Transvaal and Afghanistan, were evidences of Gladstone's marked dislike of imperialism, with which he had as little sympathy as he had with the new Socialistic ideas of the younger generation or the radicalism of Chamberlain. The "grand old man" and the whole Liberal Party were, in fact, getting out of touch with some of the major currents of the time. Still interested in social reform and above all in the Irish question, he cared little for colonial problems and therefore was inclined to delay in decisions regarding them. We find another example of this in Egypt, although in the last two decades of the century British administration in that country was to be a model for the world and one of the finest accomplishments in British overseas history. Ironically it was to be Gladstone who was to bring about the occupation of the ancient country of the Nile, in spite of his having bitterly denounced Beaconsfield's forward imperial policy in the Midlothian campaign.

II. THE CRISIS IN EGYPT

Egypt was theoretically subject to the Turkish Sultan but practically had long been semi-independent and governed autocratically by its own rulers, the Khedives. Earlier in the century the Khedive Mehemet Ali had spent vast sums and had used tyrannical methods in attempting to Westernize the country according to his ideas. He had also engaged in costly military adventures, including the conquest of a large part of the Sudan. His successor, Said Pasha, had continued the expensive Westernizing and it was he who had authorized the building of the Suez Canal. The next Khedive, Ismail Pasha, had still greater ideas, including a wide extension of control in the vast area of the Sudan, filled with fierce and restless tribes. In this work he secured the aid of two Englishmen, the latter of whom was Charles, or "Chinese," Gordon, who did much to abolish the slave trade and to bring a certain amount of order out of the welter of native anarchy.

The English have always been peculiarly successful as leaders and administrators among savage or primitive races, far more so than in governing aliens of high culture. In this work none has ever been greater than Gordon, a man of saintly character, deeply religious, although erratic and hard to handle by higher authority.

Ismail had been fantastically reckless in his personal and state expenses and in thirteen years had increased the national debt from £3,000,000 to about £100,000,000. Most of this money had been derived from bonds sold chiefly to French and English investors. He had also replaced Gordon by an incapable Egyptian, and both the Sudan and Egypt were rapidly going to pieces, with much consequent misery for the common people. In 1876 the Khedive suspended payment of debts, and France, which was much more active than the British Government, which wished to hold back, insisted on a Commission, the so-called *Caisse de la Dette publique*, which would receive directly a part of the national income for the benefit of bondholders without its passing through the hands of the corrupt officials. It was only two years later that the British moved and joined the French, sending as her two representatives to Cairo, Sir C. Rivers Wilson and Major Evelyn Baring, who is better known as Lord Cromer and who was to prove one of the greatest administrators the world has known.

If Egypt, and especially the Egyptian poor, were to be saved it was clearly necessary to assume control of Egyptian finance. Two Controllers-general were appointed for that purpose, one French and one British, but Ismail merely intrigued and fomented revolution. As a result, the Turkish Sultan was induced to depose him and place his son Tewfik on the Egyptian throne. There had already been secret conspiracies and revolts, chiefly under the lead of a native Egyptian, Arabi Pasha. After the Sultan's intervention he led a nationalist movement directed against Turks and foreigners, fanning the flames of both religious and racial hatred. Finally Arabi and his forces surrounded the palace and forced the Khedive to increase the army from 4000 to 18,000 men to be under Arabi's own command. The Khedive was now helpless, and the Franco-British Commissioners in a critical situation. Later, in 1882, Arabi practically made himself ruler.

Months of negotiations followed between the French and British as to how to meet the situation. Arabi and his followers showed no ability in governing and the mob and discontented soldiery were getting out of hand. The country was approaching anarchy, and with great reluctance Gladstone agreed with the French Premier, that the two nations should send a joint fleet for the protection of foreigners. The combined fleets arrived at Alexandria to maintain order, but the Egyptian answer was a massacre of some fifty Europeans, including the British Consul. Arabi was now the dominant power and began building shore batteries threatening the fleets. Warned to desist, he refused, and the British fleet opened fire, destroying the new batteries in about ten hours. Meanwhile there had been a change of ministry in France, and the French fleet was ordered to retire, leaving the British alone. France, which had been the leader in intervention and had urged Britain to join her, now simply scuttled off and ceased to play any part in Egyptian affairs other than to help defend the Canal.

Even that slight promise of aid was withdrawn after another Cabinet crisis in France, and after the Sultan of Turkey had also declined to do anything to maintain order in his suzerainty. Britain then announced that she would undertake the task alone but without any thought of annexation and would withdraw when the authority of the Khedive was restored. The Gladstone government now moved swiftly.

About 1870 the British army, together with its expenses, had been much enlarged. Even more important, its character and morale had been greatly improved by the efforts of Edward Cardwell, who had been appointed Secretary for War in 1868. By his reforms, including the abolition of the degrading custom of flogging, except in war, he had made the army a career for decent men instead of the last refuge of the lowest strata of the population. He had also encouraged the colonies to raise forces of their own for local defense and had brought home regulars from them, increasing the army in Britain itself by these and other means to about 20,000 men. This had all been done in opposition to the traditional teachings of Wellington and to the wishes of most of the officers. The results of the Cardwell reforms were now evident. Put to the test, Britain was able without delay to ship 13,000 men, under Sir Garnet Wolseley to Egypt, and in September, 1882, he completely routed the forces of Arabi at Tel-el-Kebir, finishing the job at Cairo, where Arabi and his remaining followers were taken prisoners. Arabi himself was banished to Ceylon.

The quick transfer of so large a force over a sea route nearly 2500 miles long, and the immediate and complete victory, established British prestige at a high point, at which it was to remain until the Boer War. France, with the fruits of nearly seventy years' efforts in Egypt at stake, had completely withdrawn. Britain had quelled the revolt single-handed in about two months, but much remained to be done. As a result of the Arabi revolt and of mismanagement by several generations of Khedives there was no government left.

France, which was thenceforward to play the part of the dog in the Egyptian manger, was now vociferous in demanding British withdrawal. Nothing would have suited Gladstone better, with his anti-expansionist mind, but the situation was too complex. British forces had gone into Egypt and they now remained the only dike against the flood of anarchy. Quite apart from the interests of the international bondholders there were other interests at stake, such as the Canal, which the French refused to defend, and the welfare of the Egyptian people themselves.

Europe wanted a settled Egypt, and the nations except France were quite willing that Britain should undertake the task of restoration. Indeed they would have been willing to have her annex the country or declare a protectorate over it. The government did neither, and so created an anomalous position for itself which was to cause many difficulties in the future. Baring, who had been in India since 1880, was called home, knighted, and sent back to Cairo as British Agent to perform a most difficult task. In Egypt itself he had no official status except his British commission and Britain had no status other than that of any other foreign nation except that she had an army in occupation. The Sultan would do nothing, except occasionally interfere to make trouble. The Khedive could or would do nothing save on the same terms. The *Caisse de la Dette* remained in existence, in control of half the revenue of the country, and made trouble, as did also the French. Baring, who nominally could do nothing but offer advice, remained twenty-three years and in spite of every impediment rehabilitated the country.

Meanwhile, the Gladstone Ministry had made a fatal mistake. The Egyptian Government had misgoverned the Sudan so atrociously since dismissing Gordon that a very serious revolt there under the leadership of a native who called himself a Mahdi, or Messiah, had blazed up, and two Egyptian armies sent to quell it had been defeated. The Egyptians obviously could not reconquer the vast territory and the revolt would have to be overcome by the British. This might take years and delay evacuation. The only alternative was to abandon the Sudan. The latter course was chosen, but there were scattered garrisons of Egyptians, in some cases under British officers, who could not be left to the mercy of the natives, and the problem was how to get them out. Against Baring's advice Gordon, who was in London, was chosen for the task and left immediately.

Gordon reached Khartoum, the center of Sudanese administration, but, as Baring had feared, he did not obey orders. Instead of evacuating the garrisons at once he delayed while he bombarded Baring with contradictory telegrams as to policies. Meanwhile the Mahdi's forces were gathering and Gordon was hopelessly besieged. The new problem was now how to extricate the hemmed-in extricator. In London the Cabinet hesitated over alternate suggestions, and drifted from the first of April to August. Far too late Wolseley was ordered to proceed to Egypt and undertake an expedition for Gordon's relief.

Hardly any preparations had been made, and in spite of valiant fighting and marching over the desert the force did not reach Khartoum until January 28, 1885. The place had been stormed by the Mahdist forces and Gordon killed two days earlier. Although the unfortunate leader had courted disaster by his own delays, the chief blame must lie with the Cabinet, who chose him and then delayed for months to send him succor. The responsibility was placed squarely on the shoulders of Gladstone, who had been immersed in domestic British questions and had dallied in the Sudanese affair, and no other act of his so adversely affected his popularity and influence. Whether to abandon the entire Sudan was now the question. This was promptly settled by Russian moves in Afghanistan which threatened an Anglo-Russian war. The Sudan was left to the Mahdi and his successor, who it is said reduced the native population in a dozen years by millions of lives.

Although this year marked the end of Gladstone's second Ministry we may glance forward another ten years to complete this phase of the Egyptian question. Baring and the group of British administrators and officers saved Egypt from bankruptcy and rebuilt the quality and morale of the native army. By means of irrigation they laid the foundations of prosperity and restored that of the long-oppressed *fellaheen*. The national budget was actually balanced by 1888, which permitted the continuance of public works on a large scale. All parts of the administration, including taxation and justice, were cleansed and rendered honest and efficient. Schools, hospitals and railways were built, and Egypt which had for generations been a sink of iniquity and misery became in less than two decades of British control a prosperous and happy land, a performance unrivalled in history. The remainder of the story belongs to a later period.

We may also note the long-felt international repercussions of the handling of the Egyptian question by the Gladstone Ministry. It had drifted into the problem without wishing to and without foresight. France was to remain estranged for twenty years with serious effects on Britain's role in European diplomacy. When in 1885 an Egyptian loan of £9,000,000 was required, the Ministry declined to guarantee it, with the result that there was an international guarantee by most of the powers, six of whom obtained seats on the *Caisse*. Of these, Russia and France were in constant opposition to England, throwing Britain into the arms of the Triple Alliance and making friendship with Germany particularly essential. Bismarck had won all the moves in his game.

III. IRELAND AND THE HOME RULE QUESTION

The problem which overshadowed all else in these years was that of the perennial Irish question. We have already spoken of the great influx of American wheat. The effect was transformation on a large scale of corn land into grazing, resulting in agricultural distress in both England and Ireland but more especially in wholesale evictions of tenants in the latter country. In spite of the Act of 1870 the land problem yet remained unsettled, and the Irish Land League, with Michael Davitt at its head, and in receipt of large funds from both America and Australia, adopted a policy of terrorism against the landlords. Although there was much violence, this in itself was of less importance than in forming the background of English opinion with regard to Ireland. Ricks were burned and cattle were cruelly maimed, although life was spared until the brutal murder of Lord Mountmorres. "Captain Moonlight" stalked through most of the island in his errand of spreading terror.

To some extent Parnell joined in this campaign, and even became head of the Land League because he realized that he must have all parties behind him as far as possible in order to achieve the one end to which he from now on devoted his life. Parnell, who in 1880, at the beginning of Gladstone's Ministry, began his career as one of the dominant figures in the House of Commons, was a man of iron will, except for one weakness; a fanatic, with supreme contempt for anything which stood in his way; without great constructive ability and with only one object, Home Rule for Ireland. He cared nothing for the means by which it might be achieved, whether peace or violence, the wrecking of Parliamentary government, the granting of local self-rule or complete independence. A Protestant of the landlord class, he gained complete ascendancy over the Catholic peasantry.

At the opening of Parliament in 1880 the policy of the new government was seen in the statement in the Queen's speech that the Coercion Act passed by the Conservatives would be allowed to lapse at its expiration. The policy of governing Ireland by normal British methods in the larger island could have succeeded only if immediate relief were given for the conditions prevailing in the more unhappy one. The origin of the troubles there was "sheer misery," and sheer misery is impatient of delayed reforms. In that same year over 10,000 Irish peasants were evicted from their homes and there were about 2500 violent outrages in return. It is said that 100,000 tenants were in heavy arrears of rent and so liable to be deprived of their land under the 1870 Act. A bill to compensate those evicted was rejected by the Lords. The rising storm resulted in the passage of two Acts the following year: one a Coercion Bill doing away with civil liberty, and the other a Land Act aiming at fair rents, fixity of tenure and the right of the tenant to sell his interest in his lease.

The outrages, however, continued, and Parnell was clapped in jail by Forster, Secretary for Ireland in the Cabinet, in spite of Parnell's prediction that with his influence gone the situation would become worse. This proved the case and in 1882 Gladstone threw over Forster and released Parnell. For a few hours it appeared that possibly the way was now open to settlement, but two days later one of those fatal mischances occurred which seem to have always dogged the relations between Ireland and England. As Forster's successor, Gladstone had sent to Ireland Lord Frederick Cavendish, a man for whom the English people had something of the affection they had for Gordon. Almost on his arrival he was murdered in broad daylight while walking with Burke, the Under-secretary, in Phœnix Park, Dublin.

The assassins belonged to a small organization called the "Invincibles," or more popularly the murder club, and it has been said that they intended to kill Burke only, but they had been opposed to Parnell's more conservative policy and it has also been said that they wished to balk this by an act which would make reconciliation impossible on any terms. If the latter were the object they succeeded. The fact that Lord Frederick, a son of the Duke of Devonshire, was a man of noble character, and the errand of conciliation on which he was bent, both lent a peculiar horror to his murder. It threw the English into a paroxysm of

239

anger and made them feel that whatever they tried to do, nothing would satisfy the Irish.

Parnell, who had broken with the extremists and had replaced the Land League by a National League whose only object was Home Rule, was horrified and offered to resign his seat in Parliament. He told Davitt that he felt as though he himself had been stabbed in the back, and in fact the murder club had temporarily ruined his cause. A new Crimes Act obviously had to be passed, and it was provided in it that the police should have right of summary arrest and that even grave crimes could be tried by three judges without a jury. On the other hand the policy of appeasement was still pursued, and Acts were passed for cancellation of arrears of rent. Parnell wished for a period of peace and to a considerable extent suspended his policy of blocking the operation of Parliament by the Irish members. Yet the reign of violence continued, including many murders in Ireland and dynamite outrages in London.

In spite of the failures recorded, the Ministry had important domestic reforms to its credit, such as the Act making employers liable for damages in case of accidents to their employees, and the Act finally abolishing flogging in both army and navy. The Married Women's Property Act, which for the first time gave a married woman the same control over her own property that a spinster would have, was passed in 1882 and was one of the milestones in the woman's movement.

The great Act of the Ministry, however, was the third Reform Bill (1884), which gave more citizens the franchise than the earlier two Reform Bills had together. The first had given the vote to a large part of the middle class; the second to a large part of the workers in the towns and trades, but the rural population had been neglected. In vivid contrast to the great popular excitement in 1832, there had been little general interest taken in the matter, although Mr. G. O. Trevelyan had continually maintained the cause in the Commons. In that House there was no opposition to the measure when it was introduced but as usual it was blocked by the Lords, who, however, agreed to a compromise after conferences between Gladstone and Salisbury and the exertion of influence by the Queen. This called for a second bill, redistributing Parliamentary seats, which was passed the following year.

In general the Reform Bill of 1884 brought fairly complete democracy, except for the women's vote. It gave the franchise to practically every male head of a household, and greatly improved the position of the farm laborers, who had been unsuccessful in gaining any advantage by formation of labor unions, by giving them a certain measure of political power. The value of such power was shown in the next twenty years by the changed attitude of landlords and the larger farmers, and the greater consideration bestowed on this form of labor. The Redistribution Bill, which divided all Britain into approximately equal election districts, each represented in Parliament by a single member, altered the historic nature of representation and by making the districts artificial instead of natural or historical tended to increase the importance of party machinery.

There were two other important effects. The extension of the franchise to Ireland on the same terms as in England, meant that Parnell would be supreme and control a party which would be much more important than the number of Irish constituents would warrant. Also, the alteration in the historic mode of representation in England itself meant the end of the Whig power, though neither of these effects was contemplated at the time of the passage of the bill.

Although these measures had to some extent restored the popularity of the Liberals, the tragedy of Khartoum followed almost immediately and Gladstone was defeated on the Budget. Parliament was not dissolved but in any case a general election was due in about seven months. Gladstone resigned and a new government was formed with Lord Salisbury at its head.

The new Prime Minister, whose successive terms of office were to constitute the longest tenure held by any man since the first Reform Bill, being a year longer than Gladstone's, was an aristocrat of the old school, careless of what people thought of him and heartily despising modern methods of publicity. Grave and distinctly intellectual in type, he had character and principles although lacking in broadly constructive views and with little interest in democratic reforms. His great service was to be later in the international partition of Africa, but his first Ministry, which lasted only until the election, was marked by little except the annexation of Upper Burma to the Empire and the passing of an Act to facilitate the purchase by Irish tenants of land from its owners.

We have already spoken of the solid block of Irish votes in the House and the controlling influence of Parnell. During the few months the Conservatives were in power they gave the impression that they were favorable to the Irish cause, and before the election Lord Carnarvon, the Conservative Viceroy in Ireland, with Salisbury's knowledge, gave Parnell the impression that if elected the party would be in favor of some kind of home rule for the island. Gladstone also was moving toward the same sort of settlement but he made no statement, and Parnell therefore backed the Conservatives. Gladstone had asked the voters to give the Liberals a majority which would enable them to control Parliament without the Irish bloc, but the returns, although they showed a Liberal majority over the Conservatives of 86, also showed that Parnell had secured 86 members out of 103 in Ireland pledged to Home Rule. This gave the Conservatives and Parnellites combined four more votes than the Liberals and made Parnell the deciding factor between the two British parties. The fact that the Irish, outside of Ulster, had returned 86 members pledged to Home Rule as against only 17 unpledged, so clearly indicated the wish of a united people that Gladstone now believed some sort of Home Rule to be inevitable if Ireland were to be governed in peace.

So intent was he on securing this result that he offered Salisbury his aid if the Conservatives would bring forward some measure to gain the end in view, but the Prime Minister rejected his advances. Convinced of the necessity for action and that the Conservatives would not take it, he allied himself with the disillusioned Parnell and with the help of the Irish defeated the Government, which resigned. Gladstone, now Prime Minister for the third time, at once introduced a Home Rule Bill, including a separate Parliament for Ireland and a plan for buying out the Irish landlords at a cost of £50,000,000 to settle the land question on a grand scale. Meanwhile, he had been deserted by a large part of the Whig section of his party and of the radical wing under the lead of Chamberlain, and the bill was defeated by a majority of 30. In his desire for a political and Irish national settlement he had overlooked or neglected the problem of Protestant Ulster.

He had now to decide whether to resign or to appeal to the country in a second election in nine months. He chose the latter course, and at seventy-seven years of age he threw himself into the campaign as a holy cause. By doing so he split his own party definitely into Liberals and Liberal-Unionists. He himself was accused of destroying the party for the sake of personal power, and the British electorate was not interested. The old man, as wonderful in eloquence as ever, had lost followers by lack of tact and of understanding of the new forces of the times, especially that of imperialism. The more conservative of his followers were coming to regard him as a demagogue, much as conservative Americans regarded Bryan in the campaign of 1896. To be a Gladstonian was almost to be socially ostracized.

On the other hand, labor and the radicals were following the imperialist Chamberlain. The English thought of the Irish in terms of the assassination of Cavendish, of "Captain Moonlight," of the innumerable agrarian outrages, and of Protestant Ulster left to the mercy of an Irish Parliament with a Catholic majority. In the general political background were the dark shadows of Majuba Hill and the needless death of Gordon. The people voted against Gladstone, and returned a majority of 118 Conservatives and Liberal-Unionists as against the combined strength of the remaining Liberals and the Parnellites. Home Rule appeared to be killed, but it was to have an even more dramatic ending, for the nineteenth century at least, within the life of the old man now so signally defeated for the time.

As a result of the election, July, 1886, Lord Salisbury again

243

became Prime Minister, retaining office for six years, when he was once more to be replaced by Gladstone. Of the imperial aspects of the Salisbury Ministry we shall speak in the next chapter. In England it enacted some useful measures, such as the Education Act of 1891, which at last made education free in all elementary schools; a new Factory Act which reduced the hours of work for women and indicated the conditions still prevailing for the poor by forbidding the employment of children under the age of eleven; useful Acts improving the character of local governments, and which, with one other Act a few years later, made possible many of the reforms of the next generation. Cities, particularly London, had grown up in haphazard fashion and the confusion of overlapping and inefficient jurisdictions had paralyzed efforts toward improvement for which the way was now cleared by the Ministry of 1886-92.

But, as Lord Salisbury said in 1887, the situation was still such that "politics are Ireland." Parnell wished to end the reign of violence, which he felt could only retard the coming of what was his one single object, Home Rule. That secured, the land and other questions could be dealt with, but others in Ireland were not of his opinion and put the other questions first. "The Plan of Campaign" put forward by agrarian agitators included both non-payment of rents and other unlawful proceedings. It was met by a fresh Crimes Act, and, although the Ministry tried to offer relief in the way of land legislation with one hand, the other was still the mailed fist. By-elections in Britain were beginning to indicate that more of the electorate were becoming converted to Home Rule, when certain events in the last four years in the life of Parnell altered the possibilities completely. As we have seen so often in our story, in spite of the faults, we may say crimes, which have marked England's undeniable failure in Ireland, Anglo-Irish relations have been deflected again and again by accidents and personalities for which the blame cannot be placed on Britain.

Gladstone, who was again to become Prime Minister in 1892, had now but one thought in mind, the securing of Home Rule for Ireland. That was also the sole thought of Parnell, who had

244

struggled for it so long and was now himself to defeat all hope for it. In 1887 *The London Times,* the most influential journal of the day, published a letter in facsimile and apparently in Parnell's hand, approving in part of the murder in Phœnix Park. It took two years to prove that the document was a forgery by another Irishman which had almost inconceivably been accepted and published by *The Times* without proper investigation as to its authenticity. In the revulsion of feeling on the part of the public, Parnell became almost a hero, and the prospects for Home Rule at the next election were brighter than they had ever been. Then the final blow fell.

Parnell, one of the great figures of his day, taciturn and apparently much of a recluse, was a lonely but not a licentious man in the years he spent in England. About ten years before the explosion which blasted him he had met and fallen in love at first sight with a Mrs. O'Shea, wife of a spendthrift Irish captain in the Hussars, daughter of an English baronet, sister of Sir Evelyn Wood, afterward Field Marshal, and otherwise well-connected. O'Shea some years earlier had ceased all marital relations with his wife. As he failed to support her, she was wholly dependent for the present and future on the whim of an aged aunt, who gave her about £3000 a year and who would presumably provide handsomely for her in her will. This she eventually did, leaving her niece £144,000 when she died after an unexpectedly long life.

Meanwhile, Mrs. O'Shea and Parnell had lived as man and wife for ten years, with the full knowledge of the husband, who blackmailed them, and who occasionally stayed at the house in order to keep up the semblance of married life in the eyes of the aunt, who knew nothing of the liaison. When the aunt died, O'Shea offered a divorce for £20,000, but the aunt's will was disputed by the Wood family, including Sir Evelyn, and the couple could not raise the money to buy off the husband, who then brought suit for divorce from his wife, claiming he had been deceived for nine years. Named as co-respondent, Parnell could not and would not defend himself. The result was the most resounding scandal of the time, which profoundly affected the relations between England and

Ireland. We have to consider not only the largely hypocritical morality of the Victorian Age, but the unmistakably sordid aspects of the case.

Gladstone, sensing public opinion and believing that if Parnell remained the leader of the Home Rule group of Irish the cause would be lost and that his own life was nearing its end, insisted on Parnell's retirement. The Irish statesman in his long career had always appeared as coldly calculating, unswayed by any emotion which would deflect him from his almost mathematical reasoning in politics, but now he flared into a frenzy of anger and misjudgment. He would not bow to English prejudice as to his private life, though that prejudice in his earlier days he would have recognized as a political factor of the first magnitude. He refused to resign his leadership even when a majority of his own devoted party of Home Rulers abandoned him and the Catholic Church in Ireland pursued him. His action split all Ireland into warring parties of Parnellites and anti-Parnellites and the cause to which he had devoted his life was ruined by himself. Although his death in the following year produced a reaction in his favor, the bitterness of faction had been too deep to be assuaged.

In the general election of 1892 the Gladstonian Liberals and Irish Home Rulers secured a small majority, and Gladstone became Prime Minister for the fourth time, but a Home Rule bill passed in the Commons was rejected by the Lords. The indomitable old man, now eighty-three, would have gone to the country again for a mandate but the party leaders knew it was useless, and in 1894 Gladstone retired from public life in which he had been a dominant figure for sixty-three years. From then, until it was defeated in 1895, the disintegrating Liberal party, headed by Lord Rosebery, accomplished some reforms, such as the disestablishment of the Welsh Church, but the day of the party was over and there was only dissension and no strength within it.

Salisbury again returned to the premiership with a combination of Conservatives and Liberal-Unionists. There is a school of historians who refuse to take the influence of individuals into account and believe only in social forces, but there seems good reason to believe that if it had not been for Parnell's weakness for Mrs. O'Shea, the character of her worthless husband, and the miserable family lawsuit, the relations of Britain with Ireland might at long last have taken a marked turn for the better and the crises of the next century been avoided or minimized. Neither the Liberal Party nor Home Rule were dead but both passed out of the sphere of practical politics for a decade. It is true that in Salisbury's third Ministry, in which he at last included some of the Liberal-Unionists, an effort was made to conciliate Ireland and to "kill Home Rule by kindness." Local county government was much improved, and Sir Horace Plunkett's co-operative enterprises and other means of solving the agrarian problem did much to restore a degree of prosperity, but the desire for Home Rule remained, and as we shall see later was, after the turn of the century, to give rise to the sinister Sinn Fein movement.

IV. BREAKDOWN OF LIBERALISM AND RISE OF LABOR

We have already spoken of the Whigs and Radicals as discordant elements among the Liberals and before passing to the story of the Empire outside the United Kingdom in this period we may review briefly that of Radicalism and labor. From 1880 to 1885, there was constant friction even in the Cabinet between the two wings of the party, Joseph Chamberlain being the chief leader of the Radicals within the Government. An astute Birmingham businessman, an ardent imperialist and later to become Colonial Secretary in Salisbury's Conservative government in 1895, he was in the early 1880's regarded as a demagogue and a dangerous man. Although a member of Gladstone's Cabinet he did not hesitate to put forward in the election of 1885 an "unauthorized program," as it was called, of his own with which his chief had little sympathy, and which included such planks as free education for all, disestablishment of the English Church, denunciation of the House of Lords as in the way of social progress, a progressive income tax bearing heavily on the rich, and a vast agricultural readjustment which would give rural laborers land of their own. The

247

campaign slogan of "three acres and a cow" recalls to an American the earlier one after the Civil War of "forty acres and a mule" for emancipated slaves.

After the failure of the Chartists, Socialistic ideas had almost disappeared, but in this period they were revived. Karl Marx and Friedrich Engels, who were to have such vast influence on the development of Continental Socialism, had long been living in England, but partly because of a personal quarrel between Marx and H. M. Hyndman, the leader of English Socialism in this period, the English Socialists were but little moved by the Marxian theories. The Socialism of the period was, indeed, of a mild type and meant rather an extension of social services by the government, such as education, factory legislation and such matters, than the inevitable class war of the pure Marxian doctrine.

Chamberlain's own brand was of the "gas and water" variety, that is, municipal ownership of certain public utilities and not nationalization of all resources. Hyndman did try to impregnate the laboring class with Marxian ideas but made little headway and if we have succeeded in our effort to illustrate the British character the answer is not far to seek. Class war and violence are not in the English tradition. Another group of Socialists, of whom William Morris was a member, were rather Utopian dreamers of a happy social order for the future as pictured in Morris's still delightful *News from Nowhere*. In 1883 yet another type emerged in the formation of the Fabian Society, named for the Roman general whose method was "slow but sure," and which, under the guidance of Mr. and Mrs. Sidney Webb, aimed at gradual improvement of social conditions, in a collectivist direction to be sure, but without revolution. Far more influential than Marx was the American Henry George, whose lectures and volume *Progress and Poverty* made a profound impression. As yet, however, although a more equitable distribution of wealth was much discussed, the sources of wealth and the modes of its acquisition were rather taken for granted as forever to remain what they were at the time.

After the successes of Trades-Unionism in the 70's the movement had become more or less atrophied, and interested in sick and old-age benefits rather than in fighting employers. In 1888 Sir William Harcourt, a Gladstonian Liberal, might say jokingly that "we are all Socialists now," but in fact the government was not moving very fast even in the direction of what we have described above. On the other hand, genuine Marxian Socialism had been making such rapid headway in the autocratically ruled Germany that Bismarck attempted to take the wind out of its sails by means of government measures providing insurance against sickness (1883), accidents (1884), and old age (1891). Britain was far behind in such legislation, and the United States Federal Government did not embark on any such course until a half century later.

Possibly the failure of the British Government to act hastened the change which now occurred, ushering in what is called the "new Unionism." Among Trades-Unionists who were dissatisfied with the lack of union action were Tom Mann and John Burns, both of the Amalgamated Society of Engineers. The latter declared that the "reckless assumption of the duties and responsibilities that only the State or whole community can discharge, in the nature of sick and superannuation benefits, at the instance of the middle class, is crushing out the larger unions by taxing their members to an unbearable extent. . . . The result of this is that all of them have ceased to be unions for maintaining the rights of labor, and have degenerated into mere middle and upper class rate-reducing institutions."[1] Not only was there a more militant note sounded than by the old Unionism, but the new was especially directed toward organizing the weaker trades and the unorganized manual laborers.

Public opinion in general was sympathetic rather than hostile. The trade depression of the 70's had given way for a brief period to a mild prosperity between 1881 and 1883, but then had bogged down again. To use one index, the tonnage of ships built annually fell from 1,250,000 in the latter year to only 473,000 in 1886. The suffering of the working classes was intense and was beginning to be recognized by those above them in the economic scale. A series

[1]Cited by J. F. Rees, *Social and Industrial History of England 1815–1918*, London, 1932, p. 134.

of Reports by Royal Commissions displayed shocking conditions. Arnold Toynbee, who had wished to learn of these at first hand, moved from his post at Oxford and settled in the slums of the East End of London in 1883, establishing the first "settlement" among the very poor. Four years later William Booth, a great organizer and one of the world's noted religious leaders, had founded the Salvation Army to work among those at the very bottom of society, and in a few years was to arouse the people to what was going on, in his *Darkest England*. Although the finical might object to some of the crude emotionalism of the methods employed by the "Army," they were successful in rescuing to a better life and hope millions of human beings in the course of the Army's subsequent work, and the movement has proved one of the greatest in the history of Christianity.

Still the government did little to ameliorate the conditions of the poor, and in 1888 the new Unionism swung into action. Mrs. Besant, who had been deeply shocked by discovering the abominable conditions under which the poor girls of London who worked on making matches were forced to labor and live, wrote a scathing article, thinking they could do nothing to help themselves. To her surprise some of them read her article and 700 of them went on strike. Apparently among the most helpless creatures in the great city and with no chance, they finally won against their employers, with the financial aid of Mrs. Besant and others. Some months later the newly organized gas workers struck for an eight-hour day, and won, but the greatest struggle came in August, 1889.

The dock laborers, among the lowest-paid and most sweated labor in London, were organized by Mann, Burns, and Ben Tillett and went on strike. They asked only for sixpence an hour for their casual work and for some minor reforms, but the employers would not even confer with them, thinking that the workers were wholly within their power, as they lived on the edge of starvation. Day by day they marched peaceably through the streets, usually ending at Hyde Park, and carrying stuck on pikes samples of the horrible food which was all they had to eat. After two weeks their resources were exhausted and as a last desperate throw they asked for a general strike, though there was no chance the request would be heeded.

Then one of the most dramatic events in the history of Empire labor occurred. Far off in Australia the dock workers of Brisbane met to consider what to do to help their fellow workers in London. Although the Port of London had had to be closed for the first time since 1797, the employers had remained adamant, counting on starvation of the workers. Then came the amazing response from Australia. The British island-continent went wild with sympathy. Money was collected from every direction, and the unimaginable sum of £30,000 was cabled to the strikers. The desperate employers resorted to every means to bribe, coerce or bring on conflict with the strikers and refused mediation until in September they had to yield. The victory was not for the dockers in London alone, and it gave an enormous impetus to the Labor Union movement throughout the whole country. It also marked the beginning of an alliance between the Union and the women's movements which was to bear fruit in the future.

Moreover, the victory, instead of increasing the revolutionary movement, which had never been strong in labor ranks, had the reverse effect. Revival of trade and the increased strength of the Unions led labor to look to increased representation in Parliament, with possible eventual control of the constitutional machinery of the state, to secure their ends. Three Socialists were elected in 1892, John Burns, J. Havelock Wilson, representing the sailors, and Keir Hardie, the last arriving at the House escorted by a brass band and wearing a cloth cap and a red tie. A new day had evidently dawned and a shudder went along Pall Mall.

All three of the new members were Socialists but not Marxians or revolutionaries. They realized, however, that a mere infiltration of Parliament by a few of their own kind might not bring results for generations. Hardie made up his mind to form a new party devoted solely to the interests of labor and established the Scottish Labor Party, the first Labor Party in Britain. It was decided, however, to establish one for the United Kingdom, and in January, 1893, representatives of Trades-Unions, the Fabian Society, the

Scottish Labor Party, and other organizations met at Bradford. The Fabians and some of the other withdrew, but under the lead of Hardie the Independent Labor Party then came into being. Two years later, in the election of 1895, it put forward twenty-eight candidates, but not one was elected, even Hardie losing his seat for a while until returned in 1898 for Merthyr in Wales, which seat he held for life.

Coming to the fore in the movement now, however, were such men as Philip Snowden and Ramsay MacDonald, although owing to renewed apathy on the part of labor in general as to Socialism and its methods, the party had still long to wait for the control of which it dreamed. In fact the "I. L. P." was scarcely a party as yet, coming really into being in 1900, but the foundations had been laid, and chiefly by Hardie. He was a portent of which the comfortable classes failed wholly to grasp the meaning. Set to work in Glasgow at seven years of age, he toiled in the coal mines from the time he was ten until twenty. The manner of his arrival in Parliament noted above was not intended to be either a demonstration or an affront, but the press and upper classes made it out to be such. Feeling with the whole depth of his sensitive nature the misery of his own class he moved an amendment to the Address to the Throne at his first session, asking that some attention be paid to the 1,300,000 people then out of work, which again brought a storm of disapproval from the Conservatives.

The next year, 1894, the Duchess of York gave birth to the future Duke of Windsor and 260 miners were killed the same day in a disaster. The next, the French President was assassinated. When the House was asked to pass a resolution of sympathy for the French, Hardie asked for another for the families of the killed miners, whose dangers and lives he knew so well. Harcourt refused and turned off the request casually. Hardie, infuriated by what he thought callous indifference, then opposed the message congratulating the Duchess on the birth of a future heir to the throne. The storm which then broke on him indicated how little Britain's governing class still understood the people it governed, and the new forces which were to mould their world.

252

CHAPTER XII

THE NEW IMPERIALISM

I. Change in Imperial Feeling

IN THE last quarter of the nineteenth century there was an outburst of imperial zeal in Europe which can be compared only to that of the seventeenth century. As in the earlier period England, France, and Spain had contended for empire, so another group, Britain, France, Italy, Germany, and others seemed no less intent on staking out claims to what available acquisitions remained. Many factors were at work in the international rush to appropriate the remaining lands of the world inhabited by backward races. One was the enormous increase in population which had been one of the most marked and important features of European development in the century since the industrial revolution. The increasing desire to control sources of raw materials and markets for manufactured goods was another. Among yet others were psychological ones, such as the pride engendered by the new nationalism, which had been growing since the Napoleonic days. As a rich man builds himself a great house and spends much of his money in ostentation, so the new and even older nations felt the urge toward the ostentation of imperial possessions to show how great they were.

For Britain, at least, history and poetry also played their parts. In 1884 Seeley published his book, *Expansion of England,* which reviewed the growth of the Empire for three centuries in a way to stimulate the pride of the nation in its imperial work and achievement. Much shorter and written in a far more popular fashion than Dilke's *Greater Britain* of nearly twenty years earlier, it caught the popular imagination and was of vast influence. Another fillip to the pride of the British in the part they had played in world affairs was afforded by a book by an American naval officer, Captain, later Admiral, Mahan on *The Influence of Sea Power in History*, which for the first time demonstrated the overwhelming part played by the British navy in the history of the globe.

This was a work for statesmen and scholars, but the great reading public lapped up the emotional appeal for the new imperialism in the volumes of Rudyard Kipling, both prose and verse. His work was enormously popular and made the blood of a seagoing and imperial race pulse as the war tom-tom did that of the savages in the jungle.

If there was much that was crude, blatant and mercenary in the race to "paint the map red," we must not forget that this had also been true in the glorious days of Elizabeth. There were, however, some of the finer motives which had likewise been present in the earlier era of expansion with which the new movement had much in common. After a long period of paying little attention to overseas empire, the British suddenly felt the old emotions stirring. There was much of the adventurous and even buccaneering spirit and the British were enthralled when Kipling sang:

"You have heard the song—how long! how long!
Pull out on the trail again!"

. . . .

"The Lord knows what we may find, dear lass,
And the deuce knows what we may do—
But we're back once more on the old trail, our own trail, the out trail,
We're down, hull down on the Long Trail—the trail that is always new."

There was a new feeling, as in the days of Queen Bess, of adventure, wealth to be gained, somebody's beard, though it was not now the King of Spain's, to be singed, and the glitter of imperial spoils. Like the "Manifest Destiny" of the United States to expand across the American continent to the Pacific, Britain had rediscovered its imperial destiny to govern more of the globe than any other race.

The Conservatives, under Salisbury, formed the party of advance, but among the Liberals, though the party was split, the Radical wing was rapidly reviving the creed of imperialism, particularly in the form of some sort of Imperial Federation. This was doomed to failure, for it savored too much of the doctrinaire and "blue print mind," which has always been alien to British character. There were, indeed, ample difficulties in managing the group of colonies, large and small, now scattered all over the world—to say nothing of the peculiar problem of India. For one thing even those which had received local autonomy and responsible government were neither independent nations nor did they have a voice in the foreign policy of the Empire, though deeply affected by it. Moreover, as we shall see, some of them had ambitions of their own which ran counter to what the controlling powers in London might desire or consider wise for the Empire as a whole.

Such problems of conflicting interests between the colonies and the home country, or even between the several colonies and dependencies, bring vividly to mind much the same difficulties, of policy, local interest, contribution to their own and imperial defense, and so on, which wrecked the first Empire in the days of the American Revolution. The problems remained to a large extent unchanged. What had changed was the broader spirit in which such problems were now treated in Westminster and in the colonies themselves. Imperial Federation was no more a solution than a small Parliamentary representation of the American colonies would have been in 1776, but although the movement could not succeed, it did do much to focus attention on the Empire. It brought realization of the fact that the Empire no longer consisted of a mere disconnected group made up of Great Britain and a lot of scattered dependencies, but was something far greater than that, a gigantic imperial unit which in territory, population, resources, and power surpassed any Empire of which the world had yet dreamed and made even the Roman seem insignificant in comparison. To the making of this "Third Empire" in British history, as Professor Ramsay Muir calls it, there went all the inheritances and influences of raiding Danes and Norse, of Normans and feudalism, of growing sea power and trade, of political training for near a millennium, of dogged character, with its good and bad, and all the other events and factors of Britain's long history.

II. Victoria's Jubilee

In 1886 a Colonial and Indian Exhibition in London interested the populace in the resources and products, as well as the extent, of the Empire, but an event of incalculable influence was that of the Queen's first Jubilee the following year. When fifty years earlier, as a young girl, she had gone to the Abbey to be crowned, it had been a local British event, though naturally celebrated in the colonies. The celebration of her half century of rule demonstrated the changes which had taken place in the public mind. In 1837 little thought had been given to the colonies, and the Crown itself had sunk to perhaps the lowest point of public respect and interest in its history. But by 1887 the Crown had become not only the center of an almost religious devotion on the part of the people of Great Britain, but the symbol of unity of a great Empire of which the people had become aware. It is almost impossible for us to realize the wave of emotion which swept through all classes. Merely from her age it was not thought that the Queen would live many years longer, and, without realization of the future, she seemed to sum up in her own person a half century of marvellous achievement, both material and spiritual.

The ceremonies also brought vividly home the pinnacle which the Empire had then reached. In the procession from Buckingham Palace to the Abbey, where a thanksgiving service was held, there were representatives of almost every nation in the world. As the Queen-Empress drove in state, the procession which followed her was one of the most remarkable in history. Members of most of the ruling Houses in Europe, envoys from far countries over the globe, fighting forces from every part of the Empire, and above all the retinue of Indian Princes, made a spectacle which surpassed any of the triumphs in the days of Rome. It vividly impressed masses who saw or read about it, with the might, pomp and majesty of Empire. Every hamlet in Great Britain shared in the thrill in local celebrations and that night bonfires blazed on hilltops from the Shetland Islands to Land's End, lit as the blaze from the initial one in the Malvern Hills was seen, from hill to hill throughout the whole of Britain. A few weeks later, beside army reviews, there was a great review of the naval forces held at Spithead, and, although the number and size of the vessels seem small to us now, it electrified the world.

III. BEGINNING OF IMPERIAL CONFERENCES

Among those who had come to give homage to the Queen were representatives from all the self-governing colonies, and the opportunity afforded for consultation was taken advantage of and resulted in the first "Colonial Conference." It was to prove of tremendous import for the future that the responsible heads of the colonies should meet with the British Prime Minister not as subordinates or as mere colonial agents but on terms of equality. The spectacle in itself gave to both the British and colonial peoples a new sense of what the Empire was and meant. Nothing concrete of great importance was accomplished but that infinitely important thing in British history and government—a precedent—had been set, and that alone would have made the Conference a milestone in our imperial story.

The agenda had been prepared in advance with great care and tact, and a wise understanding of what at this stage could and could not be discussed to advantage. Imperial Federation was not to be mentioned. The meeting was held under the shadow of the fear on the part of the colonies of the more aggressive ambitions of other European powers in the rush for overseas possessions, and as Lord Salisbury told the members the object was not to form a Union or a *Zollverein* but a *Kriegsverein*, a combination for imperial defense. The only definite result at the time was the agreement of the colonies in Australia to provide in part for the additional ships which were to be stationed in Australian waters.

Salisbury's further statement was not only to prove true but was typically English in its approach to possibly great political changes. Speaking of federation and possible developments in the Empire he said they were "grand aspirations," "matters for the future rather than the present," and that although they were "doubtlessly hazy, they are the nebulous matter that in the course of ages—in much less than ages—will cool down and condense into material from which many practical and businesslike resolutions may very likely come." Unlike the neat plans for federation, this slow moving forward step by step and finding the solution for a multitude of immediate problems as they might successively present themselves was to transform the imperial structure as the same method through the ages has transformed the political one of England herself. At the moment it was enough that a new organ of imperial government had been found in the idea, now first put in practice, of the Imperial Conference.

Another step was taken seven years later when a Conference between the self-governing colonies was held in Ottawa, the capital of the greatest of them, the Dominion of Canada, with merely an imperial representative present from London to show the sympathy of the mother country and provide information. It was largely trade matters which were discussed, including tariffs and possible imperial preference. Naturally there were differences of interest between England as an old manufacturing country and the colonies desiring to establish domestic manufactures of their own, but the most important aspect of this second Conference was the spirit prevailing. The mother country now acknowledged that her children had come of age and could discuss their own affairs, whereas they, on the other hand, showed a just sense of the difficulties and point of view of England. Colonial statesmen who as colonials wanted protection admitted that if they were in Britain they would want free trade.

The Conference of 1887 had shown home-keeping statesmen who had no first-hand knowledge of the Empire, that in its far-flung states there were men who were their own equals. Tact, discretion, and personal intercourse were making rapidly for an increase in mutual respect, a sense of mutual dependence, and a broader viewpoint on the part of Britain and an increasing loyalty on the part of the colonies, which were to be put to most desperate test in a few years in the Boer War and later in the World War. Mutual dependence may count for much, but it must also be recognized that, although affection may be only an emotion and the flag and the Crown only symbols, they were to prove of far more binding force than trade advantages or a written imperial constitution.

IV. RACE FOR EMPIRE

We have already spoken of the strong feeling on the part of Gladstone and his Liberals not to embark on new adventures and indeed to draw in the boundaries of empire. In this they had not been in sympathy with the changing temper of the people and it was left to the Conservative Lord Salisbury to align national policy with the new spirit and to add enormously to Britain's imperial possessions. We have mentioned the parallel between the imperialism of these years and those of the days of Queen Elizabeth. It is rather odd that Victoria, in the time of England's second great expansion, was being served as Prime Minister by a descendant of the two Cecils, including the first Earl of Salisbury, who had served Elizabeth; and also that there was a wholly unconscious revival of the use of chartered mercantile companies which were now to do much the same work in imperial expansion which their predecessors had done nearly three centuries before in Tudor times. Among the more important were the East Africa Company, already mentioned, the Royal Niger Company and the South Africa Company. Of the particular work of Rhodes we shall speak later, but may here glance briefly at the general partition of Africa among the great powers. It was perhaps Salisbury's greatest triumph that he secured it peacefully.

The rush for territory had begun in the 1870's. Before the end of the 90's practically all of the African continent, with the chief exceptions of Abyssinia and Morocco, was in the possession of one or another of the leading European powers. The earliest attempt

259

at a settlement of conflicting claims had occurred under Gladstone, when Dilke, Under-Secretary for Foreign Affairs, drew up a convention with Portugal, which the government approved. Portugal had the largest if also the least substantial of the claims. Naturally France, Germany, and Belgium objected to a determination of the fate of the vast Congo region without being consulted, and the Gladstone government, which at the moment was courting Germany on account of the Egyptian situation, had somewhat ignominiously to cancel the Portuguese agreement, in June, 1884. In the autumn of that year a conference of fifteen nations, presided over by Bismarck, met in Berlin, and the most pressing questions as to the Congo were settled, but the greatest scramble was in the five years following during which Salisbury and Bismarck, until the latter's fall, were the leading figures among the statesmen and did most to avoid war.

Although, in the heat of the race, that was a great accomplishment, the various agreements signed in 1890 contained the seeds of future trouble, due in large part to the short-sightedness of Bismarck with regard to the value of African colonies. Britain had done the major part of the exploration and opening up commercially of the Dark Continent, but France had been the first of the great powers to realize the future. In the settlement she obtained the largest share, including the great island of Madagascar, to which the British had far the more valid claim.

Indeed, the French had none, but for some years during the Gladstone Ministry had been ousting the British traders and had established a protectorate by force. The Gladstone Ministry had let France have her way partly because of the Liberals' lack of interest in expansion and partly because of not wishing to antagonize the French too far while involved in the Egyptian imbroglio, which colors much of the international policy of the period. Although a large part of the Congo had already gone to Belgium, France also secured in that section a rich territory larger than all Germany's African colonies put together.

The grandiose historical claims of Portugal were finally settled by ultimatum. She was given a somewhat larger strip on the coast than claimed, but her shadowy titles to Mashonaland and Nyasaland were yielded to the British, who in the general 1890 settlements also acquired Zanzibar, Kenya, and Uganda, the boundaries of the latter two being so drawn as to block the German push toward the Upper Nile. In this Egypt was again a determining factor, as it had been in the change of attitude in allowing the Bismarck government to develop its East African claims. In the west, Germany got little but a strip of the Cameroons and a small extension of its Southwest African colony, which would connect it with the Zambesi River, whereas Britain secured title to the extraordinarily rich trading region of Nigeria, though there was to be trouble later with France over boundaries.

If Germany was far outdistanced in the African scramble it must be remembered that it was chiefly due to her own policy. England had not put impediments in her way, but, as we have said, Bismarck was less interested in colonies than in consolidating the position of the new empire he had erected in Europe. Britain had something which the military leaders of Germany, even after Bismarck's dismissal, considered important enough to trade for vast possessions in Africa. To compare the tiny and almost uninhabited island of Heligoland in the North Sea, which England had owned since 1807, with the vast territories changing hands in Africa seems at first sight absurd, but, fortified, it not only commanded the mouths of the rivers Elbe and Weser, but also the western end of the Kiel Canal, which Germany had been building. Germany considered it the key to her future position as a naval power. England, without foreseeing its eventual importance, agreed to cede it to Germany as part of the African negotiations. The transaction gave that nation a grievance for the future in the claim that she had not had her just share in the partition of a continent and a "place in the sun," and also immensely strengthened her military position for both defense and offense.

In the African settlement Austria-Hungary did not participate at all, and Italy was in part balked of what she thought was her prey. She had, with British support, secured her colony of Eritrea and proclaimed a protectorate over a large part of Somaliland, the first bordering on the Red Sea and the latter jutting into the Gulf of Aden, and so both abutting on Britain's shortest route to India. Between and back of these was Abyssinia, the only native Christian and partially civilized state in Africa. After some years of fighting, Italy had made a treaty with the Emperor which she construed as giving her a protectorate over his country, but subsequently the Emperor denounced the treaty, and in renewed fighting the Italian forces were so heavily defeated at Adowa in 1896 that Italy gave up her effort at conquest. Later both Italy and Britain were to guarantee the independence of Abyssinia, but the earlier episode is of interest not only as leading up to Mussolini's conquest, but because in the partition of Africa the Abyssinians were the only race that proved able to beat off the spoilers. Conquest awaited the day of aeroplanes and poison gas, which were among the fruits of European culture in the next century.

The partition was not a mere staking out of claims. It was followed in each case immediately by occupation, administration, and in some cases exploitation. The methods adopted by the different nations varied greatly. They were at their worst in the Belgian Congo, where King Leopold, who had started with high motives, yielded to the desire for rapid wealth and, by means of forced labor and other methods, afforded perhaps the worst example in modern times of the control of a backward by an advanced race. The Belgian Congo was to become an international stench. The French have always got on well with savages and barbarians, and their treatment of the natives was far better than Leopold's, although they were to regard their natives as cannon fodder for war. As they also considered their colonies as closed preserves for French trade only and endeavored by high tariffs to close them to all other, their development was slow. The Germans never made their colonies pay, and with their overemphasized ideas of discipline and efficiency were unduly harsh in their treatment of the blacks, with the result that there were frequent insurrections.

On the whole, although the record of the British is far from being without spot or blemish, I think it may fairly be said theirs was the best and that it was well for Africa that the greater part of it was in British hands. They had had by far the greatest experience of any nation in the administration of subject races under all sorts of conditions, and although they draw the color line in social and marital relations, as the French do not, they have developed a sense of trusteeship with regard to lower races which have come under their flag to an extent which no other people have except the Americans who have followed them. This statement is far from meaning a record of perfection in either case, and is only comparative. On the whole, the uncountable millions in Africa under British control have been reasonably content and have been allowed a greater degree of freedom in living their accustomed lives than under other rule. In addition, the markets of British Africa have been freer to all the world than those controlled by other powers.

The experiment is still comparatively new but in general the overrunning of Africa by Europe may be deemed as a blessing to the natives, who had beyond memory been sunk in the lowest and most cruel and degraded barbarism. The native wars and the slave trade, which formerly took their tolls by millions, have been almost wholly stopped; many horrible customs have been abolished; many tropical diseases conquered by modern medicine; hospitals, schools, and railways and steamboats on the rivers have brought civilization to the jungle; and the natives have learned that wealth may be earned by peaceful industry instead of by plunder in barbarous war. The picture is not without its deep shadows, but if we could look down on the life of the native African from the Cape to Cairo a century ago and again survey the whole human scene today I think that, aside from any profit to European exploiters, there would be seen an immense human profit to the natives themselves.

As in the earlier great period of exploration and exploitation in the sixteenth and seventeenth centuries, the fever which had got into the blood of Europe at the end of the nineteenth led men to all parts of the world. Africa, with its enormous extent, riches, and a population estimated (1920) at 180,000,000, naturally occupies the center of the scene in the division of the world a little more than a generation ago. But the Far East and the islands of the

Pacific were also goals in the international race. Britain obtained a protectorate over the Malay Peninsula, annexed the whole north-east coast of Borneo, and over a hundred islands in the Pacific, many of which were given over to the administration of New Zealand, which thus became an extensive island empire. We shall speak of New Guinea later in connection with Australia. Other nations were also busy, including the United States, which at the time of the Spanish War in 1898 had a brief spasm of imperialism, though the Americans as a people have never cared for overseas possessions or responsibilities.

At the end of the race the world, as well as the Empire, had entered upon a wholly new phase. In the Empire the fervor of imperialism had almost entirely conquered the hesitation of the Gladstonian Liberals to undertake responsibilities or expense for the sake of expansion. Britain, which had been used to a dominant world position and which had as yet scarcely realized, outside of certain high circles, that she was steadily falling behind in comparative figures for world trade, was still successfully competing in the race for new territory. The potentiality of Japanese power was not understood, and China was considered negligible. What counted were the great European powers and the United States.

Of the great powers, as then established, five only owned half the earth by 1899. The British Empire was well in the lead with some 12,000,000 square miles; next came, in succession, Russia with 8,-500,000; the United States with the third largest population but only 3,500,000 square miles; France with 4,500,000; and Germany with only 1,250,000 but a virile and drilled population of 70,-000,000 and developing intense resentment because in a now practically closed world she had not earlier staked out her claims. Heligoland, for which imperial possessions had been sacrificed, now looked insignificant for the moment as a symbol of either power or prestige.

V. Changed European Alignments

Meanwhile a new and important alignment of the European powers among themselves was under way. In trying to write a brief running narrative of the Empire we are limited much as is a biographer who in telling the story of one life cannot write a history of the times, and although foreign policy and the policies of foreign countries naturally were important for the development of the Empire they can be touched upon only lightly. Without going into details, therefore, we must content ourselves with pointing out that so long as he remained in power Bismarck was the center around which the intricate, frequently secret and often immoral system of treaties and alliances revolved.

As a result of Egypt and the consequent hostility of France, Britain, as we have seen, was led to court and back the German Chancellor. His intriguing and secret treaties had built up the Triple Alliance of Germany, Austria-Hungary and Italy, with Russia uncertainly involved by other secret treaties. Troubles in the Balkans, with a remaking of the map in that quarter, enlightened the Czar as to the fact that, in any conflict of interests, Germany would be on the side of the Austrian Emperor and not on his. In the pressure toward the Black Sea and the Dardanelles Austrian and Russian interests were in direct conflict, and Britain, trailing along with the Triple Alliance, feared Russian designs on India. The situation made France and Russia obvious allies, an alliance made all the more necessary after Bismarck's fall in 1890 by the policy of Kaiser William II. Bismarck in 1887 had suggested to Salisbury in a personal letter, in words that sound strange today, that Germany, Austria-Hungary and Britain were now all contented and wholly satisfied powers while France and Russia would be the aggressors. Two years later he asked for an Anglo-German alliance but against France only, it being his belief that Germany could not risk a war on both fronts at once and therefore he must keep on good terms with Russia, though the treaty he had made with that country, and which ran counter to that establishing the Triple Alliance, was unknown at the time. As Russia and not France was considered the greatest potential enemy of Britain, Bismarck had really nothing to offer and Salisbury declined joining the Triple Alliance as a fourth power, though there was for some years a defensive treaty between Britain and Italy.

Although it is not easy to follow the mental windings of Bismarck's diplomacy it may be that he was sincere in describing Germany as satisfied. In a generation a great nation had been welded together, and he himself was supreme in the diplomacy of all Europe. As we have said, he was more interested in seeing the Germany of his creation the most powerful state on the Continent than in world expansion, and he had little or no jealousy of Brittain's world empire. Nor did he dream of the young Emperor William's ambition as expressed in his statement in 1896 that "Germany's future lies on the water." In the close connection which he had cemented between Berlin and Vienna the seeds of Pan-Germanism, which were to blossom into the poison flower of Hitler's "pure race" in our day, had been planted, but if Salisbury did not understand what Bismarck was doing neither did Bismarck himself understand where the forces he had called "from the vasty deep" were to lead his own country under the untutored and inexperienced lead of the young Emperor. But yet in what we have so briefly described, we of today can see the "shape of things to come" already taking form.

Not only was the world divided up so that great empty spaces and unpre-empted riches could no longer afford a safety valve for the ambitions of new nations, but the "concert of Europe" had given place to the two armed camps of the Triple and Dual Alliances with the modern instruments of war and great conscript armies. This was a new world situation, fraught with dire peril. There is an American slang phrase: "all dressed up and nowhere to go," which more or less accurately describes the Europe of 1894–1914. The Old World had been saved from destruction in the earlier colonizing period by the empty spaces on the globe, as, more locally, in America, the West had served as a safety valve for the discontented and rebellious elements in the settled East so long as there was empty and free land.

Now the world was all parcelled out and in Europe there were two jealous alliances of the five great powers, fully armed but with nowhere to go unless they conquered one another, their European satellites or their overseas possessions. If there were to be expansion anywhere in the world, it meant conflict in the heart of Europe itself. Britain, across the narrow channel, maintained its "splendid isolation" for a while, policing the seven seas with her invincible navy, but, as we know now, could not fail to be dragged into any general war which might make some other nation dominant on the Continent or the globe. In trade she was losing rapidly in relation to Germany. The growing German navy, the Kiel Canal, the cession of Heligoland, the young Emperor's dictum quoted above as to the future destiny of his country, went largely unregarded.

VI. India Now a Unified Country

Meanwhile, we have to trace the development in the far parts of the Empire itself. India was now a unified country to an extent it had never been before, and the great triangular peninsula, bounded on both sides by seas on which British naval power was supreme, and on the north by the highest and most impassable mountain range in the world, might have seemed impregnable but there were, so to say, leaks, at both ends south of the Himalayas. In the east, the French advance in Indo-China had forced the Burmese war and the annexation of Upper Burma already mentioned. The Anglo-French clash over Burma, which France coveted although the trade had always been British, was only one of such clashes in this period which helped to breed bad feeling between the two nations. A new Burmese King, Thebaw, under French influence, disregarded previous treaties with Britain, and after imprisoning and monstrously fining British subjects, was forced to resign his throne. The ethical problem of imposing the will of an advanced race upon an inferior one, is, as we have said before, always a difficult one, but if we compare the cruel and atrocious rule of Thebaw with the increase of 20 per cent in population and 50 per cent in cultivated land in the first decade after the British took the country over, there would seem to be a case for "imperialism."

The western "leak" was the wild territory between Afghanistan and India proper through which went the famed Khyber Pass but which was inhabited by the most lawless and unconquerable native tribes in the world. During the period covered by this chapter there were a series of minor tribal wars fought here by the British, who had to employ over 40,000 troops without achieving success, and the settlement of the troubles, if it can be called such, belongs to the later Viceroyalty of Lord Curzon (1899–1905).

That of Lord Ripon (1880–84), calls for special notice, as its period covers perhaps the most important turning point in the history of modern India. The chief defects in British rule during the last part of the nineteenth century may be considered to have been the absence of any definite goal in Anglo-Indian political relations, and the racial feeling which kept the British from employing Indians in the work of government, at least in the higher posts. Lord Roberts probably expressed correctly the feelings of most British in India when he wrote that "It is this consciousness of the inherent superiority of the European which has won for us India. However well educated and clever a native may be, and however brave he may have proved himself, I believe that no rank which we can bestow upon him would cause him to be considered as an equal by the British officer."

Although in general military officers and civil servants shared this view, Viceroys and at times the home government had both advised opening the lists of higher offices to natives. The failure to do so, as well as memories of the Mutiny, and the growth of the European bureaucracy, resulted in creating practically a new caste in India, at the top of all, "the White Brahmins," *i.e.*, the British. The effect was bad on both races. The educated natives, even though they were but one wave in the vast ocean of native population, naturally resented such an attitude as that of Lord Roberts, often even more bluntly expressed and in any case excluding them from any worth-while public career. On the other hand, the small number of the British governing class developed those ingrowing qualities apt to appear in any small group which is in authority or considers itself superior to all about them. They tended to become small-minded, snobbish in the worst sense, and, worst of all for India, stagnant in their work of administration.

Ripon, however, realized that there must be some end toward which British control was working, that well on to 300,000,000 people could not be permanently kept in subjection by less than 100,000 alien rulers. He foresaw eventually the demand for some sort of local responsible government, along modern democratic lines. As he properly believed that crisis must some day arise, he boldly attempted to prepare India for it. Whether his reforms were too sudden or not may be open to question but what is not is that some such development would in time be inevitable.

One of Ripon's first acts was to reverse his predecessor, Lord Lytton, who had muzzled the vernacular press owing to the violent attacks it had been making on the government and on British control in general. Although the educated and even the literate part of the population was only a small fraction of the whole, a free vernacular press was to be of enormous influence in forwarding the nationalist movement which dates from this period in its modern form. Another step in the democratic process was taken by Ripon in the setting up of local self-government in the shape of District Boards in municipalities and rural areas with the idea of giving the natives training in administration. These, however, were more or less nullified and blocked for a quarter of a century by the Indian bureaucracy and the home government.

Still another proposed reform was connected with the administration of justice. In India Europeans had had the right to be tried by British magistrates only, but in 1883 Ripon proposed to do away with this privilege and to abolish the distinction between British and native magistrates. Feeling was so strong that the bill which had been introduced in the Legislature had to be withdrawn, but the result of the controversy was greatly to embitter racial opposition. The British had been enraged at the suggestion of placing them at the judicial mercy of natives, and the natives felt that the withdrawal of the plan was an insult to themselves.

More important was Lord Ripon's educational program. Hitherto Indian education had been almost wholly in the hands of

269

government or the missionaries, but under the new system the number of students was increased and both schools and colleges were placed largely under native control. It is true that in proportion to the population, which was increasing by about 10,000,000 each decade, the next twenty years may not have increased the percentage of literates, but the number of college students was nearly doubled, and the combined effect of the number of leaders educated under native influences, with the vernacular press, was profound on the Nationalist movement. Also in spite of the use of native languages, the increasing knowledge of English had for the first time given the educated classes a common medium of communication in all parts of the country. The daily and weekly newspapers began now to play a great part, such as *The Hindoo Patriot, The Bengalee, The Maratha,* and others.

The vast mass of the population was reasonably content, but a foreign governing class must in time inevitably arouse opposition and nationalist aspirations on the part of the governed, and there were several groups in India who resented domination and whose members were seeking careers for themselves on a par with the outsiders. In the 1880's a politically minded middle class, which believed that a "white collar job" was the right of any educated person of the higher castes, and who were offended by the attitude of superiority assumed by the British, began to organize opposition. At first, under the lead of such men as Gokhale, they were occupied chiefly with moderate reforms and content with a slow rate of change, much as were the Liberals in England. The first of the Indian National Congresses, which were to have so great an influence later, held in 1885, was essentially a meeting of Moderates. The members were not politically elected representatives from districts, but voluntary attendants representing many local organizations of all shades of opinion. The progress of the annual meetings was slow, and in the early days the resolutions passed and demands made were of a mild nature, largely such as asking for rights similar to those granted in the self-governing colonies.

Although the programs were inspired chiefly by Western ideas there were also strong currents of religion and race, and the streams

of Westernism and anti-Westernism met and swirled tumul-
tuously as time went on. Such leaders as Swami Vivekananda and
Saraswati taught the superiority of Indian civilization to that of
Europe and demanded a return to primitive Indian thought and
ways. The mass of Indians was largely untouched by the movement, and among the educated who knew about it there was much
diversity of opinion. There were those who believed in the West
and those who decried it; those who were loyal to the British and
those who wished to throw the hated foreigners out. Aside from
the attitudes toward the outside world, as always in the welter of
races and religions which make up India, there were internal differences.

As Nationalism grew stronger, however, the Moderates lost
control and the Congresses came more and more to represent the
more violent anti-Western elements. In some of the native peri-
odicals, lying propaganda of the worst sort and extreme Nationalism swayed the minds of increasing numbers. In Bombay an Indian, Tilak, who founded the paper *Kesari*, voiced the belief of
many that the propaganda in the struggle was that of war time and
that no statements made need be true. The result was as usual, the
dissemination of a great mass of misinformation and the growth
of unreasoning hatred. In 1896 the unrest already existing was
increased by drought, famine and a severe epidemic of the bubonic
plague, and a new phase of the anti-foreign campaign began with
the assassination of two young Englishmen who were fighting the
plague at Poona.

The English hatred of violence, and especially of secret and
cowardly violence, is something which those peoples who believe in
the efficacy of "frightfulness" seem never to be able to take into
account. So far from frightening the English it merely stiffens
their backs and hurts the causes for which those who employ the
method may be fighting. The increase in political assassination in
India belongs in the next period, but that country was obviously
on the eve of great changes, though the conflict, as in Japan, between the parties—that which wished to develop on Western lines
and that which wished to keep to the old ways and culture—was

obscured for a while in a common opposition to the mere fact of foreign influence or domination.

In 1892 the British tried to make an effort toward leading India on the way which the colonies had travelled toward self-government by admitting a certain number of natives as representatives in the legislative Councils, but as was shown in the case of the early American colonies and in the discussion of Imperial Federation, mere representation in a body in which the representatives are a small minority to be outvoted at any moment can be no solution of the problem. The only case, I think, in which such an arrangement has been peacefully accepted has been that of the continental Territories of the United States, which have been represented in Congress by one member who cannot vote, but in that case territorial status, with the handicaps which go with it, has always been recognized as constitutionally merely a stage on the way to full statehood when certain conditions as to population and so on have been complied with.

VII. The Stability of Canada

We must now turn to the other side of the world and the first Dominion of the Empire, Canada. Each of the great self-governing colonies, a term which as applied to them was to disappear after the end of the century, had developed a character of its own. In Canada there was little of the Socialism and radical social experimenting which were to be so characteristic of Australia and New Zealand. Canada, indeed, has shown a marked stability combined with progress. This has been indicated in part by her political history. Not only in the Dominion Government, but in those of many of the Provinces, the Ministries have been of very unusual length. Sir John Macdonald was in power as head of the Conservative Party from 1878 until he died in 1891, and the Party itself continued to govern for five years more. The Liberals who came in under the lead of Laurier in 1896 remained in office until 1911.

Canada, with its vast expanse and resources, was intent on its own development, and with its chiefly small-farming population, wealth was fairly equally distributed. The main differences in opinion between the classical Liberal and Conservative Parties were economic, the Conservatives favoring protection, whereas the Liberals inclined to free trade or low duties. There were other economic issues, such as those connected with the building of railways, but there was no Labor Party and almost none of the cleavage between labor and capital which was beginning to show in England and which was already so prominent in Australia and New Zealand.

When the Dominion had been formed, British Columbia had been promised, in 1871, that a transcontinental railway would be built within ten years, but due to the inertia of the Mackenzie government only 300 miles had been built at the end of the stipulated period. In 1880 Macdonald and several of his collaborators went to England to interest British capital and succeeded. A syndicate was formed, later known as the Canadian Pacific Railway Company, of which the leading members were George Stephen (later Lord Mount Stephen), Sir John Rose, James J. Hill, a Canadian who was afterward better known as a great railway builder and magnate in the United States, and Donald A. Smith, who was to become Lord Strathcona. As in the United States, the terms offered by the government to those who dared to risk their money in building transcontinental lines, several thousand miles in length through mostly uninhabited territory, had to be very liberal in the eyes of some at the time and of later generations who think of the country and traffic as they became subsequently and not of the wilderness waste in which tens of millions had to be sunk.

Opposition developed, and another company, with less assured backing, offered to accept lower terms, but finally the Canadian Pacific syndicate was allowed to begin operations, and in 1885, less than five years after they began, the road was completed to the coast, although they had to ask the government for two additional loans, aggregating $27,500,000. In due course these were repaid. Macdonald may be considered as one of the builders of greater Canada, even though it may be true that he was primarily a politician rather than a statesman. One critic has said that he spent much time on thinking how to retain power but perhaps never a half dozen hours on how to build the Northwest or to stop the steady exodus to the United States. This seems hardly fair, for at the crisis of the affairs of the railway, on which the union of Canada from the Atlantic to the Pacific largely depended, and when its fate hung on the last $5,000,000 to be borrowed from a reluctant government, Macdonald forced his followers to agree to the loan, and the enterprise was saved. In a young country, as Americans can bear witness, politics tend to become a trade. Without social ranks or inherited wealth, most people are too busy climbing the economic ladder to care much about the usually ill-paid political offices. If Macdonald was primarily a politician it was largely because he had to be one with the material he had to work with, but he organized a great party, saved the Canadian Pacific Railway, and was the initiator of the policy of protection for Canadian industry. The Canada of today is largely the result of his work and policies.

During the period now under consideration, protection was particularly important as directed against the impact of the United States. The Canadian Liberals, during most of the time, were inclined to an economic union of the two countries under a joint tariff or a reciprocity agreement which would have had much the same effect. Macdonald, however, sensed the general feeling of Canadians that they did not want that result and, as has been proved ever since, to the satisfaction of themselves and of the Americans, they preferred their own national independence within the British Commonwealth of Nations. That dual status entails plenty of complications, and because the Canadians and the Americans divide almost the entire North American continent between them their relations are peculiarly close. As we have already pointed out, Canada has not only the protection afforded by the Empire, but also that of the United States, which would never allow a foreign country to conquer a neighbor occupying more than one half of the continent on which it is itself dominant. The question was more open in the 1890's, and there were somewhat acrimonious and prolonged controversies over such matters as the seal fisheries in Bering Sea and the fisheries on the east coast which, with new differences, were not to be settled until after the turn of the century. The ordinary citizens of both nations, however, were being drawn more and more into the orbits of their own nationalisms and becoming less and less inclined to desire either a peaceful union or one by force. Canada was rapidly growing up to the belief, later expressed by Kipling that

"Daughter am I in my mother's house,
But mistress in mine own."

On the other hand the earlier occasional demands by small groups in the United States for annexation had faded out entirely. As far as nations are concerned, Canada and the United States were to become neighboring households living on exceptional terms of friendliness with one another and affording an example to the entire world of what such an international relationship could mean. Whatever expenses the two nations may incur for armaments, neither spends a cent on defense or offense against the other.

Macdonald would have been glad to retire from public life in 1885 when he was past seventy and had achieved all he wished to, but a second rebellion had broken out in Northwestern Canada under Riel, the leader of the earlier insurrection. The building of the Canadian Pacific had aroused fears among the Indians and half-breeds, and the government had been lacking in tact in handling the situation. Riel put himself at the head of the movement, and when captured was hanged. The revolt in itself had not been of much importance, but Riel had French blood and was a Catholic, and his sentence was utilized to stir up racial and religious questions again by the Liberal Party with Edward Blake at its head. Probably the most important consequence of the whole affair was that in the election of 1887 the Liberals were defeated, though not heavily, and Blake resigned the leadership of the party, opening the way for one of Canada's ablest men, Wilfrid Laurier. Although French and Catholic he was to win the confidence of those of both races and both religions, and by his superb command of both languages, his clear mind, great ability, and courtly manners were to be reckoned among the dominant forces in the new Empire now developing. In 1896 he was made Prime Minister of the Dominion and held office during critical years, supported by possibly the ablest group of men Canada has ever had in one Cabinet, to whom we shall return later.

Perhaps his dearest ambition was to unite the two races, French and British, in a harmony of hearts and of purely Canadian patriotism. Toward the end of his life, through circumstances beyond his control, a cleavage was again to come, and he took the side of his own blood, but so long as he was himself in office Canada was singularly free from the racial animosities of before and after. French and British remained the two great groups, but, as the prairies were settled, there was considerable racial mixture as contrasted with Australia and New Zealand, although Canada was never to be the melting pot which the United States became nor to have the native problem of South Africa. There did come, however, Jews from many lands, as well as Swedes, Norwegians, Icelanders, Germans, Russians, Ruthenians, Hungarians, and many others. In the fourteen years after 1897, under a government-fostered immigration policy for the purpose of filling up the great empty spaces, the number of newcomers received annually rose steadily from about 20,000 at the beginning to a third of a million by 1911, while the outward flow to the United States had become heavily reversed.

American capital, however, continued to be invested in Canada in large amounts, and, with increasing business between the two countries, Canada has become one of the most important links in the chain of understanding between America and the Empire as a whole. If Canada is the eldest daughter of Britain among the Dominions she is, in a sense also, a younger sister of the United States on the continent they share. In 1895, when Mr. Olney, the American Secretary of State, sent an unexpected and wholly tactless note to Lord Salisbury with regard to a boundary dispute between Venezuela and British Guiana, it was evident to most Americans that the words almost inexplicably used by Olney could not apply to the possessions, such as Canada, already a part of the

Empire. The whole incident, with its sudden threat of war, averted by the calm statesmanship of Salisbury, probably brought about, with the sigh of relief with which the settlement of the question by arbitration was ended, a better understanding on the part of even isolationist Americans of what the Empire meant. A large share in the improved knowledge came from the example so near at hand of our peaceful neighbor over our northern boundary. If Britain suddenly realized that war with the United States was almost unthinkable owing to the close ties between them, so Americans realized that a war with Canada would be equally so.

VIII. THE BOLD EXPERIMENT IN NEW ZEALAND

One of the most fascinating aspects of British imperial history is the extreme diversity which has been allowed within its loose but thoroughly substantial unity. Passing from Canada to New Zealand we find an amazing contrast. Like its elder sister, New Zealand was indeed a country still chiefly inhabited by small land-holders using their lands for farming or grazing and with a comparatively negligible industrial or labor problem. Nevertheless, the most striking feature of New Zealand history, especially after the depressed years of the two decades or so before 1895, was the bold experimentation of its statesmen, especially Richard Seddon, who was Prime Minister 1893–1906, with social legislation of the most advanced type. When the Liberals came into power in 1891, the trades-unions had begun to put up Labor candidates, and the Seddon Ministry favored the unions and labor legislation to a remarkable extent in a predominantly agricultural country.

Most of the experimenting of this period and a few years after appears to have had for its object the use of governmental machinery to maintain a high standard of living for the people, together with the prevention of great differences in wealth as between individuals, and the maintenance of a pure race. Although trades-unions were favored, strikes were frowned upon, and Conciliation Boards, composed of representatives of both capital and labor, were established to settle industrial differences without violence. Should they fail to do so, the cases went to the National

Arbitration Court, which could arbitrarily settle all questions of hours, wages and other points in dispute, both parties having to accept the decisions under severe penalties for not observing them. While this interesting and bold experiment, among a people even more independently British than the homekeeping British themselves, has not wholly succeeded it has done so to a large extent, and the decisions in general have been very favorable to labor. Wages were kept high, helped in part by a high tariff which likewise provided some of the heavy taxation called for by other experiments.

Several of these had to do with the prevention of the accumulation of large fortunes. The small landowner, up to 500 acres, was not taxed at all on his land, whereas the progressive tax on larger holdings made their ownership, especially if lying idle, very costly. In addition there were special municipal taxes on unimproved property in urban districts, as well as progressive income taxes and heavy inheritance taxes on large estates.

All these and other devices, such as renting Crown lands instead of selling them, government ownership of railways, coal mines and other utilities and resources, together with old-age pensions, placed experimental New Zealand in this period in strong contrast with conservative Canada and the slow-moving mother country. Again, in order to maintain living standards at the expense of rapid development, New Zealand took a course precisely the opposite of Canada's and instead of stimulating immigration legislated largely to prevent it, even from the British Isles. Asiatics and Polynesians were excluded in 1899. We have already spoken of intermarriage with the Maoris, and it is rather odd that the group of British which has taken the most pains to keep the race pure is the only one which has accepted the natives on a basis of social equality, even allowing for the extraordinarily high type of the original savages they encountered.

With all the efforts to maintain a high, if more or less evenly balanced, standard of living the local industries would not have allowed of it had it not been for an invention which developed entirely new industries and made the declining sheep ranching into practically a new one also. The development of refrigeration changed the whole scene; and the long depression was followed by the rapid development of the later 80's and 90's, which permitted the social legislation. The first ship to carry frozen meat to England sailed in 1882, and although much experimenting had to be done and prejudices overcome, the opening of the home and foreign markets to New Zealand meats and other products such as butter and cheese made a complete transformation in the life of the islands. One of the important results was, in time, to be the dominance of the dairying interest and the small farmer, the diffusion of population, the absence of large cities, the decline in the labor movement, the change from two sharply divided and hostile classes of great and small landowners, and a whole economic and political system and outlook quite unlike that of Australia. Whether these results have all been good socially we shall have to leave for later comment, but we may here note that it was not the small farmers but the wealthy landowners who in the 80's had the money and the initiative and showed the courage to experiment with the refrigeration from which the whole population was later to derive its standard of living and its large increase in aggregate wealth.

IX. THE LABOR MOVEMENT IN AUSTRALIA

During all of this period, until the federation in 1900, Australia remained a geographical expression with six distinct colonies around the coast. Before discussing briefly the story of these we may note their relations with some of the Pacific islands, which throw an interesting sidelight on the growth of the Empire. To the northeast of the Australian continent, separated from it only by Torres Strait, lies New Guinea, the second largest island in the world if we consider Greenland the largest. Its size, close proximity and supposed great natural wealth made it an object of interest to the Australian colonies, particularly those on the east coast. In the 1860's and 70's several of them had tried to induce the British Government to annex the island but without success. New Zealand, some 1200 miles away, cared nothing for the project, having her eyes on other islands nearer home. The administration of the Fijis had cost Britain more than had been expected and, as the Australian colonies avowed themselves unable to support or even contribute to that of New Guinea, the government at home, in a period of imperial retrenchment, refused to have anything to do with further Pacific expansion. Meanwhile, Australia became anxious to secure for the future other groups of islands which she considered as lying within her eventual sphere of influence, such as the New Hebrides.

There are a number of interesting points to be noted in the long discussions and procrastination shown in enlarging imperial possessions in the Pacific. One is that though Britain has come to own a quarter of the globe she has not been the insatiable grabber of lands which she is sometimes said to have been. The Empire has grown piecemeal from all sorts of local causes and in all sorts of ways, extension having sometimes been willing and sometimes most unwilling. The Empire, indeed, has been somewhat in the position of a great landowner who may not want more acres but here and there finds himself forced by circumstances to add to his holdings to protect what he already has. Not only this factor but many others, such as protection of established trades in lands which if annexed by other nations would be closed to the British who had opened them, varying in each case, have been the moving causes which have brought about the immense spread of British imperial rule. In such expansion the interest of one part of the Empire has sometimes had to be sacrificed to another, as in the classic example of the lost American colonies.

Another pertinent point is that just as the Empire as a whole has been forced to expand, so portions of it have tended to become little empires within the larger one. This has been the case with both New Zealand and Australia, which have developed their British civilizations far from the rest of the Empire and have had to watch with a jealous eye the acquisition by foreign nations of bases or colonies from which, without great military resources of their own, they might be attacked.

This was particularly true in the case of Australia and New

Guinea. Both France, which had the habit of closing to others colonial markets in its possession, and Germany were feared by the British in the Antipodes, but the home government did not take the menace seriously. Suddenly, in German fashion, in December, 1884, the bomb burst when Bismarck informed the British Government that the Germans had taken possession of New Guinea. If the Gladstone government was unwarrantably surprised, the Australians were furious. In vain Gladstone reminded Bismarck that the northern part of the island had been reserved for a general settlement of Pacific problems. Bismarck admitted that there had been a "misunderstanding," but insisted on retaining what he had seized, and finally Britain had to give way, agreeing that the Germans should have the north coast and they would be content with the south, facing Australia.

Once again Gladstone had been worsted in imperial policy and for the same reason—Egypt. "It is really impossible," he wrote to Granville, "to exaggerate the importance of getting out of the way the bar to the Egyptian settlement," and as part of the price paid for Germany's friendship in Egypt as against the hostility of France, Germany received in that and the immediately following years, half of New Guinea and a considerable colonial expansion elsewhere in the Pacific. New Zealand, which had pressed her claims to Samoa and the Tonga Islands, was asked to abandon them and to recognize "the good claims of a great friendly power." The naïve trust placed in Germany by successive British governments, in spite of Bismarck, the Kaiser and Hitler, is one of the most curious threads running through British foreign policy for a considerable part of the past two generations.

Although there were local differences among the six Australian colonies the uniformities were far more noticeable, especially after gold was discovered in the desert of sparsely settled Western Australia, and the colony grew so rapidly in population as to be self-governing by 1890. In general the course of development was so similar fundamentally in the various colonies that although not united till 1900, we need not attempt to describe the course of affairs in each, but may speak of general Australian characteristics.

One of the most notable of these as contrasted with Canada or New Zealand was the fact that for a new country, and one still largely agricultural, grazing and mining, an exceptionally large part of the population was gathered into the larger cities, such as Sydney, Melbourne, Brisbane and Adelaide. The result was that, in contrast with New Zealand in particular, the political life of the country was dominated by the industrial instead of the farming citizens. Trade-unions were very strong, but for a time, when the deep depression of the 90's succeeded the somewhat false prosperity of the 80's, there was constant use of the strike instead of conciliation. We have already noted the intense enthusiasm of the Australian unions in the cause of the London dockers in 1889, and the following year there was an almost universal strike in Australia, including even the sheep shearers on the ranches.

Although there were additional ones during the decade, which was one of the most disastrous in Australia's history, they were not in general successful. Several years of drought, an almost complete collapse of credit and stoppage of immigration, due in part to legislation and in part to lack of faith in Australian opportunities, made a background for revolution perhaps but not for success in the use of strikes. True to national instinct the Australians turned naturally to the method of legislation. By 1891 a Labor Party had appeared in New South Wales, always one of the more · radical states, and was soon followed by the formation of the same party in the other colonies. From the first the party has been developed strictly on class lines and the labor conflicts have been notably bitter. In South Australia it was even ruled by the party that none but manual laborers could belong to it. Outside of the cities, where there were loose organizations of skilled workmen, the nationwide organizations, such as the Australian Workers Union made up of migratory sheep shearers, tended heavily to lower the intellectual standard of a movement which in England had been started and controlled by the more intelligent labor wing. The party was also at first so organized as to prevent any free discussion among its members of its policies, to which all members had to pledge themselves in advance as determined upon by the leaders. Although around the turn of the century both in the separate states and in the then newly formed Commonwealth, labor legislation to some extent modelled itself on the lines of the Conciliation Boards of New Zealand, the Labor Party in Australia tended to be narrow, uncompromising and bitter. Its attitude had not a little to do with the growing reluctance of foreigners to invest capital, and so with the financial and commercial collapse of the 90's.

X. The Diamond Jubilee

The story of final federation belongs in the next chapter, to which we may also defer the events in South Africa in this period, as they form the immediate prelude to the Boer War and may be better considered in that connection. Jameson's raid, however, had already occurred and it was realized that war clouds were gathering when Queen Victoria celebrated her Diamond Jubilee in 1897. The same glorious pageantry was enacted as ten years before, but the enthusiastic imperialism and optimism of the earlier occasion had to some extent evaporated. Many had begun to feel the more sordid side of imperialism, which had been marked in the scramble by all nations and which some of the British felt, as in South Africa, was tarnishing their own Empire. The Queen, who had now reigned for sixty years, was old and feeble, and her end could not be far off. The nation felt instinctively that an epoch as well as a century was drawing to a close and there was foreboding as to what the next might bring to pass. The anxiety would have been replaced by horror could the full vision of the next generation have been vouchsafed to the crowds who loyally acclaimed the worn and frail old Queen driving slowly from the Palace to the Abbey to lead the nation in thanksgiving.

Even the Empire seemed less united than it had ten years before. Advantage was taken of the presence of Prime Ministers from eleven colonies to hold another Imperial Conference, but the decade had made it clear that uniting the Empire involved apparently insoluble problems and more than the emotions of 1887. Three methods of bringing about closer union had now been discussed for some years, and at the Conference, presided over by the Colonial Secretary, Chamberlain, he advocated his own method, which was imperial federation with some sort of central representative body, but the colonies had been coming more and more to pride themselves on their growing self-sufficiency and their local self-governments. They feared some diminution of these should an Imperial Parliament be set up, and the plan was buried under a Resolution which merely stated that "the present political relations between the United Kingdom and the self-governing colonies are generally satisfactory under the existing condition of things."

Nor were other approaches to unity more successful. The first had been political. The second was military. The question of sharing in the cost and other burdens of imperial defense has been an unsolved problem from the earliest days of the first Empire and has not been solved yet. The Admiralty stressed the necessity of a single imperial fleet, under a single command but supported to some extent proportionately by all the colonies as well as the United Kingdom. Other than Cape Colony, which offered to give one first-class battleship, and the Australian colonies, which offered a small grant in cash, the feelings of localism and separatism were too strong and no colony would commit itself to any definite program. Finally, the economic approach yielded little more than the others. Chamberlain's idea of an imperial *Zollverein*, based somewhat on German precedent, left the colonies cold, while their own scheme of Imperial Preference raised too many difficulties to make it practical.

The Conference, however, was by no means a failure. The mere gathering in itself, including such men as Laurier of Canada, Seddon of New Zealand, Reid of Australia and the others, was a significant event in the development of the Empire. In the usual British fashion they were groping their way, instead of attempting to establish new institutions by resolutions. One resolution, however, that to have the Conferences held at intervals in the future instead of being casual meetings depending on some event such as the Jubilees, did go far to make an imperial institution through which there has developed slowly means for much closer understanding between the home and the colonial and Dominion governments. In spite of the refusals to accept any ready-made plans for closer union, the unity of Empire was growing, as the events of both the Boer War and the World War were indubitably to prove.

CHAPTER XIII

THE REACTION FROM IMPERIALISM

I. THE BOER WAR

AT THE very end of the century there was to be a great crisis in the Empire. It was more dangerous than even the Indian Mutiny, because it threatened to divide the English people and their power at a time when they stood isolated without a single ally in a hostile world. It did result in a serious cleavage of opinion among the most sober-minded Englishmen on the subject of imperialism little more than a decade before they had to sail into the hurricane of the World War as a united nation. For some time many Englishmen, especially among the Liberals, had been seriously searching their hearts as to the ethical aspects of the new type of imperialism which the international rush for empire had brought into being.

We speak casually of British, French, Germans, Americans and others as though they all belonged to a single stereotype of character and thought. Of course they do not. Biological analysis and careless thinking mislead us. From one standpoint individuals are the cells of the national body but unlike the cells of a physical organism they differ among themselves immensely in opinion and outlook. The cells of a biological organism do make a stereotype, but not those of a nation. A lion of today is precisely like a lion of a century ago but the essentially peace-loving "France" of today is quite unlike the "France" of Napoleon's time. In telling the story of any nation we have to bear such differences in mind. In

England the drift toward imperialism had already received a severe set-back when the news of Jameson's raid on the Transvaal confirmed what had come to be the opinion of an influential part of the British nation. It marked dramatically a change in national thought. To understand it and the events flowing from it we have to go back a few years prior to the end of the previous chapter.

We have already spoken of the character of Paul Kruger and of the Transvaal Boers. Old "Oom Paul" was a dictator but there was a good deal of opposition among the more progressive of his subjects, though in general the civilization and level of culture were still those of the seventeenth century. The whole situation, however, had been changed by the discovery of gold in 1884 and in 1886 of the gold-field of the Witwatersrand, still after forty-odd years of exploitation the richest gold deposit in the world. It was stated only the other day (1939) that the gold still in the ground there exceeded the huge hoard held in the United States, more than half the mined supply of the globe.

At once the gold rush brought into the Transvaal a huge immigration, chiefly of British and Australians. The government, from a condition of bankruptcy, suddenly became wealthy and in a position to equip itself for modern war. The simple farming population of the seventeenth century found itself plunged into the power politics of the most sordid and imperialistic financial period of the late nineteenth. Briefly, the foreigners had in a decade built cities—Johannesburg from a hamlet had grown to 100,000 by 1896—and threatened all the old ways of life, including the supremacy of Kruger, shrewd, narrow and stubborn. The Boers themselves were supposed to have defeated him for the presidency in 1893, but in spite of the belief that there had been a deliberate miscount of votes he was declared elected by a small majority. He was still in power and able to enforce his policies.

These had included not allowing any votes, even in municipal elections, to the foreigners who had made the wealth of the country, and who, although they were heavily taxed at his will, were allowed no voice in government. Even their children, almost wholly British, were required to be taught only in the Dutch language

in the schools supported by British industry and taxes. The 100,-
000 British in the almost wholly British-made and British-popu-
lated city of Johannesburg and the thousands elsewhere in the
country were in the hands of this one old man, whom even his own
people wished to throw over, and who employed Dutch and German agents to assist him in making the most of the wealth the
British had developed. These conditions, which irked the more
progressive Boers, naturally appeared intolerable to the British,
who were practically not allowed to become even citizens and were
merely used as milch cows.

Meanwhile, stubborn and strong-willed as Kruger was, there
was another man in South Africa who was equally so. In the history of empire the figure of Cecil Rhodes will always loom large,
in spite of his mistakes. If he phrased the leading principle of
what should guide the empire building of his day as "philanthropy plus 5 per cent" and seemed at times to be wholly possessed by the desire to acquire the vast riches which came to be
his, nevertheless he was not merely acquisitive but the dreamer
of vast imperial dreams. Wealth for him was an essential lever
to power, not an end in itself. Possibly the main flaw in his thought
was that with that lever he could accomplish anything, though
his ambitions were for the Empire and not for himself. In his
somewhat clumsy way he fumbled with the belief in the divine
mission of the British race, and devoted himself and his wealth
to forwarding it. For a while, as the dominant figure in the
Kimberley diamond fields, in mines, as Managing Director and
practical dictator of the British South Africa Company, and as
Premier of Cape Colony, he moulded the destinies of the southern part of the vast continent through which he dreamed of an
all-red strip from the Mediterranean to the Cape and of his Cape
to Cairo Railway, British owned on British soil.

When the racial question was acute Rhodes believed in equality
between the Dutch and British as the only solution and formed an
alliance with Hofmeyer, leader of the Afrikander Bund in the
Cape Colony. He also took an active interest in education and the
fair settlement of the native problem. In Cape Colony not only

were the Dutch and British in possession of equal political rights but the blacks also had the franchise. That Colony and Natal and the Orange Free State united during his term of office in a customs union, and with the development of the territory under control of his South Africa Company, named Rhodesia in his honor, he hemmed in the backward Transvaal.

There the foreigners, called Uitlanders by the Boers, had become desperate. Rhodes firmly believed that the future of the South African empire which he had in mind could be achieved only by the hearty union of Dutch and British under the lead of the latter, and that he himself was the one destined to accomplish this result. Of his great practical ability in affairs there can be no question. He had also many of the qualities of the great statesman, but he lacked one essential—patience. He was always making wills, embodying his ideas (of which the Foundation for the Rhodes Scholarships was one), and was haunted by the thought of the brevity of life.

It was this trait which caused him to make the great mistake of his life. He was impatient at the intransigence of the Kruger regime, which seemed to be blocking his plans. The Uitlanders planned an armed rising against the Boer Government to force the righting of their grievances. Rhodes unfortunately lent himself to these plans, and his friend Doctor Jameson, administrator of Rhodesia, was to hold himself in readiness at the border to rush in to the help of the Uitlanders when they rose in Johannesburg and Pretoria. Aside from the madness of the scheme the timing went all awry, and the rising did not take place as planned. In spite of this and a countermanding of orders by Rhodes, Jameson and his small force crossed the border on what could be considered only as a feeble and unjustified attack by British on a nominally friendly power. The force was ignominiously routed, captured and the leaders of the proposed insurrection arrested.

The cards were now in old Kruger's hands. Rhodes, whose implication was beyond question, at once resigned as Premier of the Cape and his political career was at an end, as well as his statesmanlike dream of a union of races. The Boers of the Transvaal again rallied around their President, and gained the sympathy of their fellow racial elements in the Cape and the Orange Free State. Rhodes went to London to face a Parliamentary enquiry, which was handled in a way to increase Dutch suspicions. We shall speak of Anglo-German relations later in this chapter, but may here note that the Kaiser sent a cablegram to Kruger which the latter interpreted as meaning he could count on German help.

The Jameson forces had been defeated January 2, 1896, and the conditions rapidly deteriorated in the next three years. The Dutch had now been largely united against, and not with, the British. Kruger by means of his taxation of the British people and industries in the Transvaal had the means with which to arm heavily and with modern weapons. In January, 1899, about 21,000 British subjects in that country petitioned the Queen for a redress of their grievances, including the lack of equal political rights for all white men such as existed in every British colony.

The laxity of wording of the Convention of London, already alluded to, now made itself felt. Just what the relations were between Britain and the Kruger government had been left uncertain. The British Ministry did not feel it could interfere with the domestic affairs of the Transvaal and yet was unwilling to admit Kruger's entire independence. There was a deadlock. Kruger, believing in German help and practically certain of the aid of the Free State, felt sure he was more powerful than the British, and demanded in an ultimatum that the British withdraw all armed forces from the neighborhood of the Transvaal within forty-eight hours. Britain realized that it had blundered into a serious war, though how serious it did not yet recognize. The curtain had fallen on the first act of one of the most disastrous dramas in the history of the Empire, though the mistakes were to be nobly retrieved before the end.

In spite of the series of Imperial Conferences the real strength of the Empire in a crisis was still unknown. There were the United Kingdom, India, and a group of globe-encircling self-governing Dominions and other colonies. Otherwise Great Britain had worked herself into a position of complete isolation. She did not have a friend or ally in the world. What would the loose agglomeration of "possessions" scattered round the earth mean to her? Would they prove assets or liabilities in the then nebulous constitutional and sentimental relations subsisting and amid a world of enemies? Those were questions to which the men of Britain could find no sure answer as they faced the situation, and we may pause here a moment to trace briefly the causes of Britain's isolation.

II. BRITAIN'S ISOLATION

These were partly moral, if we can still use such a word in speaking of international relations, and partly political. In the New World Britain had nothing to fear. There had been, as we have seen, a marked reaction in the United States from the temporary asperity of the Olney Venezuelan incident, much helped by the obviously friendly attitude of England in the Spanish-American War. Anglo-American relations had never been so good since long before the two countries had separated in the eighteenth century. But it must be recalled that if a quite considerable proportion of the British themselves, with the smell of the Jameson raid still in their nostrils, regarded the Boer War as forced on a small white nation merely because it stood in the way of imperial advance, the same impression might much more readily be made on nationals of other countries who thought Britain always ready to pay more attention to the "5 per cent" than to the "philanthropy" of Rhodes' phrase. Americans were at the moment going through a certain phase of self-righteousness because of their having given Cuba to the Cubans and paid $20,000,000 to Spain for the Philippines and Puerto Rico in spite of their easy victory over that decadent nation. There was a feeling across the Atlantic that England was playing a rather dirty game and that her fight against the Boers was a sample of *fin-de-siècle* commercial imperialism at about its worst. But there was nothing to fear from America.

In Europe it was different. Britain has for long had to play a difficult dual role. From one standpoint her policy must be that of an island center of a world-flung empire with practically no possessions in Europe. From another, owing to the fact that she is only twenty miles from the European continent she must be affected by the power and alignments of the great nations there which not only covet her outlying possessions but are such close neighbors as to make a thrust at her heart, the home island of Great Britain, a possibility. How great that threat is at present is indicated by the fact that the British Prime Minister takes his daily walk with a gas mask slung on his back. Before the present generation and the day of planes and aerial bombs the navy could hold the narrow seas, but even so the Continental powers could exert tremendous and threatening influence on British policy.

As the crisis of the Boer War impended, the five great powers were lined up in the two groups of the Dual Alliance—France and Russia—and the Triple Alliance—Germany, Austria-Hungary and Italy. Britain was wholly isolated. She could try either to re-establish the concert of Europe, that is the six great powers interested in European questions working together by the method of conference and peaceful settlement of disputes, or ally herself to one or the other group as seemed most promising.

Both methods failed and the only alternative left was to try to negotiate standing disputes and points of friction at a disadvantage. Problems in Armenia, Crete and elsewhere showed how difficult that would prove. Russia was thinking of a push toward the Mediterranean which would give her a "warm water" port, and Germany was beginning to dream of both naval supremacy and the *Drang nach Osten*, which would allow her to control the Near East. The Berlin-Bagdad Railway plan was an ominous portent. Should Russia be allowed to control Constantinople or the Germans the Persian Gulf? These were merely some of the problems which deeply affected British lines of communication.

Germany, whom practically alone British policy had counted on to maintain her position in Egypt, was becoming restive. The Kaiser was thinking in terms of the navy and overseas empire. In the middle of 1897 Admiral von Tirpitz had become Minister of Marine and lent himself whole-heartedly to a great increase in the navy. The first thing picked up on the road to the new German

Empire was Kiao-Chow in China. Russia followed by appropriating Port Arthur in Manchuria. Britain approached the German Emperor for an alliance under terms of strictest secrecy, and the Kaiser promptly betrayed the negotiations to the Russian Czar.

The Czar, however, proposed a conference, held May and June, 1899, to which all governments were invited, to reduce armaments and revise the rules of war. Except possibly Russia no nation in Europe really wanted limitation of armaments, and Britain killed the proposal of the United States for immunity of private property on the high seas. The only result of the meeting was the formation of the Hague Court of International Arbitration, a real step, though only a minor one as it has since proved, in the direction of the peaceful settlement of international disputes. In 1940 "power politics" rule the world more strongly than even in 1899. In the summer of 1898, Joseph Chamberlain, who had steadily been working for a German alliance, negotiated a treaty with that country. This provided that Germany should be allowed to secure a large part of the claims of Portugal to Africa should Portugal be willing to dispose of them, and in turn she was to release any claims to the Transvaal. When in November of the following year the Kaiser came to Windsor for the birthday of his grandmother, Queen Victoria, Chamberlain renewed his plea for an alliance, but Bülow, the German Chancellor, suggested a triple one to include Germany, Britain and the United States. This was unpopular in England, and any statesman who understood the isolationist sentiment in the United States with regard to Europe would have realized that it could not have been accepted in America. Chamberlain backed the proposal in speeches, only to be turned down and snubbed by Germany.

III. Germany and France

Tirpitz secured, for the Kaiser, the passage of a bill in the Reichstag doubling the scale of naval increase of two years earlier. It was only the incident of the Boxer Rebellion in China, where Germany was somewhat at the mercy of Britain, that kept the

German Government from giving encouragement to Kruger when he visited that country and France in search of aid in the Boer War. The old Boer had been officially received by the President of France, but the Kaiser refused him the same honor. Meanwhile, affairs otherwise had not been going well with the French Republic, one of the largest empires in the world and within sight of the cliffs of Dover.

That country, as we have noted, had deserted Britain at a critical moment in Egyptian affairs, leaving the British in the lurch and refusing to accept any responsibility for maintaining order in the country of the Nile, and since then had played the part of dog in the manger and had steadily opposed the hegemony of Britain in Egypt. It was this which had forced England into the arms of Germany. Egypt had, as we have also seen, formerly claimed the Sudan, but had had to abandon it owing to the failure of its finances and armed forces.

Lord Cromer's marvellous administrative achievement at last made it possible not only to reconquer it but to re-establish order in it. The importance of the huge region is evidenced by the fact that more than half the length of the Nile, which alone sustains the life of Egypt, is included in it. The fanatical Mahdist natives had brought about there both a state of anarchy and a resumption of the atrocious slave trade with the farther interior. After most careful preparation, Sir Herbert Kitchener, later Lord Kitchener of Khartoum, Sirdar of the Egyptian Army, waged a two and a half years' campaign with final victory at Omdurman, not far from the city which gave him his title. In spite of the fact that Britain alone had remade Egypt, the international status of that country was still complex and subject to dispute. This was not true of the Sudan, which was subject solely to joint British and Egyptian rule and control. However, some French explorers had penetrated to a point, Fashoda, on the Nile even higher up the river than Khartoum, and France, just at the time when relations between the two countries were strained by the avowed British sympathy for Captain Dreyfus, chose the moment to put in a claim to territory which was disallowed. The "Fashoda incident" of

1898 was part of the European background to the Boer War and the isolation of Britain at the time.

IV. End of the Boer War

That war, to which we may now return, began in October, 1899, and was one of the most critical in which the Empire has been engaged overseas. Everything had played into the hands of Kruger. The British, as has so often happened, were wholly unprepared, and had merely drifted into the conflict. The Boers invaded British territory and laid siege at once to the cities of Mafeking, Kimberley and Ladysmith. In one month the forces directed to the relief of each were defeated. The imperial optimism of a decade before gave place to deepest gloom. France, Germany and other leading European powers were hostile. The Empire had not been tested, and Britain was being defeated by the despised Boer farmers whom they had considered as dangerous foes. They were, however, magnificent fighting material under the conditions under which the war was fought. Nevertheless, the British fleet still held the seas, and the answer of the Empire to the need of the Mother Country came like a bugle blast to arouse both her and the world. Canadian and Australian troops first rallied to the cause. The strength of the imperial ties became apparent.

The Boer advance had also spent itself, notable as it had been. In England, where an easy victory had been expected, men's faces became set, and the British settled down to the job. Kitchener and Roberts were placed in high command. How intense the anxiety had been was shown by the marching crowds in English cities and towns the night the word came of the relief of Mafeking by a force under the lead of Baden-Powell, later founder of the Boy Scout movement in the world. More important military events were happening, but Mafeking had become a symbol and the intense revulsion of feeling when it was saved gave rise to a new word in the language, "mafficking," to express the extravagant and quite un-British behavior of the crowds celebrating the event, though the Oxford Dictionary, with more accustomed British restraint, states that the word is no longer used!

The details of the campaigns, which lasted some two and a half years more, need not concern us. The Boers put up a magnificent fight. Roberts and Kitchener, in command of the greatest British forces Britain had ever put in the field, swept across the Boer states. The Presidents of both asked for peace but none was granted. Kruger finally fled to Europe and the British annexed both the Transvaal and the Orange Free State.

Britain, however, had become sobered. The raw imperialism of the 1880's and 90's had passed. The real defeat of the Boers was followed by a period of guerrilla warfare before the final peace came. Rhodes, a dying man, said, "You think you have beaten the Dutch! It is not so. . . . What is beaten is Krugerism, a corrupt and evil government, no more Dutch in essence than English. No! The Dutch are as vigorous and unconquered today as they have ever been; the country is still as much theirs as yours, and you will have to live and work with them hereafter as in the past."[1]

Finally, May 31, 1902, the Boers accepted the peace treaty of Vereeniging and became British subjects. Few treaties, if any, have ever been so generous to the vanquished, and if that of Versailles could have been negotiated in the same spirit the world would have been spared the possible destruction of its Western civilization. The people incorporated into the Empire were granted not only full guarantees of liberty and civil rights, self-government, and safety of their property, but also a grant of £3,000,000 to re-establish their farms. With all the dark spots which can be pointed to in the growth of the British Empire, and they are many as we are all human, I doubt if any other nation in history would have made such terms after such a struggle.

Thereafter both races were to have equal rights and that is all that Britain gained, though the statesmanship of the next few years was to win her also the loyalty of her late enemies. The Union of South Africa belongs to the next chapter, but we may here note that the Boer leaders, Botha and Smuts, came to the fore in effecting a real and lasting peace of hearts and not merely of arms. The long story of South Africa which we have touched upon

[1]Quoted by G. M. Trevelyan, *British History in the Nineteenth Century*, 1922, p. 421.

at times in our narrative was bound to leave a certain amount of bitterness. Yet the way was at last open for the various governments there to become united as a great Dominion in the Commonwealth of Nations which form the Empire today, and that it should become a loyal member of that Commonwealth was due to the wise magnanimity of the British, the breadth of vision of the Boer leaders who came to the front after Krugerism was destroyed, and to the respect which each side had gained for the other in the desperate fighting which they had waged against each other. In broad racial terms they were one. The Boers themselves had realized to some extent the changes in the world which have involved us all, willing or not. The part South Africa took in the World War and the stand it has taken today in the new World War are the best evidences possible of genuine loyalty to the Empire because of fair treatment by it.

V. The Imperialism of 1900

The venerable Queen Victoria had died, January 22, 1901, before the ordeal was over, an ordeal more sobering to the British people than almost any which they had before faced. The War of the American Revolution had developed into a World War, for that time, and the Napoleonic struggle had involved all Europe. The Boer War had been envisaged as merely one of the innumerable "little wars," frontier and other, in which the Empire had been engaged for centuries. That it taxed the strength of the entire Empire, took years, and was opposed on ethical grounds by some of the soundest of the British people themselves, was a sobering fact.

On the other hand the substantial unity of the Empire had been shown. If Britain had had no allies and scarcely any friends, the Dominions and colonies had stood by her to an unexpected extent. All the self-governing colonies voluntarily despatched contingents of various size overseas to aid in the fighting, though Canada held back at first, largely due to the hesitation of the French Canadians, which Sir Wilfrid Laurier helped to overcome. At Capetown the government, sustained by Dutch votes, refused any official action, but South Africa provided some 30,000 volunteers, Canada sent nearly 16,500. It was an impressive exhibition of imperial strength and almost the only bright spot in a period of otherwise unalloyed gloom and disillusionment.

The change of policy from that of force, which had lost the first Empire, to that of loose control and giving the colonies the greatest possible measure of self-government as soon as each became ready for it, had borne fruit. Affection, common ideas, freedom shared among all, and a sense of strength from unity, had proved themselves the strongest of possible links.

During the war the process continued and a new self-governing Dominion came into being with the final union of the six Australian colonies in the Commonwealth of Australia. Such a plan had long been mooted but, like the early American colonies, those in the far-away continent were jealous of one another, and, in addition, were in some cases far separated. Improved communication, a better realization of the problems of continental extent which could not be solved by the colonies acting individually, and also the growing menace to the dream of a "white Australia" from the rise of Japan to a world power, all contributed to bring about what the more far-seeing statesmen had advocated without avail for two decades.

VI. UNION OF THE AUSTRALIAN STATES

The flexibility with which the Empire was growing was shown in the differences between the Act passed for the union of the Canadian provinces already noted and that signed by the Queen in 1900 and which went into effect January 1, 1901, for the Australian "states." The difference in nomenclature between provinces and states was of more than verbal significance. We have already described the Canadian constitution. That for the Australian Commonwealth differed from it in that it followed much more closely that of the United States in strictly limiting the powers of the central government and reserving those not specifically delegated to it to the several and jealous states.

There was, however, provision for easier amendment than in

298

the American model, and the fundamental British idea of responsible government, that is, of an executive directly responsible to the control of the majority in the legislature, was preserved. Even in a unitary state the lack of such a system is a serious handicap, as we Americans have discovered at many critical moments, but its importance is even greater in a complex of semi-independent nations such as the British Empire has become. That each of the daughter nations, however they may have differed in other constitutional points from Britain or each other, should all have maintained this essentially British feature in constitution making, has been and will be of enormous importance. It is obvious how greatly the fact that the executive of each can speak, knowing that he speaks for a majority in the legislature of his country, facilitates any business between them whether gathered in Conference in London or consulting by cable in a crisis. Americans perhaps can appreciate even more than the British the advantages of this British invention, experienced as they are in governmental deadlocks due to an executive having to deal with a hostile majority in Congress or the paralysis between the election and the inauguration of a President should there be a change of party. Nothing shows more clearly the political sagacity of the British, with all their "muddling through," than the unanimity with which the race, in all parts of the world and under very varying conditions, has clung to this fundamental idea.

With the opening year of the new century three daughter nations—Canada, New Zealand and Australia—had thus come to maturity. Of the development of South Africa, more swift and happy than could have been thought in 1900, we shall speak in the next chapter, and may now turn briefly to India. We may mention here that, although we have spoken of many smaller colonies from time to time, we do not wish to create the false impression that the Empire is made up only of Great Britain, India, and the Dominions because, of necessity, we have had to devote most of our space to them. It is impossible to tell how and why every bit of land shown as red on the map of the world was acquired. A glance at that map will correct the false impression, if such has been gained, that the Empire consists only of the parts which have been specially mentioned. Every splash of red has its own story, sometimes sordid, often heroic and thrilling, always human.

Before passing from South Africa to India we may note a link between the two which was to have serious consequences as we shall have to observe when we come to Ghandi and the present day. In a new country the labor problem is always likely to be a difficult one. In America, for example, it was solved in various ways. In the beginning there were the so-called "indentured servants," who agreed to serve for a definite number of years in order to secure their transportation to a new field where there appeared to be more opportunity than in England. Slavery was also tried, which proved profitable in the South though not in the North, and has left the states with the serious problem of some 12,000,000 of an alien race. Later came inducements to other races, some easily assimilable and others not. The American Government, in time, however, could and did close the door. In the British Empire the problem is different because the races, desired or not in certain parts of it, are British subjects and citizens in other parts, which complicates the question.

We have already spoken of the racial problem in South Africa—the leading two white races of British and Boers, and the vast native black population. To this was to be added a fresh complication. In Natal, especially in the sugar-growing belt along the coast, the whites would not labor and the native Bantus were not considered satisfactory. So, as early as 1860, indentured labor was brought in from the teeming millions of India. With occasional scruples, this was continued, with the aid of government grants, for more than a generation. Eventually, as America had found with its Negroes, the racial problem of both indentured and free Indians became a threatening one, not only in Natal, but to a lesser extent in the Transvaal, especially as the free Indians, with a lower standard of living, entered into competition in various lines with the dominant whites. The ideal of a "white Australia," of an American Pacific coast excluding Asiatics, was repeated in South Africa, only with the important difference that in the last case the people to be discriminated against and excluded were not foreigners but citizens of another part of the Empire, indeed of its most populous and richest dependency. A nation may close its door to foreigners, but it is far more difficult, without arousing possibly deep animosities, for an empire to prevent citizens of one part from moving freely into another.

VII. CURZON IN INDIA

Turning now to India itself, we find the old system of government and the old imperial relations at perhaps their very best during the Viceroyalty of Lord Curzon, 1899–1905. The lean years and the famines just before his arrival had come when India as yet had but 22,000 miles of railway and meager equipment. In the later great droughts of 1906–7 and 1918–19, the railways had been greatly extended and improved so that food could be more easily moved to the districts in which famine was worst. Nevertheless, though Curzon had his distinct limitations, and his partition of Bengal into two provinces was a bad error of judgment, he did greatly improve the administration and for a number of years was popular among the educated classes in India at a time of dangerous transition. He had not only, in spite of his constant and severe physical suffering, of which few knew, an enormous power of work, but he loved detail, and deeply believed both in himself and in what could and should be done for India.

The Achilles heel of India, both in respect to the native tribes and relations with Russia, was the Northwest Frontier. Here Curzon erected a new province, withdrawing British troops, who had irritated the natives, from the contact areas, replacing them by the "Khyber Rifles," native troops of fine fighting quality and unquestioned loyalty. The system worked well, and under the notable reorganization of all the military forces undertaken by Lord Kitchener, the Northwest Frontier was made the key to the whole of Indian defense. The menace of Russia continued and when that country was known to have sent a mysterious mission to the yet more mysterious land of Tibet, isolated in the Himalayas, Curzon countered with an expedition of his own, which had to cross passes 19,000 feet high to penetrate the forbidden land and make a treaty with the Grand Lama.

Curzon's weakest point was his failure to understand the strength of the native and growing nationalistic sentiment. Cold, austere, efficient, he did not realize the outrage to Bengali feelings by his division of their province, and in his attempted reforms of education he again ran counter to Indian feeling. The educational system badly needed overhauling, but to increase English control was merely to antagonize the new class of Westernized Indians who had been encouraged to manage the system themselves. Far more helpful was his aid to scientific agriculture and irrigation, helped to no small extent by gifts of American money, and his encouragement of the movement of building up Co-operative Societies on English lines. Whenever it was a question of lavish grants of money, of increasing efficiency, of reorganizing the bureaucracy, of energy, Curzon succeeded, and India's economic position improved.

He did not, however, understand the people whom he ruled. He did not realize what they were thinking or the influence of the vernacular press, which he despised. He thought the Congress a mere passing phase of unimportant political agitation which could be ignored. It was not that he was indifferent to the people or their history. More than any other Viceroy he undertook the work of restoring the historical monuments and architectural glories of the race. He simply did not understand the deeper currents of racial and national feeling which were stirring below the surface. Possibly he was a little intoxicated by the magnificence of the ceremonies of the Durbar which he arranged for the proclamation of the accession of Edward VII as King-Emperor in January, 1903. It was, perhaps, the most gorgeous spectacle which India had ever witnessed, and the loyalty of the reigning Princes may have obscured for the Viceroy the thoughts in the minds of less resplendent persons whose destinies were less obviously bound to the British Crown.

The old Queen-Empress had died, January 22, 1901, after

reigning longer than either Elizabeth or George III. So long had she occupied the center of the public stage and been the symbol of imperial power and stability that it was almost as though Westminster Abbey or the Houses of Parliament had disappeared. Not living to see the final victory in the Boer War she died at one of the darkest moments of imperial history. Although her popularity had somewhat declined, due in part to her rare public appearances, the mourning was sincere. No race loves stability more than the British or more dislikes change. It was felt that something sure and stable had gone out of British life. In truth it had, though it was not merely the Queen as person, monarch or symbol. The entire world was to change so rapidly in the next few years and to become so different from that of the nineteenth century, that those whose personal memories do not go back to the 1880's or 90's simply cannot understand what the change has meant.

CHAPTER XIV

THE EDWARDIAN PERIOD

I. Last Years of Victoria

VICTORIA was dead, and with her the "Victorian Era." It had been one of the greatest in British annals. If after almost a generation of reaction we are returning to it in costume and other minor modes it is not merely nostalgia, but to some extent it expresses our desire to recover a world not only of seeming solidity but of observed decencies as well. It is easy to draw up a long indictment against the Victorian period, but it is quite a different and much milder indictment than that to be drawn against what we may call the Hitlerian period of today. Jigsaw architecture, poor taste, the horrors of the "what-not" in the drawing-room corner, and all the customary criticisms of the period seem rather insignificant now in view of the breakdown of civilization in our own day.

We speak of the Victorian period, but in truth there were several, all covered by the life of the one woman who, without either great character or intellect, had made the Crown respected throughout the Empire, cemented that Empire together, and who had quashed, by what she did and even more by what she did not attempt, the nascent movement toward republicanism in Britain which would have meant the end of Empire. Britain itself might be a republic but the Empire could never hold together under an elected President chosen in an election held by a quarter of the earth's inhabitants and of all races. Changes had already set in many years before her death, and not only did the Boer War carry over from her reign to that of her son, but the transition was marked in other ways also by no sharp cleavage.

The more or less complete unity of outlook and classes of the mid-century had begun to crumble rapidly by its last decade. The lack of unity and also the change in spirit make the picture somewhat inchoate, but we may mention some points before passing into the more or less complete chaos of the Edwardian and Georgian periods preceding the World War.

The old standards were rapidly passing. We have already mentioned the decline in religious observance and the change from the old Sunday to the new "week-end," but all along the line old bonds were loosening. The clergy were losing influence and changing in character. Among the nonconformists new careers were opening to the intellectual and ambitious youth who had previously found his opportunity by entering the ministry, and even in the established Church the decline in agriculture had seriously impaired the economic position of the clergy with the result of a change in the social and intellectual grade from which it was recruited. The country parson, with his wife and household of children, who set certain standards, was lessened in influence. Science, literature, new social customs, were rapidly secularizing thought and ways. Cheap railway excursions for Sunday, and the opening of the public museums on that day, were among the signs in the late 90's of the change in attitude.

The broadening of the franchise and various social legislation had also helped to break down the former unity. New groups and whole classes were beginning to taste power and to strike out on unaccustomed paths. The old stable social structure was in ferment, but on the eve of the Great War the movements had gone far enough to portend its complete breakdown, a point which, in its misleading of Germany, never clever at understanding the psychology of other peoples, in itself contributed to bringing on the conflict.

It was the *fin de siècle* years which saw the most momentous alteration in the press, the beginning of which we noted in the previous chapter. The Harmsworths emerged as great newspaper proprietors, and besides their earlier ventures established *The Daily Mail* in 1896. The new form of journalism which was now to develop, and not in England alone, but in its birthplace, America, and elsewhere, was to have sinister aspects. It was based not only on the fact there was a new literate, though not educated, public but on two other points which were to be of great influence. One was the change of support from subscriptions to advertising profits. The other was that the new public had gained political power through the franchise. The fact that the new journalism was to depend on advertising and that advertising rates depended on circulation made circulation all-important in the building up of great properties and newspaper fortunes. The lowest mental common denominator came into play, which was emotion, and preferably a "good hate." War would enormously increase circulation, and it came about that a characteristic of the yellow press everywhere was to be, all too often, the promotion of international ill-feeling.

There are yet great journals which maintain high traditions, but the rise of a group of powerful papers which catered to the newly enfranchised classes would seem to have been one of the strongest influences making for the new barbarism of the twentieth century. Propaganda is not new but it received a tremendous impetus from the yellow journalism, and the dictators who have played on hatreds of minorities or foreigners in peacetime learned many of their lessons from great newspaper proprietors in many countries in the decades preceding.

Literacy had been assured, but literacy meant as yet merely placing dangerous weapons in the hands of irresponsible men unless the masses became educated in a real sense. Later such weapons were to consist also of the moving picture and the radio, which lend themselves still more to emotionalism and do not even require that the victim of propaganda should be literate. But in the earlier period now being discussed, education was losing in the race for genuine democracy and world peace. It is true that the opportunities for "book learning" were being increased both by improvements in the schools and the development of the free-library system, but that is not enough. Men cannot govern themselves and live in a free society with their fellows unless they have character, the old English instinct for compromise and fair play, and a sense of responsibility. It was the last of these which was to be conspicuously lacking in the period on which we are now entering.

Literature was changing rapidly. Kipling was still writing at top speed, but in the 90's Thomas Hardy, Stevenson and Meredith all published their last notable works. With the new public had also come the "best sellers" of vast circulation, such as those of Marie Corelli and Hall Caine, but the newer novelists were not great and reflected often without genius the more sordid aspects of the period. It was characteristic that there was much demand for books on trade and economics, and in these years the Webbs produced their monumental and still standard researches on *Trade Unionism* and *Industrial Democracy*.

American influence was felt in the establishment of public libraries, the Scotch-American, Andrew Carnegie, having been the leader in that movement. Interest in art was reviving, and the foundation of the National Portrait Gallery, the Tate, and the Wallace Collection, among the most important of London's museums, all date from the last decade of the century. There were others also, which either date from this period or were greatly enlarged and enriched, such as the National Gallery, the Victoria and Albert Museum, and many in provincial cities.

Publishers' figures show that the largest percentage of increase in books published was in the field of poetry and drama, though in the first department this was more of an indication of public taste than of the development of poetry, which, like that of fiction, produced little to compare with the earlier Victorian period. Drama fared better. Pinero and Arthur Jones were producing their plays, though Bernard Shaw, who had published ten, had not yet seen one on the stage. That Shaw was eagerly read, however, shows how changed the Victorian era had become, and the revival of English music was marked, both in composition and public interest. Among the new composers, who were many, Edward Elgar easily led, and his *Dream of Gerontius*, composed during the South

African War and while the old Queen was still living, illustrates the many conflicting currents at work which became more obvious in the reign of Edward.

II. Edward VII

Ascending the throne in his sixtieth year, when a man's mental habits are set, the new King was in many ways unprepared for his task. Victoria had made the Crown not only the symbol but the very keystone of the arch of Empire. That perhaps was her greatest achievement, though the actual political power of the Crown had declined. She had, however, exerted very considerable influence within a narrowed constitutional field owing to her expressed personal reaction to matters of state, though never trespassing over the borders of her constitutional position. To do this she had to know affairs and she did know them intimately from painstaking reading and consideration of state papers throughout her entire reign. During her long retirement after her husband's death, living in her widow's dress and much in solitude, she was familiar with all matters of national policy, and statesmen knew it. If she could not command, she was consulted, and her often excellent advice was frequently taken. As a symbol her age and the length of her reign had to offset her lack of social brilliancy and her infrequent public appearances.

In both these points the new King offered a strong contrast to the late Queen. Partly because of the temperament and character of Victoria and partly because of those of the Prince, he had not taken his father's place in his mother's counsels as he grew older. The positions of both a Prince Consort and an heir to the throne are difficult. As Edward went through early manhood and middle age with the glare of publicity on him but with nothing serious to do, his natural disinclination to mental effort increased. He never had cared for reading or study and, shut off by his mother from any real participation in public affairs, he had more and more devoted himself to his life as a mere man of fashion and the world. Both before and after his mother's death he performed with consummate tact and charm the social duties which devolve upon royalty and which his mother had abandoned.

The result was that during his brief reign the real power of the Crown tended to decline, but he gave it additional prestige and splendor as a symbol. His knowledge, wide rather than deep, was acquired mostly by conversation, and his tastes, though not highly cultured, were such as to make him popular. Even though he spoke English with a German accent, the last of his house to do so, he was accepted as a thoroughgoing Englishman. Even the scandals connected with his name were rather willingly accepted in a society fast changing and in revolt against the rigors of Victorianism. The British like pageantry and costume, which for them is not a mere show but symbolically links their whole past to the present, and they like also the romance of royalty and high life. Deeply as the old Queen had been revered, her long abstention from public life had hurt her popularity. For nearly twenty years she had not even opened Parliament in person in the fine old ceremony, and it was characteristic of Edward that he did so, driving from the Palace to Whitehall in the glass coach, and with all the display of former days. Splendor and a man who was perhaps the leading social figure in Europe had replaced the quiet retirement and almost commonplace life of the old Queen as symbol of Empire. That splendor was to continue, but it is probable that the real influence of Edward on governmental, and especially foreign, affairs was formerly overrated. In any case, the ten years of his reign would have been troubled ones.

Turning first to the Empire, we may note its increased importance in the eyes of Britain by the addition in the title of the new King of the words "and of the British Dominions beyond the Seas" to that of "the United Kingdom of Great Britain and Ireland" and Emperor of India. Disraeli's rather flamboyant conferring of the title of Empress on Victoria had never really pleased the public. It had somehow an un-British ring to it. Edward's title really expressed something new which had come into British consciousness, the feeling of a genuine imperial unity. This was due far less to the type of imperialism of the 90's than to the bond which had developed from the brotherly aid given in the crisis of the Boer War, although the word "Dominions" was not used technically, but meant all the colonial possessions of every sort.

III. END OF THE BOER WAR AND SETTLEMENT

The King had come to the throne in the midst of that crisis of the Boer War and in spite of the generous terms of the treaty of peace, the war had left causes for even deeper cleavage than before. In its final phase it had been an affair of guerrillas. This had made it necessary to divide the country into districts and comb them for persons in arms, who, when captured, were placed in concentration camps. These were not regular troops but civilian men, women, and even children who were continuing the fight and preventing any order from being established. The concentration-camp system is always bad, and in Cuba under the Spaniards its abuses, though exaggerated, had done more than anything else to goad the United States into war on Spain in 1898. In South Africa there seemed to be no other method available for bringing peace, but there also the system worked with appalling results. The death rate in the camps ran up to about 6 per cent of the total interned, and some of the leading British statesmen and others at home raised their voices against it, especially Campbell-Bannerman, who was to become Prime Minister at the end of 1905, following the three-and-a-half-year Ministry of Balfour. He was bitterly attacked for denouncing the horrors of the concentration-camp policy, but he had won the confidence of the Boers, who felt that he was a genuine friend.

This undoubtedly was a main factor in the remarkable settlement which ensued. The war ended with intense bitterness in 1902. In general, after a good fight, the British do not nourish a grievance, though their treatment of the United States and of Americans after the Revolution a hundred and fifty years ago forms an exception. Within three years after the Boer War it was suggested that representative government be granted to the conquered republics. Although this seemed dangerous, after Campbell-Bannerman became Premier a much farther-reaching plan was put into effect, giving first the Transvaal and soon after the Orange Free State full responsible government. The courage required for this step was immense, but it was well repaid. Although the British had won the war they allowed Dutch majorities to be elected not only in the conquered Republics but also in Cape Colony. There was, however, no flaring up of racial feeling. Instead there was a demand at last for unification. By 1910 a unified state had come into existence by legislation of the four colonies, confirmed by a statute of the imperial Parliament, and South Africa took its place in the British Commonwealth as a Dominion beside Canada, Australia, and New Zealand.

It was one of the bravest and noblest experiments in statesmanship in history. There are few more dramatic moments to record than when Lord Gladstone, the British Governor-General, handed the seals of office to the first Prime Minister of the new nation, General Botha, late commander of the Boer armies who had fought the British. The story of the Empire, like that of any nation and of almost every individual, has had in it much that was sordid, selfish or unwise, but there has also been much that was brave and idealistic, and this act of statesmanship deserves to rank with the great deeds of Britain's leaders of its navy and armies. Its success speaks equally well for the character of the Boers. On the part of the British, moreover, it was not an act of mere generosity. It was the strongest possible proof that the nation of marauders in early days, and of "shopkeepers" in later, had learned the lesson that the only worth-while life must be based on liberty, and that security comes from freedom and not from force.

There had been times, during the first Empire, when various American colonies, later to revolt, had attempted to give military aid to the Mother Country in her wars, but English political thought was then provincial, and efforts at co-operation brought about ill rather than good feeling. Two centuries, more or less, had wrought great differences, and both during the Boer War and in the years intervening between that and the World War, the attitude of the Dominions and the meaning of Empire were better appreciated. Partly as a result of the Imperial Conferences and partly because of the better understanding by both England and the Dominions of what the seemingly loose but really strong ties between them meant, Canada, Australia, and New Zealand had all offered contributions to the defense of the Empire. Canada, which was immensely prosperous and adding rapidly to her population, had developed plans for a Canadian navy to be used in co-operation with the British fleet in time of war, and reorganized her military forces. Australia and New Zealand both adopted universal military training and added important naval contributions. A new sense of responsibility and maturity of outlook was developing. Without freedom there would have been mere resentment against too long prolonged control, but with it came a sense of unity, which was to prove of inestimable worth in the two World Wars.

IV. EGYPT

The problems in Egypt and India were of a different nature. The populations were ruled by the British, but were themselves of an alien race. Among the main currents of the nineteenth century and our own have been racialism and nationalism. These helped to bind the British portions of the Empire together, but at the same time they tended to create trouble in the non-British portions. English rule in Egypt had wrought great improvements, but more and more that rule, simply because it was alien, came to be resented by the native politicians and their followers. The religious question also complicated the problem. Egypt, with a modicum of nominal self-government, was really controlled by the British agent, but it also was nominally under the authority of the Turkish Sultan, Abdul Hamid, and was Mohammedan in faith. There have been few less admirable rulers of great empires than Abdul. He was, however, powerful and resented the increasing European control of the Mohammedan world by the partition of Africa and by British rule in Egypt and India. To counter the increasing demand for reform in Turkey itself, he realized that he could utilize the wave of religious enthusiasm, which had been started by certain Mohammedan reformers, to buttress his own political position.

The new doctrine of Pan-Islamism, which was fostered by Abdul, was essentially anti-European with one important exception. That was Germany, and to a minor extent Austria. The other great powers had long controlled, or recently acquired, power over Mohammedan peoples. The Germans had not, and the Kaiser suddenly proclaimed himself the protector of the Mohammedans. The political motives of this odd situation may have been obvious enough, but the Sultan needed Western aid in reorganizing his army and administration, and he gladly employed German experts, enlisted German support, and aligned himself against Russia, France, and England. The new form which the perennial "Eastern Question" now took was to have important repercussions in the future. For the present it meant mainly that the racial, religious and nationalistic movements in Egypt as directed against England could look to Turkey for support. There were rioting, assassinations of high officials, and more or less disorder, but a new relation between Egypt and Britain was to wait until after the end of the World War.

V. Imperial Problems

The steady increase in decentralization in the Empire and the granting of local responsible governments in the Dominions has done much, as we have seen, to bind the Empire together by the bonds of similar ideas, sympathies, aspirations toward liberty, and a feeling of brotherly help in place of the old rigid control of an Imperial Parliament. It has also brought a multitude of problems, some of which are too unhappily familiar to citizens of the federated United States. A division of sovereignty or power, without attempting to define the terms too minutely, raises difficulties. The British Empire is not a federal union of states. The "Commonwealth of Nations" is a form of government *sui generis,* but it involves some of the difficulties which the United States has experienced.

In the early days of the Empire the clash of interests between its various parts was almost wholly economic, as between New England and the sugar islands of the West Indies, but with its vast

313

later extension have come racial problems as well. It is conceded that the Dominions have the right to prescribe their own limitations on immigration, but although the prohibition of Asiatics, as exemplified in the "white Australia" slogan, followed by New Zealand and Canada (as well as the United States), made trouble when Britain was in alliance with Japan, the real difficulties thus far have come from *inter-imperial* racial movements. When the Union of South Africa was formed the biracial white problem was solved. That of the Negroes remained but was in process of solution. We have already spoken of the problem of the Indians who had been imported, and when, to prevent further complications, the government of the new Union limited additional Indian immigration and placed certain restrictions on the Indians already within its borders, trouble began which was to have far-reaching effects.

Among those in Africa was M. H. Ghandi, now generally known as Mahatma Ghandi, who, like Samuel Adams in the Massachusetts of the eighteenth century, was to prove one of the most forceful agitators in history. We have already spoken of the rapid development of the nationalistic and to a considerable extent the anti-Western movement in India. When Ghandi returned to India he had the specific grievance to exploit that if Indians were citizens of the Empire, they should have the right to live and move about freely in any part of it. By 1901, there were nearly 2,500,000 Indians scattered about in other parts of the Empire, practically all of lower castes and laborer class, as the higher castes rarely permitted emigration.

As the problem grew with the growth of nationalism in India and elsewhere, it could be handled fairly well (though not wholly to the satisfaction of Indian nationals), as the colonies were still wholly under the direction of the central Imperial Government in London, but the cases of the semi-autonomous Dominions offered much greater difficulties, chiefly in South Africa. The disputes have never been satisfactorily adjusted, and Ghandi, who was at first on the side of the British, became disaffected with immense later repercussions on Anglo-Indian relations. These were set against the general background of rising religious discontent, already mentioned, on the part of the whole Moslem world. Various Mohammedan peoples were being absorbed or brought under control of the Christian nations of Europe, and the British had been playing their part or had been making no protests in the gradual absorption of Morocco, Persia, Tripoli, and other Moslem countries.

VI. India

Another Indian cause of complaint was the increasing pressure on the soil due to the steady increase of population in the cultivated areas. These areas had been increased by irrigation and modern methods of dry farming, and the additional pressure on the land could not be considered the fault of the British. Nor could the blame for increasing population be placed upon them for abolishing certain evil customs which had helped to keep down population, improving sanitation and justice or reducing the former huge losses from plagues and famines. Nevertheless, the pressure was intense. It has been estimated that in 1911 some 217,000,000 persons lived on the produce of 260,000,000 acres, of which only about 85 per cent was annually planted. The rise in population had distinctly altered the relation of the peasant to the land for the worse in the preceding two generations. It was another cause contributing to the general uneasiness, and in the decade from 1901 to 1911 the number of landless laborers in the Deccan rose by about 28 per cent.

Another topic of controversy, though largely among agitators in India and England rather than among the general public, was the continued receipt of taxes from the sale of opium within India itself. In the twentieth century reformers everywhere were more and more becoming insistent that it was a duty of government to interfere with the habits and even morals of peoples for their own good, another evidence of the general passing of *laissez faire* in the philosophy of the times. There are many who consider that the government should prohibit the use of alcohol and that opium is far more deleterious. The fact that the government did not prohibit it, and even made a revenue from it, afforded an easy weapon of attack. Without defending the use of opium there are certain points to which the reformers did not give due weight.

In India opium is almost universally eaten, a practice far less harmful than the Chinese method of smoking it, except when given to children. Its use in India is very ancient and even more widespread than the use of wines and other alcoholic beverages in Europe, and it is much easier to prepare illicitly. The failure of Prohibition in the United States would indicate that any attempt to prohibit the use of opium in India would merely result in widespread illicit consumption and in disrespect for law. The revenue had been becoming unimportant, and a convention had been entered into with China to reduce exports to that country until they should have ceased entirely by 1917. It was considered wisest, however, to consider the tax system within India as the best means of regulating and cutting down the traffic. The failure of the American Prohibition experiment and the fact that after exports to China ceased in 1914, and China herself had tried to suppress domestic production entirely, illicit production rose to the highest figures on record, would indicate that the British system had some justification. That did not prevent severe criticism and the use of the topic as a weapon of agitation. Meanwhile, the Congresses became more radical. Bombing and passive resistance increased, and in the years before the World War it appeared that Britain might have serious trouble in maintaining her position in her largest possession.

VII. THE EMPIRE DRAWING CLOSER TOGETHER

In general, however, the Empire was drawing closer together. At the Imperial Conference of 1907 it was agreed that Conferences should thereafter be held each fourth year, and be presided over by the British Prime Minister and not the Colonial Secretary. The problem of Imperial Defense made progress and plans were developed by the Dominions for their contributions, as also for closer co-operation with the military policy of Britain itself. As a milestone in the story of status it may also be mentioned that at this Conference it was agreed that henceforth the term Dominion instead of colony should be used for such self-governing colonies as were attending the Conference. Although Newfoundland was represented, it has at present lost its status as a Dominion and has reverted to the position of a colony, owing partly to its small size and more especially to its temporary political and financial difficulties.

At the next Conference, in 1911, the representatives from the Dominions were frankly and fully consulted as to foreign policy. It was right that they should be. If they were to join in the defense of the Empire they had a right to know what foreign events might suddenly make their aid necessary and why. The clouds were gathering rapidly over Europe and it was fortunate that when the storm broke three years later the Dominion statesmen were already informed and in close touch with those of the Home Country. They could thus advise and guide their several peoples and Parliaments with a speed and authority which would otherwise have been impossible.

Of the diplomatic affairs and their background which occupied the imperial statesmen in 1911 we can speak only briefly. The world had been becoming more and more uneasy. There were ample signs, as there had been for some years, that the world was entering upon a new era of possibly major disturbances and readjustments. Germany and Austria had become dominant in the restless Balkan region, having edged Russia out of what she considered her special sphere. Turkey was rising again to power in spite of her losses, and we have noted the Pan-Islamic movement which was stirring storm waves in all the Mohammedan world.

The rise of modern Japan was also beginning to have effect on anti-European racial feeling in the East. In China, the nations had quarrelled over staking out their claims. Russia was angry at the Germanic powers in Europe and feared Japan on her Far Eastern front. The Boxer Rebellion against foreigners in China ended in its suppression and the usual demand for indemnities and concessions. The game became more furious, rousing many animosities.

Only Britain and the United States protested against the partition of the nation with an ancient civilization, a situation which Britain considered far different from that of Africa. Both the English nations demanded the policy of the "Open Door" and rights of trade for all, but the United States refused to involve itself in a general war.

VIII. INTERNATIONAL AFFAIRS

Then in 1902 came an event of far-reaching importance. Britain formed an alliance with Japan, each agreeing to maintain the *status quo* in the Far East and to go to the aid of the other if attacked by more than one nation. Three effects were at once visible. If Japan fought Russia or China she would have to do it alone, but if any other nation joined—which in the circumstances meant Germany or France—they would have to face the British as well as the Japanese. But, second, in view of the overwhelming power of the British fleet neither could reach the Far East. Thirdly, Japan now ranked as one of the great world powers.

Two years later Japan did fight Russia and won a great victory, increasing enormously her own pride and Oriental prestige by having conquered single-handed the largest and most populous state in Europe. It is difficult now to value the Anglo-Japanese alliance of 1902 and we can point only to its effects. It solved for the moment the problem of China, and seemed to many to help Britain in her threatening Oriental difficulties by giving her a strong ally in that part of the world. On the other hand, many British objected to such an alliance with the most militarized of the yellow peoples, and if this was also true to a great extent of Canadian feeling it was even more so of American, which was stunned by finding the British Empire in alliance with America's greatest potential enemy in the Pacific. In addition, the treaty unquestionably helped the rise of Japan, increased the restlessness of the Orient, and in time was to have the ironical result that instead of preventing the partition of China by Europe it was practically to turn most of China over to Japan by 1939.

Meanwhile, during Edward's reign a turn for the better came

in the relations of the age-old enemies through the centuries, France and England. It was chiefly the work of the British Government, though the tact of the King and his well-known fondness for Paris, where he was always popular, assisted the work of the diplomats, aided even more perhaps by the common danger which was threatening both nations. The Entente was not an alliance, but chiefly a settlement of disputes, with an additional treaty of arbitration (1903) according to which both agreed to settle all future questions at issue by that method except those involving basic interests or honor.

Earlier, in 1899, twenty-six nations had assembled for the Hague Conference at the request of the Czar and, although the results were mostly disappointing in a world now steadily moving toward the doctrine of force rather than pacific agreements, there had been set up a permanent Court of Arbitration to which nations wishing to settle their disputes could repair. The new Franco-British agreement may be considered as one of its first fruits. In the Entente, rather than the Treaty, the two nations, besides minor questions long at issue, had agreed on the settlement of what had been some of the chief quarrels between them. The first, which in particular had made bad blood for a generation or more, was Egypt, and France now, in exchange for a free hand in Morocco, yielded any further claims to the former country.

Even if there were no strict alliance the way was paved for a good and fairly close relation between the two nations facing each other across the channel. The better atmosphere involved Russia also, as an ally of France. The moving cause of this new alignment of three of the greatest powers in Europe was the line being followed by Germany, toward whom Britain had been steadily friendly in ways and for reasons we outlined earlier. More and more, however, Germany, in company with Austria-Hungary, was pursuing a policy which was threatening instead of friendly, and which was based on Bismarck's theory of force, emphasized in many ways in Germany by historians, philosophers, and others. Although believing in his theory of blood and iron the old Chancellor had never considered that Germany's destiny was on

319

the seas. So as long as he was in power the British Empire had not been threatened, but when the new Emperor "dropped the pilot" and took affairs into his own hands, his leading ambition was to build a navy which could compete with Britain's, and at the same time continue to maintain the strongest military force on the Continent.

This was a different situation, though Britain was slow in realizing its full implications, despite blustering and successive crises at short intervals. In 1905 Russia had not only been defeated by Japan, but was for the time being paralyzed by an internal revolution, and the Kaiser took that opportunity to bully France about Morocco, apparently merely trying to force a quarrel with her, such as had led to the Franco-Prussian War of 1870. The Entente now came into play and the military leaders of its two members consulted as to possible co-operation in case the Kaiser should push his quarrel to the point of open hostilities. In spite of Germany's preference for a policy of force and bluster, the old Concert of Europe was still strong enough to settle the Morocco question by a general conference held at Algeciras, at which Germany, isolated, considered herself humiliated.

The following year (1907) the Entente was enlarged to the Triple Entente by the settlement of difficulties between Britain and Russia, though, again, there was no military alliance. The cry of "encirclement" now began first to be raised in Germany, which seemed to consider that anything should come under that term which would serve the protection of other powers or interfere with her growing and inordinate ambitions. In 1908 Abdul Hamid was deposed by a revolution in Turkey, and as a later, but not immediate, result, German influence became dominant in that country. In defiance of treaties Austria annexed the Serbian populations of the provinces of Bosnia and Herzegovina, and threatened an attack on aggrieved Serbia herself. The Kiel Canal had been constructed, which was estimated as doubling the strength of the German fleet, but, in the now avowed naval race between Germany and Britain, the increased size of battleships had called for its widening, a somewhat lengthy operation which was completed in June,

1914, a date to which we shall refer in the next chapter, on the war.

After a renewed crisis over Morocco, in the course of which the Kaiser sent a warship to the coast of the French protectorate, but again suffered a diplomatic defeat, Germany by three successive Acts in 1911, 1912, and 1913 enormously increased her army. For what? That was the question which overshadowed Europe. After another Balkan War, in which Austria deprived Serbia of the spoils of victory, while Germany was racing to become the leading military power on the Continent and to outbid Britain on the sea, there could not much longer be doubt of what was intended. The final crisis was fast approaching.

Many of the nations had been steadily striving for some sort of framework within peace which would settle the conflicting desires and problems of the Continental nations. Even the movement toward arbitration was progressing. We have spoken of the feeling in the United States against the Anglo-Japanese Treaty, a feeling not lessened by the signing of a new one when the first expired. The United States, however, has always preferred the peaceful settlement of disputes, and in 1911 the second great treaty of arbitration was made between Britain and America, though it was not ratified until 1914. It provided for arbitration of every question "no matter what it involves, whether honor, territory or money." The importance of such a treaty between two of the greatest powers on earth was of enormous importance in itself, but as a side issue there was another important treaty change made between Britain and Japan by which each agreed that it should not have to go to war with any third power with which it had a general arbitration treaty. The world, on the eve of the Great Catastrophe, might have seemed heading toward a peaceful solution of its problems. However, Germany and her ally Austria held aloof, with Germany as chief partner.

It has often been claimed that Germany, with her doctrines of force outside law, has been what she is because she never went through the training of being a part of the Roman Empire, but had always been barbaric. This explanation, however, hardly holds.

.e Scandinavian nations, which are essentially pacific and among
e leaders of modern civilization, never had been parts of the
ᵤreat lawmaking empire either. There seems to have been some
quality in the German people, made up of many barbaric races in
spite of Hitler's babblings about pure Aryanism, which leads them
in the direction of force rather than of international law or of
international co-operation and an ordered world. In any case
she was fast bringing about a world crisis though there was no-
body who was threatening her.

IX. THE CRISIS IN BRITAIN

We may now turn to a short survey of domestic conditions in
Britain and Ireland, which Germany overrated, but which undoubtedly helped to form her fateful decision.

We have already mentioned the new spirit of unrest and the
different and more violent approach to the problems of the day.
This was notable in many directions, the number of which appeared to indicate a change in the national character and temperament. The new century had opened with the famous Taff Vale
case, which arose out of an unauthorized strike by the workers on
the railway of that name. The Amalgamated Society of Railway
Servants, however, decided to come to the help of the strikers, and
in return the railway brought two suits, one to prohibit the Society
from doing anything to interfere with the operating of the road,
and the other claiming damages from the Society. It was successful
in both, and the Society was ordered to pay the huge sum of
£23,000 to the railway. Although according to strict construction
of changing law the judges were probably right, the decision made
an immense sensation, threatened destruction of the power of
the unions, and brought the Labor Party to life.

Up to 1909, however, there had been on the surface no difference in the general attitude of labor. In reality, under the influence
of French Syndicalism and of the American I. W. W., the labor
movement had turned revolutionary. In the preamble to the I.
W. W. constitution it was stated that "the working class and the
employing class have nothing in common. There can be no peace

so long as hunger and want are found among millions of working people and the few, who make up the employing class, have all the good things of life." Direct action and the general strike were advocated as means to make society over.

These ideas took hold of vast numbers of workingmen and a new group of leaders arose who preached them. From this time until the war one bitter strike succeeded another, usually ending in the victory of the strikers. In the dockers' strike of 1912, Ben Tillett, the leader of the strikers, made his famous prayer on Tower Hill: "God strike Lord Devonport dead," Devonport being the head of the Port of London authority. Some of the older type of labor leaders began to speak against the new methods, but the newer type of unionists continued them and began the formation of new and more revolutionary forms of union. By the beginning of 1914, it was feared that revolution might actually begin with the threatened tie-up of the nation by the Triple Industrial Alliance, made up of the groups of workers represented by three of the greatest of the new unions, including 1,350,000 of the 4,000,-000 trades-union members.

During the same period there developed the movement of the militant suffragettes. Some men and many women had for long been advocating Women's Suffrage, but the struggle took on an entirely new aspect in these years, which seemed to mark the coming of an era of violence and a forcible instead of an orderly change in institutions. The new Suffragettes, as contrasted with the older and more conservatives Suffragists, began a campaign of terrorism and lawlessness under the lead of the Pethic Lawrences and Mrs. Pankhurst and her two daughters. They smashed windows, burned houses, attacked policemen, chained themselves to the door steps of members of the Cabinet, and one in her hysterical enthusiasm for the cause even committed suicide by throwing herself in front of the King's horse in the Derby race. When imprisoned they tried to commit suicide by refusing food. This led to forcible feeding, and in another aspect the English nature appeared to have altered and to have become hysterical, violent and revolutionary.

In politics there was also a breakdown. The resignation of the

323

venerable Lord Salisbury on account of age in 1902 appeared to mark the end of an era. Under his successor, A. J. Balfour, leader of the House of Commons, we may notice here two Acts. One was the important measure to reform the educational system, but which was thrown out by the House of Lords. The other was the Wyndham Act for advances by the government to enable Irish tenants to purchase land from such landlords as might be willing to sell. It was a distinct contribution to the settlement of the agrarian problem, generous in its terms to both owners and tenants and worked well into 1933, when the Irish Free State held up the payments to the British Government. In 1902 Mr. Chamberlain, Colonial Secretary, helped to split the party by turning from free trade to tariff reform, which meant a mild form of protection, and the Ministry, weakened by other resignations and dissensions, resigned two years later. In the election of 1905 the Liberals still had a majority, the new Parliament being noteworthy otherwise for the decrease in Unionists by more than one-half and the appearance of fifty members of the Labor Party. Campbell-Bannerman, who became Premier, resigned on account of ill health and was succeeded by Asquith in 1908, with Lloyd George as his Chancellor of the Exchequer.

Asquith was not at all an aristocrat, though he became fond of high-society life, more as a successful businessman would be than as one born to it. This taste, and the wholly new society he was carried into by his second marriage, led to certain estrangements with earlier associates who could not reconcile the former stubborn Yorkshireman, a nonconformist and belonging rather to the left of the Liberals, with the husband of Margot Asquith and his new role. However, he had never been a man of imagination or the standard bearer of high causes. The presence of Lloyd George in his Cabinet, strong also in most of its other members, helped to keep the party in line. Two of the members now appear for the first time as Ministers, Winston Churchill and Walter Runciman. The new Parliament also began the temporary connection between Liberals and Laborites which became known as the "Lib-Labs." Asquith, although not essentially a reformer, took a notable step in passing an Old Age Pension Act without any payments by the beneficiaries.

Meanwhile, it was discovered that the previous government had allowed Germany to creep up on the British navy, and so had encouraged the German Admiral von Tirpitz to redouble his efforts to surpass it. McKenna, First Lord of the Admiralty, wished six new dreadnoughts laid down at once, which would seriously unbalance the proposed budget. Rather oddly, in view of his future interests and activities, Winston Churchill was one of those who opposed the naval extension, being then more interested in social reform than in naval matters or foreign policy. When the people learned of the situation, demand was at once made up for an increase which would keep the lead well over Germany, and Lloyd George had to find an additional £15,000,000, then an unprecedentedly large increase. The Chancellor determined to use the situation to advantage.

One bill after another had been passed by the Liberals in the Commons to be thrown out by the Lords, who had been preparing a crisis for themselves by their obstructionism and who appeared determined to break down all the Liberal efforts at reform. Lloyd George not only accepted the task of raising the additional money for the navy, but added much to it by schemes for social betterment—roads, labor exchanges, £200,000 a year for improving country life, and other matters. In the tremendous budget which he prepared with consummate skill for 1909, he struck right and left at the Lords, entrenched interests and big business. The Conservatives fought it tooth and claw and tried to arouse public resentment.

The Lords, already unpopular with the people at large for having come to the aid of special interests and for having vetoed many reforms, could not veto a money bill without breaking the constitution as developed for the previous two hundred and fifty years. One of the fundamental points in English constitutional development, both at home and in the early and later colonies and Dominions, had been that the lower and elected House had control of fiscal legislation. If that control passed to a House composed of hereditary members uncontrolled by popular election the people would lose the "power of the purse," which has been their strongest weapon in their long fight for liberty against tyranny.

Unfortunately the leadership in the Lords was poor. In a situation in which good temper and the characteristic English trait of compromise was called for, they displayed neither. Although the budget passed the Commons by 379 to 149, the Lords, in spite of King Edward's plea for caution, vetoed it by 350 to 75. A resolution was immediately carried in the Lower House that "the action of the House of Lords in refusing to pass into law the financial provisions made by this House for the service of the year is a breach of the Constitution and a usurpation of the rights of the Commons." In the struggle and the terms in which it was set, one is carried back two hundred and fifty years to the conflict with the Stuarts. Revolution began to seem possible.

A general election was inevitable and was held in January, 1910, the main issue of which was the House of Lords. As a result there was a considerable shift in the strength of parties, but the Liberals, Labor and Irish had the largest majority among them of any party or group since 1832, and were united in their desire to reform the Lords and to give Home Rule to Ireland. There were, however, various hitches as to procedure, and, although not known at the time, King Edward had told Asquith that he would not create more peers to end the deadlock until after another election had been held. The Prime Minister had assumed that the King would follow precedent, but had failed to obtain any guarantee from him prior to election. In view of the royal stand another election would now weight the scales more heavily on the side of the Lords. Delays prolonged the crisis until it took on a wholly new aspect owing to the unexpected and sudden death of the King after an illness of a few hours only on the 6th of May.

The stunned nation for the moment dropped controversy and awaited the turn of events. The new King, George V, was thoroughly British and the first of his House, from the time it had been brought over from Hanover, to speak English without a German accent. He had been a younger son and heir presumptive only since the death of his elder brother, when the new King, now forty-four, was twenty-six. His earlier years had been spent in the navy and he had visited many parts of the Empire while in service. This experience, as well as his relations with his fellow officers in the most popular of British services, not as heir to the throne, but merely as one of the younger sons, was a great advantage to him, but, like his father during Victoria's life, he had not been trained in the intimate affairs of state. Not a brilliant man, he nevertheless possessed a deep sense of duty to the nation and his steady devotion, and also that of his consort Queen Mary, made them in time perhaps the most respected sovereigns who have ever sat on the throne. He had, however, come to it with scarce a moment's warning and in the midst of a profound constitutional crisis.

At first he proposed a truce, and for five months eight statesmen, four from each of the leading parties, sat in conferences trying to find some solution of the problem. No plan proposed proved mutually satisfactory and in November Asquith announced Parliament dissolved and a general election ensued as matter of course. The result of the election was almost identical with the previous one and the yielding of the Lords was considered a foregone conclusion. The reform of their House as proposed in the government's bill included chiefly three points. Money bills under certain conditions were to become law without the consent of the Lords; other bills if passed thrice by the Commons and rejected by the Lords would then become law without their consent after a lapse of two years from the first introduction of the bills; and each Parliament should last only five instead of seven years.

The die-hard party in the Lords, nevertheless, continued the struggle, proposing a wholly different bill. By July it was announced to the heads of that party that the King had pledged himself to create enough new peers to ensure passage of the bill in the Lords. In spite of continued obstruction the Upper House finally yielded and passed the measure curtailing their own powers by a vote of 131 to 114. Had they been more conciliatory and, above all, had they not, as a clear breach of the constitution, held up the passage of the budget, they might have suffered a much smaller curtailment. In fact, the Liberals were very loathe to swamp the Lords with a huge creation of peers (about 250 names had been suggested) even though such a measure would have given them complete control of both Houses. The Lords had only themselves to blame for acting in a non-British fashion.

X. Factions in Ireland

Across the Irish Sea the situation also seemed to be leading rapidly to possible civil war. The new position of the Lords seemed to open the way at last to the passage of a Home Rule Bill which was pressed by the Liberals. Ireland was to have its own Parliament in control of all Irish domestic affairs although foreign policy and the army and navy were still to be controlled by the Parliament in Westminster. The difficulty was in Ireland itself, for under the lead of Sir Edward Carson the Ulster Protestants utterly declined to be placed under control of a Catholic majority in Dublin. The Irish Nationalists began arming and drilling, as did also the Ulstermen who knew they had strong backing and sympathy from the Conservatives in England. In Ulster a "covenant" of the sort which has played so large a part in British history was circulated and widely signed. In treasonable language it declared that even should the bill be passed by the Imperial Parliament it would not be recognized or obeyed in Ulster, and the smuggling in of arms and ammunition to Belfast went on apace.

Carson made it clear that the passage of the bill meant armed resistance and civil war. Asquith did not realize the gravity of the situation until after certain offers of compromise had been flatly rejected by the Ulstermen. A conference of leaders, summoned by the King, failed to agree, and it seemed as though not only would there be civil war in Ireland between its two sections if the bill *were* passed, as well as the necessity for England to make the authority of Parliament recognized in Ulster, but serious disturbances in Catholic Ireland if the Bill *were not* passed. The Sinn Fein doctrine that nothing could be expected to be gained by peaceful methods from the English Parliament had gained adherents rapidly. At the height of the crisis in July, 1914, war with Germany became imminent and in the common danger the strife mitigated slightly. Parliament passed the Home Rule Bill and at once added a suspending Act declaring that it should not take effect until six months after the end of the impending war on the Continent.

It is not strange that the Germans, who have a fatal capacity for misunderstanding the psychology of other peoples and their fundamental historic traits, should have considered the moment opportune to strike. The increasing violence of labor, the hysteria of the suffragettes, the almost revolutionary constitutional crisis between the Lords and Commons, the threatened civil war and revolution in Ireland, all seemed to Germany to indicate a demoralized and wholly disunited British nation which would be an easy prey. Moreover, the Kiel Canal had just been completed.

It is difficult to explain the state of mind of the British in the decade or so after Victoria's death. It cannot be blamed on the new classes admitted to the franchise by various Acts from the Reform Bill of 1832 onward. The un-British and violent way of confronting problems was not limited to the lower classes. It was shared by women of the upper middle class and by the most conservative of aristocrats in the House of Lords, but it did not result in a lasting change in the British character. The new century witnessed enormous strains and stresses in the whole fabric of British industrial, political, social and intellectual life as a result of forces which had been developing in the preceding one, but the Germans miscalculated when they believed the hurly-burly of the years we have briefly described meant that the British had permanently altered. There has been ample evidence since to prove the contrary in the two world crises which the Germans have brought on. What might have happened had not war come and united the nation it is impossible to say. History cannot deal with hypothetical situations but it seems probable that, aside from Ireland, the other domestic questions would have been settled in time in the same way as that of the House of Lords, by constitutional and not revolutionary methods. The entire world was in tumult and turning toward the use of force instead of reason and compromise, but now, a quarter of a century later, the Empire as a whole has still been striving to maintain compromise as the means of settlement. In spite of the great changes which the World War was to bring to every class in every land, the Empire is today staking its entire existence and risking all it holds dear for the maintenance of stability and the eventual possibility of give-and-take methods of the conference table instead of constant threats of war and revolution.

CHAPTER XV

THE WORLD WAR AND AFTER

I. The War

IN CONSIDERING the "causes" of the catastrophe which overwhelmed the world in the summer of 1914, we must distinguish between the immediate events and decisions which set the military machines in motion, and the long trends of national policies which prepared the material for the conflagration. The latter were based on fundamental human traits—jealousy, cupidity, pride, and others, which are as old as the race. Individuals have noble and ignoble qualities. Nations and governments for well-known reasons are apt to represent the lowest common denominator of the qualities of their citizens. Governments will do things which many of their individual citizens would scorn to do until played upon by the emotions of warlike passion. The longer causes of the war run far back, though we may take 1870, with the rise of modern military Germany, the world race for colonies and markets, and the new alignment of European and Oriental nations as the starting point.

With some of these we have already dealt and need not for the present discussion rehearse or amplify what we have said. A thorough examination of the *immediate* acts and decisions which led to the war breaking out when it did seems to lay the responsibility clearly on Austria and the military party in Germany. The stresses and strains due to the ambitions of those two nations, and Russia in the Balkans and Near East, had been steadily increasing to the breaking point. It had become evident to many competent observers that the end of the diplomatic method of adjustment between Russia and Austria had been reached as to the Slavic and other disputes between them, and any new incident would be settled only by war. Further it was noted that Germany would stand by Austria in any such quarrel.

On June 28 the Archduke Franz Ferdinand, heir to the Austrian throne and a friend of the Serbs, though himself disliked by many in high places in Austria who would gladly have got rid of him, was assassinated in Austria by an Austrian citizen of the Serbian race. Events then moved swiftly to what appears to have been a predetermined end. There were ultimatums, falsified documents, refusals of mediation, and mobilizations which it was claimed could not be stopped in view of the huge modern war machines. Abject offers by threatened Serbia were summarily rejected. By August 4 Germany and the Austro-Hungarian Empire were at war with Serbia, Russia, France, Belgium, and Britain. Before the struggle was to end every first class power and many minor ones in all parts of the world were to be involved.

Britain was the last of the first group of contestants to declare herself and during the anxious weeks and last feverish days had done all possible to stave off the catastrophe. It has been claimed by many that a firmer stand by Sir Edward Grey, the Foreign Minister, and the government might have caused the Central Powers to halt and that the same policy which was to lose at Munich in 1938 lost in those fatal days at the end of July, 1914. It may be said, however, that Grey was sincerely desirous of peace and that he hoped to avoid the catastrophe which was to cost the lives of some ten millions of men.

Also the crisis, although long maturing, came so suddenly at the end and with so little excuse that the British people were unprepared psychologically. All hesitation ended, however, and public opinion was crystallized by the German ultimatum to Belgium on August 2 demanding passage for her troops through that little country, whose neutrality had been guaranteed by the great powers including Britain. In 1938 Great Britain was not a guarantor of Czecho-Slovakia, but in 1914 she was of Belgium, and when the ultimatum expired on the night of August 4 Britain was in the war, as the German Chancellor said in a phrase never to be forgot, "for a scrap of paper." In a word the British people decided to stand by their treaty and keep their word, a decision incomprehensible to the German mind.

The Dominions came promptly and generously to the help of the homeland. The extraordinary outburst of loyalty shown to the Mother Country, the Empire, and the ideals and way of life for which they all stood not only staggered Germany, but even surprised the world at large. The exhibition of solidarity was magnificent and convincing. The Empire evidently did not mean oppression or trade. It meant passionate devotion to certain beliefs and to the great Commonwealth of Nations which had grown up in British fashion, linked by the symbol of the Crown and bound by neither force nor legislation. The Empire was proved to be not a tyranny or a Zollverein or a political federation, but something far more substantial and formidable—a union of hearts and loyalties. Canada, New Zealand, and Australia sent men as freely as did Britain itself, and large contingents from South Africa and India also fought in Europe. At home, unity replaced strife in all branches of the national life, and Germany was shown to have made a complete miscalculation in counting on a divided country and a disloyal Empire.

In general in the past Britain when engaged in Continental wars had made her contribution by means of her navy, financial subsidies to her allies, and usually only a small army. In this terrific struggle from 1914 to 1918 the navy played its accustomed role. Without the complete control which it exercised over the seas, neither food, supplies nor troops could have been moved. In spite of new weapons of war, such as tanks, submarines, poison gas, aeroplanes, and others, control of the seas proved, as in the past, the final determining factor. British credit also stood the strain of advancing billions of dollars to her allies. But unlike previous wars practically the entire manhood of the Empire, and we may say womanhood, was involved in the struggle. It was the first war in which the whole civil population was engaged.

For the military services alone men offered themselves from every quarter of the Empire. In Britain itself no less than 5,000,-000 volunteered, though many had to be rejected as physically unfit. The vast numbers of British troops fought not only on the Western Front in France, but all over the world—in East, South and West Africa, the islands of the Pacific, in Egypt, Turkey, Palestine, Macedonia, Italy, and elsewhere. As the struggle continued one nation after another came in, Italy, Portugal, all the Balkan countries, Japan, China, the United States (1917), and others. In some cases armies larger than any Britain had ever had in the field anywhere before were fighting in distant quarters with the need of transport of men and supplies of all sorts.

It was indeed not one war but many going on simultaneously. To describe them all in detail for the four years is impossible and unnecessary. What we are more interested in is the effect of the war on the Empire and its life and structure. We can merely skim over the military events.

At the very beginning, the Germans, having counted on broken treaties and overwhelming force for their *Blitzkrieg*, failed to get through. They quickly overran Belgium and swept down across France to within a few miles of Paris, but there they were held and turned back. With their digging in on their new line the long trench war began which was to last till 1918. They made a strike, however, to capture the Channel ports, so as to control the Dover Straits, but were repelled by the small British forces with enormous bloodshed. In the East, Russia advanced to take the pressure off France, but suffered a terrible defeat at Tannenberg, and meanwhile Turkey had joined the Central Powers, menacing Egypt, the Suez Canal, and even India. Germany, blockaded by the British navy, had to see her colonies lost. The year 1915 was a discouraging one for the Allies, though it saw the entry of Italy on their side. The costly but gallant failure of the attack on the Dardanelles, in which the Australians and New Zealanders particularly distinguished themselves, had been undertaken to relieve

Russia. In 1916 the German fleet endeavored to break out, but was forced to retreat again in the battle of Jutland. For the rest of the war the blockade was complete. The Germans were feeling the pressure and lack of food, and made a tremendous effort to get through the French lines at Verdun, with colossal loss of life on both sides and no success. Rumania now came in on the Allied side but was heavily defeated. In Palestine preparations were being made for the attacks which were eventually to cause the defeat of Turkey and her withdrawal from the war.

The Germans realized that their plans had miscarried and that affairs were getting desperate, but the Allies were also growing tired of apparent lack of progress and in Britain Asquith was replaced as Prime Minister by the dynamic Lloyd George, who had shown great driving force as Minister of Munitions. With 1917 came the desperate throw of the Germans in declaring and carrying out unrestricted submarine warfare. For a while the menace seemed overwhelming, and the losses of shipping rose as high as 600,000 tons in one month, but if food were lacking courage was not. Men instead of being deterred swarmed into the merchant marine to take the place of those who had been lost, and the rescued set sail again on the first ship they could get. New devices were found to attack the submarines and before the year was over the menace had been met, the chief effect of the policy of von Tirpitz having been only to draw the United States into the war on the Allied side.

Although slow in getting men trained and overseas, in spite of the fact that 2,000,000 were in France within a year, the immense resources of America in money and supplies were at once placed at the disposal of the Allies, and the fate of the Central Powers was sealed. The entry of America was hailed with joy and the King and Queen attended a special service of thanksgiving at St. Paul's, while the Stars and Stripes were flown from the Victoria Tower of Parliament, the only time any foreign flag has been flown over that building. Nevertheless, the year ended gloomily. In the East, Russia collapsed in revolution after great sufferings, and her new leaders, Lenin and Trotsky (Braunstein), made a separate peace with Germany at Brest-Litovsk, releasing all German troops for the West, where affairs were also going badly. The pressure on the French was terrific, and both they and the British had to send sorely needed troops to support the Italians, who had suffered a severe defeat at Caporetto, which had turned into panic and rout.

With 1918, however, came the end. The Turkish and Austrian Empires were breaking. The German people were almost starving, and the German High Command, realizing that all was lost if a quick victory could not be won, made three terrific onslaughts on the French and British. They pushed in to within forty miles of Paris and again threatened the Channel ports, but could do no more. In July the Allied armies, now under the unified command of Marshal Foch, delivered their great counterattack, with the Americans operating mainly in the Argonne. Step by step, the Allies regained what had been lost in the German drive, and by October the entire German defense was cracking. A few weeks earlier, Bulgaria, which had joined the Central Powers after the Allied failure in the Dardanelles, asked for an armistice, and was out of the war. Turkey, thoroughly beaten, did the same at the end of October. On November 4 Austria did likewise, and Germany was left alone. She also, however, collapsed. There was a mutiny in the navy, followed by revolution among the civilians, while the Kaiser saved his life and eventually most of his vast fortune by fleeing to Holland. On November 11 Germany signed an armistice, the guns at last ceased their endless firing, and the greatest war in history was over. Over 65,000,000 men had been in active service, of whom over 8,500,000 were dead and 21,000,-000 wounded. Peace had come—but to a ruined world. The flower of a whole generation had been wiped out, over 900,000 dead in the Empire and over 1,350,000 in France. Economically, socially, and politically the entire world was to enter upon a new and even yet unknown phase.

II. THE PEACE

The guns had ceased booming. Men were at least no longer being torn and mangled and slaughtered, but everywhere there were chaotic conditions and bitter hatreds. Before the end almost every nation even of slight importance, from Siam to many of the South American republics, had declared war on the side of the Allies, though in Europe Switzerland and the Scandinavian countries had maintained their neutrality. The settlement, therefore, was practically a redrawing of the map of the world and not, as at the Congress of Vienna a century earlier, of Europe only. The task was colossal and could be only tentative. The treaties, including the major one of Versailles, which emerged from the meeting of statesmen in Paris in the winter of 1918–19, were the result of the greatest united effort the world had yet made in statesmanship. No one who has not an intimate knowledge of the daily tasks of the Peace Conference can realize the complexity of the work and the conditions under which it had to be done.

It was not merely the terrestrial scope of the problem which made it so difficult, but the whole development of the previous century. The rise of nationalism and racialism introduced the question of self-determination and racial minorities. The industrial and commercial revolutions made the questions of banking, railways, raw materials, and so on, of immense importance in drawing new boundaries and creating new states. The Americans, British, and French had long had commissions at work preparing the data on which decisions might be based, but when the Conference was in session the need for haste became ever more clear. A large part of the world was in process of dissolution. As the statesmen sat in Paris the flames of red revolution seemed to be licking their way across Europe threatening to consume what the war had left of civilization and order.

There were also the conflicting ambitions of all the peoples, and the psychology of the leading members of the Conference. Lloyd George, in the election of 1918, had been elected on the slogan of "Hang the Kaiser and make Germany pay every shilling of the war cost." At one time he even talked of demanding $125,000,000,000 from her. Clemenceau was consumed with hatred and with fear for France in the future. Wilson, the idealist who had said on the eve of entering the White House in 1913, that it would be the irony of fate if he were called upon to deal with foreign affairs, was seeking a new world order by means of the League of Nations.

Although there were representatives of most nations on the globe, other than the defeated ones and the neutrals, the real negotiations fell more and more, by necessity, into the hands of the British, French, and Americans after the Italians left, displeased at the denial of their claims. In the Napoleonic wars France had overrun almost all Europe, but the statesmen of that period realized the unity of the Continent and that other nations would have to live with France; and the terms accorded her were far more generous than those now granted to the defeated Central Powers. Our story does not call for a detailed explanation of all the changes in Europe, the creation of such new states as Poland and Czecho-Slovakia, the partition of the Austro-Hungarian Empire, leaving Austria ruined and helpless, and the punitive clauses as to Germany. To her the treaty attributed the whole guilt of the war, and she was to be disarmed. In addition the huge indemnities demanded from her in cash and kind made any general European economic recovery impossible, as we shall note later.

The treaty was born of hate, fear and haste, but it was expected that the League of Nations would provide a means of peaceful settlement of the mistakes and injustices in a better atmosphere for consultation and readjustment later. The League, however, never functioned as intended. The United States declined to join it and Russia remained outside. It was a wounded bird from the start. This fact and the short-sighted diplomacy of France, in especial in the postwar years, were to prepare the way for revolution and Hitlerism in Germany. Her entire colonial empire was taken from her, and although it had never been very profitable to her commercially it had been a source of pride. Under the mandate system of the League the British Empire acquired the largest part of it, divided between Britain and the Dominions. New Zealand got German Samoa; Australia German New Guinea; South Africa received German Southwest Africa, while Britain took German East Africa and other German possessions on that continent.

The mandate system was part of the idealism of the League.

The nations which divided the German overseas empire were to hold the colonies as trustees, but the fact that Japan has insisted on holding her mandated islands in spite of the fact she has left the League indicates that ownership rather than trusteeship has again become the ruling concept. It should be said, however, that Britain has to a large extent maintained the nobler ideal, especially in such mandates as she received for Palestine, Iraq, and Trans-Jordan.

The war had had enormous repercussions in the Moslem world, which was heaving like the sea in a storm, in India; and in the Far East, where Japan, with no outlay of blood or treasure, had risen to a dominant and menacing position, particularly with relation to disorganized China. The ruin of Europe had given all the non-European world a new confidence in itself and a desire to rid itself of European influence or control. In Europe itself, semi-Asiatic Russia had withdrawn from the European system, and between that Bolshevist state and the democracies of Western Europe lay only some new and weak countries and the maimed Germany. That country of 65,000,000 people, seething with discontent, owing to economic hardship, and with hatred for her late enemies due to the terms of the treaty, became increasingly ready for any desperate experiment which might promise a way out.

III. Postwar at Home

But the victorious nations were also to suffer and to undergo great and lasting changes. None escaped. Britain indeed did not accept such a dictatorship as Italy adopted under Mussolini nor did it suffer the extreme political instability of France, yet the problems which had plagued it on the eve of the war returned, after peace, in even more acute form. One only had been solved in large degree in the final months of the struggle, the enfranchisement of women, within certain limitations. When peace came the electorate consisted of most of the female part of the population and practically all males over twenty-one, owing to an enlargement also of the male franchise. This widely extended electorate, under depressed economic conditions, was to be largely responsible for the spread of Socialism and the rise to power of the Labor Party.

As always, immediately after the end of a great war, there was a short period of illusory prosperity. On such occasions, there is general optimism, and the high war wages carry over for a brief time. The economic situation was, however, extremely bad. In spite of heavy taxation during the war, Britain had come out of it with a staggering debt on her own account. In addition she owed the United States nearly $4,500,000,000, much of which she had in turn loaned to her allies. The hope that Germany could pay the cost of the war in reparations was a fantastic dream, payments of any amount at all being finally abandoned in 1932. Meanwhile, the British Government, in the Balfour Note of 1921, had suggested that she would abandon claims on her allies except for such sums as, added to her share of the reparations from Germany, would enable her to pay her adjusted debt to America.

However, two things happened. It became evident that reparations would fail and when in 1922 Mr. Stanley Baldwin, now Lord Baldwin, went to America to arrange terms, he immediately accepted much more onerous ones than it is understood he might have obtained. That Britain was the first to suggest a settlement and to make a payment greatly raised her prestige in the States, although the debt question was later to create bad feeling. It is only fair to America to say that she had advanced the Allies over $11,-600,000,000 and had claimed no reparations or territory from Germany. She felt that the Allies had made huge additions to their nations or empires in addition to the then expected reparations to be received by them on a colossal scale from Germany. In my opinion the debts never can and never will be paid. Abstractly sound and ethical arguments may be advanced on both sides of the unhappy question, which has become heavily clouded by feeling and misinformation.

The domestic and foreign debt problems, however, were only in small part responsible for Britain's difficulties. The destruction of capital in great wars inevitably brings later a business depression, and, as this was the greatest war, involving the greatest destruction in history, it was inevitable that the succeeding secondary postwar depression would also be the greatest. There were in addition special causes operating in the case of Britain. In an earlier chapter we noted her real but undiscerned change in economic direction. This was enormously accelerated by the war and the peace. During the former she had had to dispose of the greater part of her enormous overseas investments which had come to form a large portion of her national wealth, and which were now gone.

Moreover, more dependent for wealth than any other nation on foreign trade, she had had to abandon most of it under the exigencies of the struggle, and in a world depression and against new rivals, it could not be regained to the old extent. In addition the very effort to get reparations from Germany hurt her home situation. If she got much of Germany's former mercantile marine, that meant idleness in her own shipyards; the reparations paid in coal all but destroyed her own coal industry; the need of Germany to export goods at almost any price to get reparation money flooded Britain's markets. Britain began to realize the impossibility of reparations, but the French, at least until after their fatal occupation of the Ruhr, were adamant in demanding them. Finally, under the forced draught of war demands, the industrial plants of other countries had expanded enormously, both for home consumption and export, so that when Britain was again ready to do business her markets had shrunk correspondingly. Markets for the other countries had also shrunk, with the result that they raised their tariff walls higher, which, added to chaotic currency conditions, made world trade almost impossible. In 1929, the second phase of world depression, which struck America particularly hard after a period of wild speculation, began and has lasted to the present.

The confusion of the period is shown politically in Britain by the number of governments and Ministries since the fall of the Coalition government under Lloyd George in 1922. Succeeded by Bonar Law, who in a few months was succeeded by Baldwin, the government was defeated at the polls in 1923, and the Labor Party came to power for a few months under Ramsay MacDonald, but could make no proposals to cure the country's ills. A third

341

election in 1923 returned the Conservatives again with Baldwin, who remained Prime Minister until 1929, when Labor again came in, the Liberal Party having almost completely destroyed itself. Unable again to do anything for the country, which had come to the edge of the abyss financially in the less than two years the Labor Party was in office, a National government was formed in 1931, and the Prime Ministers since then have been MacDonald, Baldwin [1935-1937], and Neville Chamberlain.

After the first flush of prosperity following peace, the labor troubles which had been interrupted by the war again developed, particularly in the coal mines, but extending to almost all branches of trade. The Miners' Federation, however, took the lead. They began with a demand for national ownership, which was followed by the great lockout of 1921 in which the miners were defeated. The workers took up the gauntlet which they felt had been thrown down to them. Membership in the trades-unions was about 6,-000,000 when, after the failure of fresh negotiations with the government and the mine owners, the miners appealed to the Trades-Union Congress for a sympathetic "General Strike," which began May 4, 1926.

Newspapers, transportation and many key as well as minor industries were stopped, but the government took a firm if not altogether wise stand, and the strike was a complete failure, owing in no small part to the way in which the ordinary citizen, from highest to lowest, turned his hand to any job he could do, running busses, locomotives, power and other plants, even men with the highest titles serving as porters at the railway stations. It was a remarkable demonstration of national character and appeared to indicate that the general strike as a weapon, revolutionary or otherwise, could not succeed. There was no violence, and the jolly fraternizing which in many places went on between strikers, public and police was typically English.

In spite of a certain amount of public fear the movement had not been revolutionary, although the government, largely under the influence of Winston Churchill, led the people to believe it was. Unfortunately, after it was broken the government and employers instead of remedying the genuine grievances of the workers did nothing except to pass legislation of drastic sort against trades-unions, which put their position back almost to that of seventy years earlier. Labor was beaten but restless.

As compared with the opening of the century, however, the standard of living for the workers was distinctly better than it had been. The working class was better dressed, fed and housed. It had better opportunities for education, including adult. It drank less and spent more money on cinemas, holiday trips and other amusements, though, like those above it, it was less thrifty. Not only the easy money of the war years, but also the various forms of social insurance, including the "dole," made laying by for a rainy day or old age seem less necessary. Also the idea of "Socialism in our day" had become much more widespread and Communism had increased to some, though not a great, extent.

The postwar years brought the problem of unemployment, which is one of the most serious for Britain as for the United States. The upward trend of population was particularly notable in the nineteenth century during which the British population rose from about 10,000,000 to about 37,000,000, with another 10,-000,000 to be added by 1937. Until the war and its vast changes this increase had been given employment by increase of home industries and by emigration, but Britain can never again occupy her former dominant position in trade and manufactures. Emigration has been largely closed by restrictive legislation, not only by the United States, but even by some of the Dominions, and unemployment, with the dole and its other social and financial by-products, promises to be permanent, at least until the now declining birth rate produces its effect.

Financially the great crisis came in 1931 in the "economic blizzard," which swept the world following the failure of a great bank in Vienna. There was a run on the Bank of England, which had resumed gold payments in 1925. The bank was forced to borrow £50,000,000 from France and America, but this was exhausted in a few days. The only salvation was to re-establish credit by balancing the budget, but this could not be done without severe cuts in

343

the cost of unemployment pay and other social services, which the Labor government then in power declined to make.

It was on this that it fell and was replaced by the National government, as noted above. On the promise of heavy retrenchments in expenses the new government was able to borrow £80,000,000 more from France and America, but before the new measures could be passed this had likewise gone, and on September 21 Britain went off the gold standard again, which has not since been restored. She was to be followed later by many other countries, including the United States, and the foreign trade of the world, on which Britain so much depended, was still further hampered by difficulties and uncertainties of exchange.

IV. IRISH FREE STATE ESTABLISHED

Crossing the Irish Sea we again encounter the centuries-old Irish problem. We have already noted the serious situation in that island at the beginning of the war, as well as its supreme importance to Britain in case of war to prevent its becoming a steppingstone for her enemies. It has been used by them in the Elizabethan days, in those of Louis XIV, in the Stuart risings, in the Napoleonic wars. In the World War there was again a rebellion, in 1916, which had to be suppressed, but at the expense of increasing the influence and power of the Sinn Feiners, who declared Ireland a Republic and set up a new Parliament known as the Dail Eireann. Owing to what was practically civil war, though of the guerrilla sort, Ireland did not render the loyal aid to Britain which the other portions of the Empire did.

England did her best to meet Irish demands and went far beyond anything which Gladstone had contemplated in his Home Rule bills of an earlier generation. In 1921 the government agreed on a treaty with the founders of Sinn Fein, Arthur Griffith and Michael Collins, to be ratified by both the British Parliament and the Dail Eireann. By its terms southern Ireland was to be practically independent with Dominion status. Unhappily a party under the lead of Eamon de Valera, an alien, born in New York, son of a Spanish father and an Irish mother, objected and started a

344

second civil war, in the course of which Collins was killed. However, the treaty was ratified in 1924, and this, with the British offer to settle the war debts, had a determining influence on American feeling toward Britain. In America the Irish have always gravitated toward political office and have counted politically far beyond their numbers. With the war debts apparently settled and with the Irish apparently satisfied, there could be no more "twisting of the lion's tail" which, on account of the "Irish vote," had been the stock in trade of many political spellbinders for a century or more.

It was considered in Britain and America that the "Irish Question" was at last settled, but in succeeding years the old quarrel continued. The treaty had given Ireland the right to raise tariffs against British goods and also had stated that the Irish farmers should continue to pay the instalments (at very low interest rates) to the British Treasury to reimburse it for the moneys advanced to enable them to buy their lands from the former landlords. There was also the question as to Ulster. Many of the Irish objected to the division of the island into two parts, although race, religion and industry did actually so divide it.

Much of the subsequent discussion has been based on legalistic quibbles, and the legal aspect of the settlement is susceptible of various interpretations. The "Dominion status" was slightly different from that accorded to the other Dominions, but rather in Ireland's favor, and the form of the oath of allegiance to the Crown has made trouble. Although de Valera has asserted that the Irish Free State would never be permitted to be used by foreign powers as a base of attack on Great Britain, it is clear that the entire independence at which Ireland apparently is aiming could not be permitted. It would be to some extent like allowing Long Island to become independent of the United States and a steppingstone for attack by alliance with or conquest by a foreign power.

There the question rests at the moment. Southern and Catholic Ireland is practically independent save in so far as she is a member of the British Commonwealth of Nations. It cannot be allowed to become a completely independent and *foreign* country. It is doubtful, the Irish being by nature what they are, and their history having been what it is, whether agitation will ever die down. Although the flexibility of the imperial structure is evidenced by the fact that the Free State is a republic, with the good will of Britain, it is nevertheless a fact that the safety of Britain requires that Ireland remain within the Empire. It is impossible to say what force might be used to prevent her complete secession, but it is certain that her other aim, the annexation of Ulster and the subjugation of the Scotch-Irish and English population of the northern counties to the Catholic and Gaelic south, could not be accomplished without civil war. In such a war Britain could not stand by as a neutral. Thus, although the citizens of the Free State have complete control of their local affairs, with also diplomatic representatives in foreign countries, and have attained a degree of independence which they never dreamed of in Gladstone's day, it is evident that the Irish problem is still far from solved.

V. NEW DOMINION STATUS

Meanwhile the status of all the Dominions had greatly changed. Just as the services rendered by British women in the war led to their securing the suffrage with scarcely a ripple in the political world, so the sacrifices made and the loyal aid given to the mother country made changes in Dominion relationship inevitable. Canada provided armed forces of about 650,000 men, or over 8 per cent of her total population, and spent approximately $2,000,000,000 on the war. Australia sent to Europe about 350,000 troops and in the Pacific her small navy rendered efficient and useful service. New Zealand, with a population of only a little over a million, raised 125,000 men and spent over $400,000,000. South Africa, although it sent far fewer troops to Europe, did valiant service in Africa itself. In all the Dominions there were minority parties opposed to the war, such as the French-Canadian party under the lead of Bourassa in Canada, which was far from representing the attitude of most of his race there, and the Labor Party in Australia, but questions were settled peaceably at the polls. In South Africa, however, there was a formidable rebellion of some of the unreconciled Dutch who did not wish to fight against Germany. This was suppressed by the South Africans themselves under the lead of the former Boer general, Botha. General Smuts, another Boer, was commander-in-chief of the forces which captured German Southwest and East Africa. The South Africans, in their fighting in the German colonies, saved Britain from having to divert any troops from other fronts, and in addition contributed about $140,000,000. We shall speak of India later.

The Dominions had indeed grown up. They had become lusty young nations, proud of their nationhood and increasing power, but the strength of the ties which bound the Empire together had been amply proven. The enormous changes which were to take place in transforming the Empire into the British Commonwealth of Nations may be indicated by the fact that in 1914, although as we have seen means had been provided by the Imperial Conferences and other methods to consult with the Dominions, it was not dreamed that Britain alone could not declare war for the Empire. In the second war with Germany, 1939, it was taken for granted that each Dominion could take part in the war or remain neutral as it saw fit, and although they went in each made its separate declaration of war.

During the World War very considerable advances were made. Although two Imperial Conferences were held, an Imperial War Cabinet was also created, consisting of the British War Cabinet with representatives from each Dominion and from India. The first meeting was held in 1917 and as Sir Robert Borden, Prime Minister of Canada, pointed out, for the first time in history the Empire was not governed from Downing Street. Ministers from six nations, each responsible to the Parliament of his own country, and each equal to the other, sat to discuss imperial policy. At this 1917 meeting a resolution which is one of the great landmarks in imperial history was unanimously passed, demanding that after the war readjustments should be made so that the Dominions "as autonomous nations in an Imperial Commonwealth, and India as an important portion of the same" should have an adequate voice in imperial foreign policy.

Although the Dominions had not been asked to declare war they were asked to make peace, and their representation at the Peace Conference as individual nations was a marked forward step. In the League of Nations, although Britain represented the entire Empire in the Council, each of the Dominions, as well as India, had seats in the Assembly. For a while, however, not much further was done, and the Conferences of 1923, 1926, and 1929, as well as the Ottawa Conference of 1932, considered chiefly economic relations within the Empire, with some danger that the real ties which bind it together might be lost to sight in wrangling for trade advantages. Moreover, the Irish Free State, which as we have seen had attained Dominion status, was straining to break as many links as possible. South Africa, the least devoted to the Empire of the older Dominions, had placed a Nationalist Party in power which did not threaten, but claimed the right of, secession. Whether or not a Dominion could secede without the consent of Britain and the other Dominions is one of the many points in the imperial structure which remain indefinite.

The British, however, have a genius for carrying on government and getting along together without crossing t's and dotting i's. The nearest they have come to doing that is the Statute of Westminster, passed by the British Parliament in 1931. This verbally established practically complete equality of status between Britain and the Dominions, all of which are now linked together only by the Crown, thus finally bringing into being the plan suggested by some American writers before the American Revolution. But even here there are constitutional questions which are quietly ignored. It may well be asked whether, if the Dominions received almost complete independence by an Act of the Parliament at Westminster another Act might not legally, at least, deprive them of it? In fact, owing to her financial and political troubles, Newfoundland was deprived of Dominion status in 1933.

Legalistic quibbling aside, however, they seem satisfied with the present flexible imperial relations, with the exception, of course, of Ireland. Nevertheless, there are many uncertainties within the structure of the Commonwealth, and some of these may cause difficulties in dealing with foreign countries, now that the Dominions are sovereign nations and have their own diplomatic representatives abroad in many cases. The situation is developing in such a way as possibly to make the same trouble which the United States (in which both the Federal government and each of the forty-eight States have sovereign attributes) has found, and which has brought her to the verge of war three times with other nations. The United States is a unit and at the same time for some purposes it is not. The same anomaly has now grown up in the Empire, with possibly, for outsiders, the same complications and misunderstandings.

VI. Government of India Act

'As we have seen, India, although not a Dominion, has come to take an increasing share in imperial policy and affairs. Considering the agitations of the years leading up to 1914, it was not unnatural that Britain's enemies should count on an Indian rising once Britain was at bay, just as they counted on the Irish and other troubles nearer home. In fact India, its peoples and Princes, proved so loyal that practically all British troops could be withdrawn from its garrisons, and not only did the Princes make lavish gifts for the imperial cause but Indian soldiers in great numbers fought in Europe, Africa and Asia for the cause.

The war, however, had its profound effect. The very efforts Indians were making seemed to call for a greater share in their own government. The Morley-Minto form of government had not achieved the results hoped for. In addition there was great and genuine distress among the common people, owing in part to the old causes and in part to sudden industrialization and rise in living costs. We have previously spoken of the effects also of the Mohammedan unrest and of the influence of the rise of Japan. The Mohammedans, moreover, were in the difficult position of having to fight on the side of their King-Emperor against the Caliph, who was their religious head. Returning soldiers brought

349

back stories from Europe not only of the nations destroying each other there but of the prosperity of European peasants as contrasted with their own poverty. Unrest had become so marked by 1917 that the British Government endeavored to revise the form of Indian government, and the bill establishing what was called Dyarchy was passed two years later.

It was a complex system of checks and balances, of responsible and non-responsible government, and probably would not have worked in any case, though the intent to reform was genuine. Owing to the circumstances at the time it was inaugurated, however, it was doomed from the start. Ghandi's influence had been steadily growing and he had developed his policy of passive resistance, gaining a huge following from his asceticism and, according to Indian ideas, saintliness. Other leaders, however, believed in active resistance and there had been a number of disorders, including the murder of a European woman at Amritsar. General Dyer, who was sent to restore order, was merciless in his methods, shooting into an unarmed crowd time after time and killing 379 persons. Also he forced all Indians who had to pass along the street where Miss Sherwood had been killed to go on all fours. Although he was court-martialled and reprimanded, racial feeling was again aflame on both sides. There was further violence and again the Afghans invaded Northwest India, but were repulsed.

When the new form of government was promulgated, Ghandi started his campaign of "non-violent non-co-operation" calling on Indians to take no part in the new government, and was later imprisoned. In view of the obvious failure of the scheme, a Commission was sent to India in 1926 to study the situation and prepare a new plan, but no Indian was appointed on it, and the feeling was so strong that fresh troubles broke out on its publication in 1928. Two years later Ghandi, who had been released, started another non-co-operation movement and was again imprisoned.

Meanwhile, the Indian Princes had agreed to join the British in some sort of federal government which should include both their states and the British provinces and which seemed to pave the way for some form of responsible government such as the Dominions enjoyed. This was to a considerable extent accomplished in the Government of India Act of 1935 which is now in effect. Without going into long detail it may be said that the Act proclaimed a Federal Union of the sixteen provinces of British India, exclusive of Burma, and of such Indian states as might agree to surrender certain of their sovereign powers for the privilege of representation in the federal legislature. The Act is very complicated but in spite of opposition of the Congress Party is the greatest advance yet made toward solution of an extremely difficult problem.

How difficult it is is indicated by the vast number of castes and religions; the fact that the total population is three quarters of that of the entire Empire; and that the states still ruled by their Princes and not by the British government of India number about 600, varying from what are scarcely more than country estates of a few hundred acres to Hyderabad, the largest, which contains 82,000 square miles. Some 90 per cent of the entire population live in about 500,000 villages scattered about in every variety of geographic and climatic conditions.

India is different from any other part of the Empire and is almost a world in itself. That it cannot yet be accorded full Dominion status and responsible government is evident but the nationalism of its people must somehow be met. Whether this new and honest effort to do so and to train its people in self-government will be successful cannot yet be forecast. The problems of every sort are both unique and colossal. The total European population is only 135,000 of whom 60,000 are troops. India may never, like the Dominions, become a "white man's country," yet besides all other reasons for retaining India in the Empire it would probably fall into the old chaos if left to its agitators and rival Princes. India is one of the greatest of Oriental countries and the British effort to educate it politically may well prove the focus of the Occidental-Oriental clash or the working out of some sort of harmony between East and West even though Kipling wrote that "never the twain shall meet."

351

VII. BRITAIN'S RESPONSIBILITY IN EGYPT

Another important postwar change was in the status of Egypt. It had never been an integral part of the Empire, but perhaps nowhere in the world, as we have seen, had the British done a finer piece of work. The nationalist movement, however, which had started before 1914, took on during and after the war a much fiercer form. The fiction had always been that the suzerain of Egypt was the Sultan of Turkey and that the British were in the country merely as administrators, although in reality rulers, but when Turkey entered the war on the side of the Central Powers it was necessary either to consider Egypt as an enemy or to sever its connection with Turkey. Consequently Britain declared a protectorate over it. The unrest was easily held down by plentiful troops during the war, but later the nationalist movement, under its leader, the impractical fanatic Saad Zaghlul, spread rapidly among the common people as well as the ambitious group, anxious for political power and plunder, who had originally fostered it.

It became evident that Egypt as a whole insisted on independence. Although Britain could have conquered her and held her down, she recognized the independence of the country she had for so long nursed into good government and prosperity, in 1922, with reservations. She kept the Suez Canal, the Sudan, which Britain alone had conquered and in which she had established order, and insisted on adequate protection for foreigners. The present situation is that Egypt is independent but Britain has the responsibility for protecting the lives and property of foreigners there should disorder arise. Whether the country will relapse into its old condition of political corruption and inefficiency remains to be seen, as well as what responsibilities may again be placed on Britain's shoulders.

According to the Peace Treaty Britain had undertaken responsibility for Palestine and Iraq, and although she is still administering the former (under mandate from the League) under difficult conditions, her tutelage of Iraq ended in 1925 when a treaty was made acknowledging her independence. Apparently Britain did

352

good work, and five years later independent Iraq became a member of the League.

VIII. LEAGUE FAILURE AND THE RESULTS

The League itself was doomed to failure, and the story of the past dozen years or so is that of its progressive decay as a means of collective security, as also of the failure of the leading powers to take over its intended function, in part, of correcting the worst mistakes of the Treaty of Versailles. There were, indeed, almost innumerable conferences, all of which failed. Hopes were high in 1925 when the one held at Locarno produced a group of treaties among the powers which Briand, the French Prime Minister, said make us now "only Europeans," an opinion echoed by the German Stresemann. Sir Austen Chamberlain declared that the treaties were the dividing line between the years of war and the coming ones of peace. This general optimism seems almost incredible in the light of the condition of the world today.

The Dawes Plan had been agreed to in order to help Germany pay the reparations with the aid of a huge international loan, but, as we have seen, by 1932, in the Lausanne Protocol, reparations had to be wiped off the slate. There were also the naval-race and disarmament conferences, such as those at Washington in 1921 and at Geneva in 1932, and in London; economic conferences in 1927 and 1933; treaties to outlaw war, such as the Kellogg Pact, or the Pact of Paris, but all were as ineffectual as the League itself. The trouble was that no statesmen had the vision to see the root of the troubles. Rampant nationalism with the new ideal of national self-sufficiency, together with selfishness and ambition, did the rest. There was also a profound moral setback. Treaties ceased to be considered binding, sometimes because of force of circumstances but often merely because new aims made it convenient to break them. The solemn and public pledges of heads of some of the leading states could likewise no longer be trusted. Italy and Japan withdrew from the League, as did Germany, which had entered in the hopeful period after Locarno. Russia was expelled after her invasion of Finland.

353

A new period of force and armed conquest set in. Japan seized Manchukuo, and then started the still continuing but undeclared war against China. Italy wantonly attacked and annexed Abyssinia in spite of the treaty guaranteeing the independence of that country, which was a member of the League. She also overran and annexed Albania. Germany seized Austria in spite of Hitler's word that he would not do so. Next came his claim on the Sudeten Germans in Czecho-Slovakia, and his faithless agreement with the British, French and Italians at Munich in September 1938, followed by the conquest of the entire country. Finally just a year later in September 1939 came his conquest, in company with his new ally, Soviet Russia, of Poland, and the start of a new war. Russia herself invaded Finland after establishing her control in the three small Baltic states. At this point history has to give place to useless prophecy.

It is impossible to confine the story of the past few years merely to the British Empire, and we have neither the space nor the knowledge as yet, to evaluate events which are fresh in the minds of all as contemporary news. Within the Empire there had been few important changes and we have already described briefly the form which it has now assumed. In Britain the economic situation gradually improved until the coming of the new war, and even in preparing for that a forced draught was set up under industry which made for profits and employment though the prosperity engendered was a false one. Once more the world is using up its remains of accumulated capital for destructive purposes, and taxation has climbed to hitherto unexampled heights. In view of the economic chaos and the profound social, political, and moral changes following the war ended only twenty-one years ago, it is impossible to imagine what another world war may mean within the same generation. One can see only that the Empire is again standing the test, that the Dominions have ranged themselves on the side of the mother country, each by its independent voluntary choice, and that volunteers are pouring in from all the Empire. Its unity and strength have again been shown on the eve of perhaps the greatest crisis in its long history, and after a great shock to the Crown, which is the one link binding it together.

IX. Edward VIII

George V died January 20, 1936. Never a brilliant man, his devotion to the country and Empire over which he ruled, and the character he displayed, had won him the affection and loyalty of all his peoples. There were, however, great hopes of the Prince of Wales, who ascended the throne as Edward VIII and who, from his extensive travels, had a wider knowledge of the Empire in all its parts than any previous monarch. Unfortunately, never married, he fell desperately in love with an American woman, Mrs. Wallis Warfield Simpson, who had already been once divorced and was at the time the wife of an Englishman. The King, who had not yet been crowned, preferred abdication (December 11) to giving up the woman he loved, and whom he married six months later after her second divorce. The difficulty was not that she was a commoner nor that she was American but, as we have many times noted, the Crown has become the link which binds together about 500,000,000 people of all lands, races and creeds. The ruler of the Empire today is not a private person, indeed scarcely a person, but a symbol of what the peoples of the Empire hold as an ideal. The fact that not only had Mrs. Simpson been previously divorced but that a new divorce had to be arranged in order that the ex-King, now the Duke of Windsor, could marry her, made an impossible situation.

X. George VI and the New World War

On his abdication Edward was immediately succeeded by his next younger brother, the Duke of York, who took the title of George VI, and it is another indication of the advance in status of the Dominions that in view of the changed line of succession, the various Dominion Parliaments passed their own Acts of confirmation. The new King was more like his father and has already won the hearts of his subjects by the seriousness of his attitude toward his new and unwished for duties, greatly aided by his popular

Scots Queen. In June, 1939, they made a tour of Canada and visited the United States for a few days, the first reigning British sovereigns ever to visit America. Everywhere they received a tumultuous and heartfelt welcome, and it was a dramatic moment in history when George VI of England placed a wreath on the tomb of George Washington, the successful rebel against his ancestor George III.

It was more than a gesture, for never before have the English-speaking races been so close. Today we stand on the threshold of an unknown world. We face not merely war but possibly a new period of barbarism and suppression of liberty of person and of thought. We know what has happened to both where the powers of Russia and Germany have trampled free peoples under foot. We know what Japan thinks of rights and treaties where her own interests are concerned. Seas and distance no longer guarantee isolation and safety. In the world of the present to whom can we better turn than to the British Empire, the democracy of France, and the sorely threatened neutrals who still believe in democracy and freedom?

We have now reached the end of our long story. In this and a preceding volume[1] we have covered some two thousand years of recorded history from the days when Cæsar first encountered the savage Britons and landed to conquer their island. We have seen the Roman civilization fade away as the shrinking empire recalled its legions from the outlying sections. Later, through the vicissitudes, the invasions, wars, the changing social and political conditions and even the change in geographical factors due to shifting trade routes and a new industrial world order, we have seen the slow development of British character and institutions building up an empire greater even than the Roman. We have seen how the British became the unique and often incomprehensible people whose nature we tried to analyze at the beginning.

Today they are facing perhaps the greatest crisis in their history, but we have seen how in the past they have encountered one crisis

[1]*Building the British Empire*, 1938,

after another which, like hammer blows on the anvil of fate, have shaped them to what they are. If they have gained a reputation for stupidity and muddling through, nevertheless they always have won through and have gained the rule of a quarter of the earth and five hundred million people. Their little nation faced extinction at the hands of the mighty power of Spain but the great armada was defeated and scattered. They faced a world against them in the war of the American Revolution. They lost the colonies which formed our United States but from apparent ruin of their empire they built one mightier than before. The genius of Napoleon seemed invincible. The whole of Europe lay at his feet. England, deserted by every ally, fought on. The struggle lasted for twenty years and at the end the fallen dictator was carried to his island exile on a British battleship, and liberty was saved. A century later, in the greatest war the world had yet known, a war of civilians and not merely of professional soldiers, not only did Britain hold firm to the end but the loyalty of every part of the Empire showed how far stronger are the bonds of freedom than those of force.

There is today a great British "folk" scattered over the globe. It is not a folk in the Hitlerian sense of a people acknowledging allegiance to a tyrant but a folk bound together by identical ideals of freedom for every individual. We see again at play the qualities we have noted in the past, unpreparedness, muddling, lack of foresight and imagination, and stupidity if you will, but, when the die is cast, a dogged determination, with no boasting, not to let go until victory is final and freedom has been saved. Dickens is the most typically English of English novelists, and one of his most widely quoted sayings is: "it is dogged as does it." If the muddling of the past decade is British, even more so, and more indicative of what the future may hold, is the calm but grimly quiet way in which the men and women of the whole Empire have accepted what they know may be the most terrible experience in the history of the race.

What, this time, the result may be no man can prophesy, but the story we have followed would seem to indicate that if the war is to be a test of endurance of nerves and character the British will not fail. If they win, the Britain that emerges will be a very different

357

one from that of today. The evacuation, for example, of great masses of children from the slum areas of the larger cities into country homes, with good food, clothes, fresh air and decent conditions of living, alone presages a great change of social outlook and aspiration. The British know this and are prepared for it. Out of the inferno, which may have to be passed through, a finer life may eventually emerge for all, unless at long last the Empire falls.

In this world crisis, we in America have a great stake. We know that stability is impossible without respect for law and order, for the honesty of the written and spoken word. Without liberty of thought, speech and press, progress is impossible. What these things mean to the world of today and tomorrow has been amply demonstrated by the negation of them in certain great nations during the past few years. Different peoples may have different ideals of government but for those who have been accustomed to freedom of person and of spirit, the possible overthrow of the British Empire would be a catastrophe scarcely thinkable. Not only would it leave a vacuum over a quarter of the globe into which all the wild winds of anarchy, despotism and spiritual oppression could rush, but the strongest bulwark outside ourselves for our own safety and freedom would have been destroyed.

CHRONOLOGY, 1783–1939

1783 Treaty of Versailles
Fox's India Bill

1784 Pitt's India Bill
New Brunswick organized
as a colony

1785 The power loom
Pitt's proposals of Parliamentary reform

1788 Foundation of New South
Wales
Trial of Warren Hastings
Convict settlement at Botany Bay

1789 Fall of the Bastille and
French Revolution

1791 Canada Act
Corn Law
Wolfe Tone founded the
United Irishmen

1792 Founding of Society of
Friends of the People
Grey introduces Parliamentary Reform Bill
French Republic and European war
Defeat of Tipu in India

1793 France declares war on
Britain
Settlement of Bengal
Irish Catholics receive the
franchise

1794 Jay Treaty with the United
States

1795 Conquest of Cape of Good
Hope and of Ceylon
Speenhamland Act

1796 British peace proposals to
France
British fleet abandons Mediterranean
War with Spain
Napoleon's trade decrees

1797 Battle of Cape St. Vincent
Conquest of Trinidad
Grey's Motion for Reform

1798 Irish Rebellion

1799 Second Coalition for war
Combination Act
Siege of Seringapatam and
conquest of Mysore

1800 Union with Ireland

1801 Carnatic annexed in India
Battles of Aboukir and
Copenhagen

1802 Treaty of Amiens
First Factory Act

1803 War again with France
War with Marathas

1805 Battle of Trafalgar
O'Connell in Ireland

1806	Death of Pitt Berlin Decree	1828	Repeal of Test and Corporation Acts
1807	Abolition of slave trade Annexation of Heligoland American trade embargo Milan Decree Orders in Council	1829	Peel reorganizes the police force Catholic Emancipation Act Foundation of Western Australia
1811	Occupation of Java Luddite riots	1830	**Accession of William IV**
		1831	Introduction of Reform Bill
1812	Orders in Council withdrawn War with the United States	1832	Reform Bill passed
		1833	Abolition of slavery
1813	Monopoly of East India Company ended in India	1834	Reform of Poor Law
		1836	Colonization of South Australia First trek of the Boers
1814	British burn Washington Napoleon abdicates	1837	**Accession of Queen Victoria** Canadian rebellions
1815	Napoleon escapes from Elba The Hundred Days Waterloo Congress of Vienna Peace with the United States and in Europe	1838	People's Charter **Anti-Corn-Law League** founded
1817	March of the Blanketeers Last Maratha War	1839	Lord Durham's Report on Canada Chartist risings
1819	Peterloo The Six Acts Birth of Victoria	1840	Canada Act New Zealand annexed Penny postage introduced
1820	**Accession of George IV** Trial of Queen Caroline Cato Street Conspiracy	1842	Ashburton Treaty Representative government instituted in New South Wales (and 1850)
1823	Monroe Doctrine		
1824	Burmese War	1843	Annexation of Natal
1826	Penal Code reformed	1846	Repeal of the Corn Laws Oregon Treaty
1827	Battle of Navarino		

360

1848 Orange River Colony annexed

1851 The Great Exhibition

1852 Sand River Convention
New Zealand Constitution Act

1854 Cape Colony Constitution
Crimean War
Abandonment of Orange River sovereignty

1855 Australian Constitution Acts

1856 Annexation of Oudh

1857 Second Chinese War
Mutiny in India

1858 Settlement of British Columbia

1860–1869 Maori wars in New Zealand

1866 End of responsible government in Jamaica
Transatlantic cable laid

1867 British North American Act
End of penal transportation to Australia
Second Reform Bill

1869 Disestablishment of Irish Church
Government buys out Hudson's Bay Company

1871 British Columbia enters Canadian Confederation

1872 Responsible government established in Cape Colony
Alabama arbitration

1874 Northwest Mounted Police established
Annexation of Fiji Islands

1876 Queen Victoria made Empress of India
International intervention in Egypt

1877 Transvaal annexed

1879 Zulu War

1880 Parnell becomes leader of Irish party
Transvaal revolts

1881 Irish Land Act
Pretoria Convention

1883 Defeat in the Sudan

1884 London Convention
Gold discovered in Transvaal

1885 Death of Gordon
Riel rebellion in Canada
British Protectorate established in Bechuanaland
First Indian National Congress

1886 Organization of British East Africa Company

1887 Jubilee of Queen Victoria
London Colonial Conference

1888 Annexation of Zululand

1889 Organization of British South Africa Company
London dock strike

1890 Tragedy of Parnell
Responsible government in Western Australia

1893 Second Home Rule Bill for Ireland introduced
Responsible government in Natal
Afghan frontier fixed

1894 Ottawa Colonial Conference

1895 Boundary dispute in Venezuela with United States

1896 Jameson Raid

1897 Diamond Jubilee of Queen Victoria
Second London Colonial Conference

1899 South African War begins

1900 British Labor Party founded
Annexation of Orange Free State and Transvaal
Australian Commonwealth Act

1901 **Accession of Edward VII**

1902 End of South African War
Third London Colonial Conference

1903 Durbar at Delhi

1904 Beginning of Franco-British Entente

1907 Anglo-Russian Entente
Fourth London Colonial Conference

1908 Old Age Pensions in England

1909 Union of South Africa
Morley-Minto reforms in India

1909 The Lloyd George Budget
Struggle with House of Lords

1910 **Accession of George V**
House of Lords yields

1911 Second Imperial Conference

1914 World War begins

1918 Armistice, and peace 1919

1920 League of Nations organizes
Irish Civil War

1921 Balfour Note on War Debts

1922 Egypt becomes independent

1923 Debt settlement with United States
Lausanne Treaty

1924 First Labor government

1925 Locarno Pact

1926 General strike
Fourth Imperial Conference

1931 Britain goes off gold standard

1932 Disarmament Conference
World Economic Conference
Ottawa Conference

1933 Newfoundland ceases to have Dominion status

1935 India Act

1936 **Accession of Edward VIII**
Abdication
Accession of George VI

1938 Munich Conference

1939 War against Germany

362

INDEX